WAR
BY OTHER
MEANS

ALSO BY JOHN J. FIALKA

Hotel Warriors:
The Press Coverage
of the Gulf War

WAR BY OTHER MEANS

Economic Espionage in America

JOHN J. FIALKA

W. W. NORTON & COMPANY

New York   London

First published as a Norton paperback 1999

For information about permission to reproduce selections
from this book, write to Permissions, W. W. Norton &
Company, Inc., 500 Fifth Avenue, New York, NY 10110.

The text of this book is composed in Bodoni Book with the
display set in Stencil and Agency Bureau. Composition by
Six West Design. Manufacturing by Quebecor Printing,
Fairfield, Inc.
Book design by Charlotte Staub.

Library of Congress Cataloging-in-Publication Data
Fialka, John J.
    War by other means : economic espionage in America /
John J. Fialka.
        p.   cm.
    Includes bibliographic references and index.
    ISBN 0-393-04014-3
    Business intelligence—United States. 2. Trade secrets—
United States. I. Title
HD38.7.F5 1997
364.1'68—dc20   96-16699
                                                      CIP

ISBN 0-393-31821-4 pbk.

W. W. Norton & Company, Inc.
500 Fifth Avenue, New York, N.Y. 10110
http://web.wwnorton.com

W. W. Norton & Company Ltd.
10 Coptic Street, London WC1A 1PU

1 2 3 4 5 6 7 8 9 0

to Deborah

Contents

Acknowledgments

Many people have helped make this book possible, beginning with my editors at the *Wall Street Journal*, Alan Murray and Paul Steiger, who gave me the time and the encouragement necessary to get the project under way. Then there are those who patiently and generously guided me through the fog that normally surrounds this subject. Nicholas Eftimiades, Steven Bryen, Kenneth DeGraffenreid, Jan P. Herring, Noel D. Matchett, Roger Molander, George Lodge, Ira Magaziner, Robert Windrum, William C. Triplett II, Deborah Wince-Smith, Mindy Kotler, and several others who cannot be named went out of their way to help make sure that I didn't lose mine. Carl Bernard, Jean-Marie Bonthous, Jean-Marie Macabrey, and Christian Harbulot helped demystify the French. Stanislav Levchenko provided the central theme, and he and William W. Geimer helped me understand some of the Russian characters. Samuel F. Wells, Jr., Charles Blitzer, and the staff at the Woodrow Wilson International Center for Scholars provided the resources, the quiet, and an excellent, supportive place to write. Then there are the Center's researchers, Kalaya Chareonying, Laura Davis, and Blake Jones, whose enthusiasm and curiosity turned up many missing pieces. Finally, I am in debt to my agent, Ronald Goldfarb, and my editor at W. W. Norton & Company, Starling Lawrence. Whatever merit *War by Other Means* has, it starts with them.

Prologue:
The Ultimate Yankee

Slender threads of brownish smoke rose from a forest of chimneypots and twisted upward into the hovering winter mist. Together they wove a dark cloak that shrouded Edinburgh as a well-appointed carriage containing an American family appeared in the gloom of the old royal city. The coachman's faint lamp barely penetrated the gathering darkness as they rattled past the outlines of the city's tall, gaunt tenements. They were searching for lodging in a strange, forbidding place that reeked of dampness, dung, and smoke. It was a perfect setting for one of the world's great spy stories.

It was December 1811. There was one thing that distinguished Francis Cabot Lowell, his wife and young children from most of the others navigating the city's narrow streets that afternoon. While the British viewed the upstart United States as a trackless land of impoverished rustics, dangerous savages, bizarre religions, indomitable ignorance, and contagious diseases, there was this trickle of wealthy American tourists beginning to challenge the myth. The Lowells had plenty of money, and it showed. Alert coachmen hustled them through the knotty traffic of downtown Princes Street and innkeepers always summoned up an extra bit of warmth.

Lowell was no mere rich man's son. A Harvard graduate, he had used his skill as a mathematician to expand a Boston docking and warehouse business. Now, at thirty-five, well dressed, and studiously self-effacing, he was a man looking for a much grander venture. Lowell quickly fit into the local prejudices by letting it be known he was in Scotland for "reasons of health."[1] Lowell's neighbors observed that as winter receded the Lowell family carriage appeared almost daily in front of the house, and Mr. and Mrs. Lowell, leaving their children behind with the governess, went on extended trips into the countryside. They often visited places as far away as Lancashire and Derbyshire to take the country air.

That was the cover story. In fact, Lowell was the most skilled economic spy of his generation, and he had ambitions to take in much more than county air. By hitching cotton-making machinery to the cheap, perpetual motion of waterpower, Britain had revolutionized the textile industry, making Lancashire and Derbyshire into places of phenomenal riches. The newly built mills had literally created the world's industrial age. Lowell plotted his tours to methodically explore this eighteenth-century Silicon Valley. Huge fortunes had been made there by replacing the skilled hand labor of many thousands with water-driven looms so simple and so reliable they could be run by a handful of unskilled women and children. The perpetually humming, swishing, clanking machines changed cheap imported U.S. cotton to bolts of fancy calico that fetched fancy prices in Paris, Berlin, and Boston. They had made rural England into a money machine that was the envy of the world.

Not surprisingly, His Majesty's Government was determined to protect the secrets of the Industrial Revolution from outsiders. As early as the 1780s, the British passed rigorous patent laws and banned the export of cotton-making technology. When foreigners found loopholes by recruiting skilled workers and luring them abroad, this was made a crime. So were the acts of making and exporting drawings of the machinery in the mills. Fortresslike walls topped with spikes and broken glass quickly grew up around the mills, and workers were sworn to secrecy. Skilled technicians who went abroad under false pretenses had their property summarily confiscated by the crown.[2]

Spies are normally associated with wartime and the theft of military technology. In the vast popular literature about espionage, there is hardly a mention of the peacetime industrial spy. One reason may be because spy stories tend to blossom when wars end. War is relatively clear-cut: there is a winner and an eventual loser; a beginning and an end. The end is normally the signal for the memoir writers to begin, but the economic struggle that attracted Lowell's stealthy genius is not clear-cut. Winners win quietly, and losers are often either unconscious of loss, or too embarrassed to admit it.

And it is a war that does not end. The stage for the studiously low-key dramas of economic espionage is set, as one perceptive French writer puts it, in a kind of perpetual limbo, where there is "neither war not peace."[3]

Moreover, because economic competition often seems peaceful, economic espionage is usually a more fruitful, less risky business. Sentries are more frequently apt to be napping. Often there simply aren't any. The work of spies in wartime is dangerous and frequently marginally useful, but the damage a clever spy can wreak in a supposedly peaceful economic setting is "often invisible and decisive."[4] And the victim—especially if he must answer to angry stockholders—is not often inclined to want a history.

Against this background, the magnitude of what Lowell achieved has few parallels, even in spy fiction. Americans generally, do not recognize his name, but we are all indebted to this shrewd, secretive Yankee. By stealing England's most valuable secret, by analyzing it and quickly acting upon it, he brought the Industrial Revolution to New England and built the economic engine that later helped drive the North to victory in the Civil War. That, in turn, laid the cornerstone for a level of prosperity that created the "American Century," and led to the formation of the world's largest and richest economy.

Yankee ingenuity being what it once was, there were plenty of prominent Americans trying to steal secrets from England.[5] But none went as far as Lowell. He was after the Cartwright loom, the crown jewel of the British textile industry. This was a water-driven weaving machine invented by Edmund Cartright, the fourth son of a country squire; a restless, seemingly unfocused man who dabbled in poetry, the ministry, and experimental farming until he became intrigued by the shortcomings of some of the machinery he chanced to observe in the neighboring Derbyshire mills. So he dabbled in machinery. The result was a loom so powerful and efficient that the British Parliament later awarded him a bonus of £10,000. The importance of the Cartwright loom to Britain's booming economy placed it in the inner ring of a pantheon of industrial secrets.

We still don't know how Lowell got the detailed plans for this tightly guarded machine, but the arrogance of the new lords of Britain's industry probably helped him. They tended to look down upon outsiders, especially the American rustics. Some, such as Edward Temple Booth, owner of a Norwich worsted mill, waived the rule that said all plants wee to be closed to foreigners. He reasoned: "When machinery is peculiarly complicated you may show it with good effect, I think, because it makes the difficulty of imitation appear greater."[6] British Customs officers, perhaps sensing something was up, went through the Lowells' baggage twice when they embarked for home in 1813. They found nothing unusual because Lowell, who is credited by most historians as having a photographic memory, probably carried the blueprints in his head.[7]

Back home, Lowell rented a Boston storefront and hired a first-rate mechanic. Together, they built a scale model of the Cartwright loom. Then Lowell hired a second man to turn a crank until they had all gears and pulleys working in the rigid, reliable mechanical dance necessary for a perpetual weaving machine. When they had it right, Lowell quickly implemented his other plans, which involved new ways to integrate labor and capital into industrial plants where raw materials were turned into finished product in the same factory. His company built its first mill at Waltham and later constructed a complex of them at Lowell, the city named for him. By producing up to thirty miles of cloth a day in a nation that then knew very little besides hand labor, Lowell, Massachusetts, provided the first big shock that jolted America into the industrial age.

The object of economic espionage, however, is not simply to gain some secret advantage over a competitor. Steps must then be taken to slow the competitor's attempts at recovery. In 1816, a year before he died at the age of forty-two, Lowell journeyed to Washington, where he persuaded Congress to impose a punishing 6.25 cent tariff on each square yard of imported cotton.[8]

From Sidney Riley to Aldrich Ames, the secrets of wartime spies are the stuff of great drama when they emerge at war's end. But economic wars don't end, and Lowell appears to have taken pains to make sure his secrets would never emerge. He kept no diary, confined his letters to family matters, and appears to have shared the method of his great triumph with no one. A man whose impact was so profound that one historian calls him "An American Newton,"[9] Lowell almost managed to erase his likeness from posterity; but after he died, a workman found a silhouette stuck behind the frame of an old picture in Lowell's office. It shows a man with a long sloping nose and a weak chin. Apart from the largest, richest, industrial economy on earth, it is all we have left to remind us of Francis Cabot Lowell.

WAR
BY OTHER
MEANS

ONE

Hollowed Ground

If there were a way to revive this faceless man, Francis Cabot Lowell, and bring him back to his beloved country in the waning days of the 1990s, the story of Rip van Winkle would not begin to describe the otherworldly shock, the endless ironies, and the frustration that this spy of spies would experience.

He would discover that during the 180 years of his slumber, his world had been stood on its head. Let us take him, stumbling, bearded, and bleary-eyed, through several of the many corridors of our economy like some Ghost of Christmas Past, and see what he would find.

First, the spark of economic life that he helped bring into being has become a beacon to the entire world. The U.S. of America, once decidedly an economic backwater, a place of dubious investment opportunities, a haven for adventurers, visionaries, and the cast-off "poor" of other cultures, has become a glistening machine that produces $6.8 trillion worth of new wealth every year. Where Lowell's Washington had politicians who had firsthand experience with the results of unheeded security threats—such as being chased out of the White House by British troops—the Washington that Lowell would find on the eve of the twenty-first century is a place where most politicians believe the threats are over. Winners of a game that has supposedly ended, they talk endlessly of the perquisites and obligations of "the world's remaining superpower." The United States has the most robust economy, the biggest single market, the richest technological treasures, the most sprawling currency system, the largest free flow of information, the most powerful military, the most admired university system, and the most elaborate and costly apparatus of protective laws, lawyers, judges, intelligence services, and law enforcement units that the world has ever seen.

But once he overcame his initial shock at millions of people whizzing along concrete freeways, at vast, brazen cities winking at him by night, Lowell, a remarkably shrewd man, would quickly sense that something was missing. The public's belief in the value of economic intelligence that made him a national hero and that triggered parades in Revolutionary-era communities when new discoveries were brought in from abroad seems to have vanished entirely.[1] While Lowell knew a citizenry that was hungry for development and preoccupied with building an economy out of scraps of knowledge brought from overseas, he would now find a different breed of Americans, born with the assumption that all necessary knowledge is here. He would find an America drifting into a profoundly introspective, isolationist, and even anti-intellectual mood.

There would be no end to the paradoxes Lowell would find. Where there was once a small elite of entrepreneurial citizen-spies like himself who rubbed shoulders with the Washingtons, Jeffersons, and Hamiltons of his day, the matter of collecting intelligence in the America of the 1990s has become a strangely professional, closed, often suspect thing. It is dominated by huge bureaucracies that are almost silent when it comes to matters dealing with the economy. Unlike Japan, Sweden, China, France, South Korea, Taiwan, and other economic powers where Lowell types still abound, U.S. citizens have the feeling they are above this sordid business and that they are somehow removed and protected from it.

Only—Lowell would discover—they aren't. The game of economic espionage continues, as it has for thousands of years, but now the scores are locked inside the nation's sprawling intelligence apparatus, which costs some $28 billion a year to maintain.[2] And there is yet another fundamental difference: Whereas Lowell's America searched the world for fresh economic intelligence, America of the 1990s seems content to stay at home. This America has become the chief target of the world's economic spies. There are quite a number of them—from at least twenty major countries—but the matter of who they are and how they do it is considered a state secret.[3]

Lowell was a shrewd Yankee who knew how to obtain secrets, so let's suppose that in an effort to orient himself he got his hands on a copy of a report by an intergovernmental working group, the National Economic Council (NEC), which includes experts from the CIA, the FBI, the Departments of Treasury, State, Defense, Commerce, and Justice, and elements of the White House. Prepared for Congress's intelligence committees in 1994, the report is stamped "SECRET NORFORN." It says: "Reports obtained since 1990 indicate that economic espionage is becoming increasingly central to the operations of many of the world's intelligence services and is absorbing larger portions of their staffing and budget."[4]

This could involve a lot of people. In the early 1980s at the height of the Cold War, it was estimated that at least 1.2 million people were involved in the world's spy agencies.[5] Lowell would see that, according to the report, nations had brought a lot of their Cold War spy apparatus with them into economic espionage, including giant computer databases, word-activated eavesdropping scanners, spy satellites, and an almost unbelievable array of bugs and wiretaps.

Economic espionage in the United States breaks down into three major styles. Agents from China, Taiwan, and South Korea are aggressively targeting "present and former nationals working for U.S. companies and research institutions." The second category is headed by France, said to prefer "classic Cold War recruitment and technical operations," which generally include bribery, discreet thefts, combing through other people's garbage, and aggressive wiretapping. Russia and Israel carry out similar spying "with varying degrees of government sponsorship." Germany is described as planning to increase the number of its Federal Intelligence Service (BND) agents in Washington to improve its collection capabilities. Japan, which does not have a formal intelligence agency but sometimes collectively resembles one, falls in the third category. It uses Japanese industry and private organizations to gather "economic intelligence, occasionally including classified proprietary documents and data." The result is an exceptionally efficient spy network that is described as "not fully understood" by the United States.[6]

The most aggressive operations against U.S. companies occur overseas, especially in home countries where spy agencies are freer to act and where, the NEC report notes, "government controlled national phone networks" and other electronic means can be used to slither inside company communications and databanks. The best places to recruit foreign nationals who work for U.S. companies overseas is said to be in third countries, where "a host country's counterintelligence services do not pose a serious barrier to effective foreign intelligence operations directed against U.S. targets. Furthermore, U.S. citizens tend to be more lax about security matters when living in countries perceived as friendly to the United States."[7]

"Lax" is probably a polite way to describe the laid-back attitudes that Lowell might find as he wandered among his countrymen today. A more recent study by the National Research Council found that one way Japanese businessmen collect information about the U.S. aerospace industry—one of Japan's current major targets—is to get their U.S. counterparts to brag. "Ego comes into play as engineers try to impress their foreign contacts. . . ."[8]

The sublime mismatch between war-trained spies and business people schooled to expect the proverbial "level playing field" has also become worrisome in Canada, where Chris MacMartin, coordinator of the technology transfer program for Canada's Security Intelligence Service, says that of five hundred companies interviewed, fully one-third brought up security problems. Many of them had discovered that people they trusted were harvesting company secrets for a foreign government.

"When you're carrying over the family jewels and you're traipsing across several countries who would crawl over broken glass to get what you've got in your briefcase, you will inevitably find that the government has far greater capability to do damaging things to you than your competitor," explains MacMartin. Naive businessmen who entrust a document in their briefcase to the hotel safe, might "just as well photocopy it and give it to the company [that competes with them], because that's where it's going," MacMartin adds.

Just how much this costs companies is hard to say. "We have seen damage in terms of lost jobs, lost contracts, and diminished contracts. We have spoken to companies who have had messages intercepted and computers penetrated," MacMartin admits, but nobody wants to talk openly about it. "Companies have very solid reasons not to make this public. They usually have shareholders who think that secrets are what make the company valuable. Invariably in all of these cases, somebody screwed up."

Canada is not about to point fingers at any specific country, but MacMartin says that 39 percent of the spy incidents occurred in Asia and another 30 percent happened in Western Europe.[9]

U.S. companies aren't much more talkative. One, International Business Machines (IBM), told a House committee in 1992 that it had losses "in the billions" from thefts of proprietary information, including thefts by unnamed government agents intent on stealing IBM's software and other secrets for competitors in their country. Corning Inc. complained of state-sponsored efforts to steal its fiber-optic technology. "It is very difficult for an individual corporation to counteract this activity. The resources of a corporation—even a large one such as Corning—are no match for espionage activities that are sanctioned and supported by foreign governments," explained J. E. Reisbeck, then an executive vice president of the company.[10]

While the need seems obvious, the question of how to mobilize U.S. intelligence agencies to inform and protect the U.S. economy has bobbed to the surface in Washington every few years since World War II. When the Truman administration assembled twenty cabinet members for a secret meeting in the CIA's cramped, makeshift Administration Building on the Mall in November 1950, they were told that because foreign economic intelligence was collected by twenty-four different agencies, many of which didn't communicate with each other, there were "important gaps in the collective knowledge of the government." The turf battles involved in reassigning areas of responsibility in information gathering proved to be too difficult for this cabinet committee, however, and a CIA committee was established to study the problem.[11]

The issue came up again in 1970 when Nixon administration officials, shocked by Japan's bold and well-aimed assault on the U.S. auto industry, told the President's Foreign Intelligence Advisory Board (PFIAB) to suggest remedies. Gerard P. Burke, then PFIAB's chief of staff, recalls that his four-man staff spent about a year studying the problem. A few organizational changes were made to bring economic officials into policy-making boards in the intelligence community, but as Burke recalls no one could find a way to address the real issue he found: While the United States was tinkering with its organizational charts, the intelligence agencies of major allies, including the British, the French, the Swedes, and the Swiss, had begun providing direct support to their businesses. "We discussed it ad nauseam," Burke remembers. "We thought U.S. companies needed it [support], but we didn't think it should be provided by the U.S. government. There were obvious conflicts of interest."[12]

Stansfield Turner, the retired Navy admiral who took the helm of the CIA six years later, during the Carter administration, raised the same problem. Beyond the Soviet Union, the major threat to the United States came from the economic sphere. "Goddammit," he remembers thundering once at a group of aides, "if this [the economy] isn't a national security matter, then what is!?"

But the aides had questions. Should you collect information for Ford and not General Motors? Had CIA agents signed up to risk their lives for a U.S. company? What about providing intelligence to a U.S. company that was partly owned by Japan? In the end, the aides' skepticism prevailed. Since that debate in the late 1970s, CIA task forces have studied the issue two more times. Each study found a problem, but backed away from practical solutions. Admiral Turner recently fired another salvo. One way to break out of this stalemate, he says, is simply to make foreign espionage assaults on U.S. companies public. "That may aid U.S. corporations less than some would like, but it also can lessen an advantage foreign corporations have over American firms."[13]

In 1985, during the Reagan administration, Michael Sekora, a young physicist working in the Defense Intelligence Agency (DIA), became preoccupied with moves being made by French, German, and Japanese intelligence operatives in the commercial area. Some of them were busy collecting ideas from U.S. universities. Why not create a database to follow key technologies, tapping the whole government for information? President Reagan's people liked Sekora's idea and wanted the database and a small staff installed in the White House. The project was called "Socrates," but the incoming Bush administration strangled Socrates' philosophy in its crib. The project posed too many questions. "You can't look at the Japanese, they said, because they're our friends. You can only look at the Russians because they're the bad guys. What we wanted to do was look at the technologies, regardless of who had them. We wanted to get to the bottom-line truth, as did the philosopher," Sekora says.

Sekora resigned and is now peddling Socrates in the private sector with mixed results. He points out that many U.S. companies, preoccupied with the bottom line and the domestic market, have cut back on research units and see no use for strategic information gathered overseas. "When I'll go into a company, sometimes an old engineer will come up and say that's what we used to do before World War II. We sent our people all over the world."[14]

Indeed they did, and it wasn't just Lowell's generation, either. "Technology-gathering missions to Europe were commonplace during the late 19th and early 20th centuries as American corporations sent their leading scientists and engineers abroad to learn advance techniques. The uncanny ability of American corporations to improve on outside innovations astonished European industrialists in a way that is strikingly similar to the way Japan's success perplexes American managers today," writes Dr. Richard Florida, a technology expert at Carnegie Mellon University.[15]

In his strolls around modern Washington, a place he knew as a tiny village where carriages often became immobilized in the sticky red clay mud that constituted the streets of the capital, Francis Cabot Lowell would find that the report of President Clinton's commission to study the overhaul of the nation's intelligence apparatus had a familiar ring. The first item on its "new agenda" says: "Increasingly, the ability of U.S. industry to compete successfully in the world market is seen as a critical element of U.S. security."[16]

In the years between 1950 and 1996, as proposals to do something about obtaining economic intelligence kept getting mired in Washington's sticky bureaucracy, three successive waves of economic espionage rolled over the country. Measured in terms of economic and strategic impact, they were all tsunamis, probably the most damaging peacetime assaults ever mounted on a nation's economy. Each, in its own way, was worse than the next. But compared with real wars, they caused hardly a ripple.

First came the Russians. In the early 1980s, just as it was about to rev up the arms race, the Reagan administration learned from the French how the Soviet economy, with all of its glaring faults, managed to match U.S. technology so quickly: The KGB had been systematically stealing information from U.S. research and development programs. "The assimilation of Western technology is so broad that the U.S. and other Western nations are thus subsidizing the Soviet military buildup," concluded a CIA report on the matter.[17]

A group known as the VPK or Military Industrial Commission, a special board of the top executives of Russian defense-manufacturing ministries, had been spending as much as $1.4 billion a year ordering technology and secrets from the West, much of it taken from the electronic brains of new U.S. weapons systems. The list, provided from a KGB spy dubbed "Farewell" by French intelligence agents, was endless, and embarrassingly familiar to the Pentagon. The Soviet "Ryad" computer had been copied from the architecture of IBM's 370.

The radars that guided the missiles shot from Soviet fighters were copied from blueprints of the radars on U.S. F-14, F-15, and F-18 fighters. Russia's space shuttle was created from documents carted away from NASA. In all, about 5,000 categories of Russian military equipment entering its arsenals in the eighties came from the KGB's efforts; about 60 percent of the blueprints and other documents was taken either from the United States or from allied nations.[18]

Farewell's reports showed the KGB had caught the United States with its barn doors wide open. While the Defense Department proved the information's authenticity, other agencies—true to the ostrichlike code of victims of economic intelligence—tried to minimize it. The CIA kept most of the evidence under tight wraps. Some former officials of the FBI—which is in charge of counterintelligence—cling to their belief that the barn was never invaded.

Big as it was, the Russian wave of economic collection was soon overshadowed by Japan's efforts. While Russia's industry outside the defense area couldn't readily assimilate U.S. technology, the Japanese economy could, and in the seventies and eighties it did so at an awesome pace. Like the Russians, the Japanese found U.S. universities to be an enormous source of free, lucrative information, and, oddly, the Japanese provided a kind of political cover for the Russian "students."

As a CIA officer, Jan P. Herring helped run the CIA's counterespionage efforts in the early 1980s. After several Russian KGB types were caught stealing secrets at universities, he recalls, the U.S. government was seriously thinking about kicking out all foreign students. "The Japanese just went ape over this, so we backed off." Later, as a vice president for The Futures Group, a Boston-based consulting firm, Herring went to universities hunting for ways to help U.S. firms compete against foreign competition—a novel idea for some of his clients. "We often found that MITI (Ministry of Japan's International Trade Industry) or JETRO [MITI's technology information collection service] had already been there talking to these people. In fact, we didn't run across too many that the Japanese hadn't talked to."[19]

When it comes to other people's ideas, the Japanese are relentless bargain hunters. Every scrap of information is collected and studied. They set up an elaborate network of small research laboratories in university towns. Gaining a sense from the universities where the new, cutting-edge U.S. technology was, the Japanese then went out and bought some forty thousand patent licenses for it at bargain basement rates. U.S. experts later concluded this was a "windfall" that gave Japan the keys to take over the television and semiconductor markets. It taught some "hard lessons" to U.S. companies, who enjoyed their royalty checks until Japan's products drove them out of their markets.[20]

U.S. economists, locked for years in an almost monastic argument over the sanctity of "free trade," have only recently tumbled to the notion that the carefully targeted, government-driven campaign Japan uses against the United States in high-technology areas is something different from the bustle and hum of free markets working. It is more like the attack profile of a smart missile: a strategic, "beggar thy neighbor" assault that targets high-tech jobs and snuffs out whole industries. Laura D'Andrea Tyson, who currently heads President Clinton's Council of Economic Advisers, estimates that Japan's aggressive efforts cost $105 billion in lost U.S. sales between 1985 and 1989, and that "the lion's share of the loss was matched by offsetting Japanese gains."[21]

What is left is a strangely hollowed-out economy that continues to function, even to boom, but it is a decidedly pale version of our manufacturing past. In constant, uninflated dollars, average weekly wages have dropped for twenty years. There are fewer, poorer, dumber jobs for blue-collar workers. It is a hollowness that will, increasingly, resonate as a life-threatening issue to politicians who ignore it. "My belief is that the decline of living standards is at the bottom of all of our discontent and a major cause of that is our decline in competitive position," says Ira Magaziner, President Clinton's domestic affairs adviser.[22]

We are losing at a game of economic jiu-jitsu where Japan, which keeps its markets closed and does relatively little research within its largely closed university system, uses one of the U.S. system's main strengths—its openness—against it. And the struggle continues as MITI targets the remaining crown jewels, the aerospace, biotechnology, and software industries that are expected to be the drivers of the U.S. economy in the early twenty-first century. While the fabled and probably fictitious "missile gap" was used politically to galvanize U.S. concerns in the sixties about the Soviet Union, the patently real "intelligence gap" posed by the Japanese has caused no outcry. But to the eye of a practiced collector, such as Lowell's, the gap would look ominous and perhaps even frightening. In 1988, Japan sent 52,224 researchers to the United States. Meanwhile, 4,468 U.S. researchers went to Japan.[23] Japanese companies invest the time and money to teach their people English and the U.S. culture. U.S. companies rarely bother.

What Japan has accomplished in the United States has caused a stir of envy in China and other Pacific Rim nations, including Taiwan and South Korea. The other Asian nations' collection efforts in the United States may eventually loom larger and more threatening than the Japanese campaign, which they appear to be using as a model. Once again, they began in U.S. universities. In 1991, 51 percent of all science and engineering doctorates awarded by U.S. universities went to students from Pacific Rim nations, with the dragon's share going to the two Chinas. Many of these students— educated largely at the expense of the U.S. government-linger in the United States after obtaining their doctorates, and a large number of high-tech companies and U.S. government research laboratories are becoming hooked on this stream of cheaper, often smarter and more biddable talent.[24] Some of these students eventually become U.S. citizens and help renew the American dream by achieving breakthroughs that mean new jobs and new markets for their new homeland. But many go back, and government recruiters from their native countries are working here to lure more home, where they become serious and sometimes dangerous competitors. Meanwhile, the faltering U.S. public education system produces fewer and fewer qualified applicants for graduate-level science and engineering.

By far the largest, most problematic player is the People's Republic of China, a nuclear power, which is using U.S. technology and some of the profits from a ballooning trade surplus with the United States to modernize its army, navy, and air force. It has begun to flex its growing military muscle in the Pacific. In a series of war games in the Taiwan Straits in March 1996, it fired its new, solid fuel M-9 missiles at target ranges situated near Taiwan's main seaports. China's prime intelligence agency, the *Guojia Anquan Bu*, or Ministry of State Security (MSS), has flooded the United States with spies, sending in far more agents than the Russians even at the height of the KGB's phenomenal campaign. About half of nine hundred illegal technology transfer cases being investigated on the West Coast involve the Chinese. The MSS recruits students. When money is not persuasive, threats against family members back home often are. And unlike the KGB, China's spies easily find protective cover in the large U.S. Asian population.[25]

Although the FBI makes an effort to watch foreign students and business people, China's flood has simply overwhelmed the bureau. "The FBI is ensnarled in a cesspool of Chinese agents and their cases are all stuck at first base," says James Lilley, former U.S. ambassador to China and former CIA station chief in Beijing.[26]

Unlike the Japanese, whose military-derived strategies are usually focused on ways to take over commercial markets, China's strategists have military goals. They covet things like missile guidance systems that can use signals from our satellite-based Global Positioning System for precise targeting information. They go after small cruise missile engines, night-vision equipment, upper-stage rockets, and nose cones for globe-spanning nuclear weapons—all items that may fundamentally shift the balance of power in the next decade and drive countries like Japan and Taiwan into full-blown nuclear weapons programs. "You're going to see an arms race in Asia that is unequaled in history," predicts Nicholas Eftimiades, the author of *Chinese Intelligence Operations*, the first open study of China's massive efforts.[27]

Despite the ominous look of things, Lowell would find that the worrying was confined to a small group of academics, corporate security experts, and intelligence analysts, and that most of his countrymen were oddly serene. They were accustomed to this seemingly comfortable new post–Cold War drift of things. In the media, the lowering of trade barriers and the influx of foreign students is often portrayed as part of a vast, multicultural economic march toward a peaceful "globalism." Increasingly, the notion of borders is dismissed as old-hat.

"In Taiwan," explained a front-page *New York Times* article, "the high-tech migration is being called the 'rencai hiliu,' literally the 'return flow of human talent.' But for the thousands of American-trained scientists, weaned on late-night pizza at the computer center and shopping at the mall, it is simply called the reverse brain drain."[28]

To the modern American mind, this might seem normal. To Lowell's nineteenth-century mind—fresh from a time when the United States fought for its borders and established its industrial base—it would raise a thousand questions. Why were foreign science and engineering students increasingly taking top graduate research posts at places like Harvard and the Massachusetts Institute of Technology? Why was the U.S. government paying for them? Why had U.S. student scores in math—a subject that gave Lowell great pleasure and great wealth—dropped to among the lowest in the industrial world? Who had let the U.S. public school system—once the envy of the civilized world—decline to such an abysmal state? Were U.S. brains being drained or starved and rejected? Was the nation's base for creating technology, the bedrock of preparedness for all wars in this century, being exported? Why?

The notion of a "war by other means" might seem foreign to some, but Lowell, a fan of protective tariffs, would probably see one looming behind the much-touted lowering of trade barriers. One effect that has been generally ignored by global trade enthusiasts has been the formation of an international mafia, an alliance between the Russian and Italian mafias and Colombian drug cartels, that has taken advantage of the relaxed sovereignty to move money from county to country much faster than national police forces can track it. According to the U.S. Treasury Department, they now send some $100 to $300 billion around the world looking for investments. Casualties of drugs flowing into the United States already closely approximate a war.[29] And the massive profits that flow out of this alliance light the fuses of future wars by criminalizing entire countries and buying elections, politicians, and officials to thwart U.S.-backed reforms.[30]

Lowell's world was Darwinian: You could keep what you could protect. It is still Darwinian when it comes to cross-border transactions, but Americans in the post–Cold War era feel they are protected in a snug, seamless, global cocoon of laws, customs, and rights. When it comes to some new things, such as the nation's galloping addiction to electronic information, the cocoon is hardly more than a fiction.

"People don't understand what's out there," explains Ambassador Anthony C. E. Quainton, who until recently headed the State Department's Overseas Advisory Council (OSAC). The Council was formed in 1985 to help U.S. corporations deal with the threat of terrorism. In the nineties, reports from some of the 1,300 U.S. corporations that OSAC communicates with shifted the group's attention more toward economic espionage.

The most aggressive intrusions come in Japan, South Korea, and China, where threat begins with the telephone sitting on the hotel room's bedstand. Quainton says he knows of entire hotels where the phones are set to receive, even when they're hung up—"The whole hotel is live." He strongly advises business people not to talk about technology, patents, or business plans in their rooms. "If they can't see the enemy, they may not think he's there, but he is."

This is a hard notion to sell to normally garrulous U.S. businessmen. Jan Herring, the former CIA counterintelligence expert, recalls making many visits to companies to warn them that when they make calls from overseas, they are "talking to the world." On the average call, Herring estimates, a "minimum" of five countries could be listening. "It always begins with your host country, then there were the Soviets, the British, the Chinese, and the Japanese." By law, he notes, the National Security Agency (NSA), America's eavesdropping agency, can't listen to Americans, but they might be tapping the second party on the line if he or she is a foreigner. While governments still hold sway over the phone lines, newer forms of communications including satellite links and cellular phones are much easier to tap, and have thus tempted thousands, perhaps tens of thousands of amateurs to get into the spy game.

And the threat is still higher when it comes to use of computers. "If you are using the Information Highway internationally, especially without encryption, you are at great risk," Roger P. Watson, an FBI deputy assistant director, recently told a group of business security executives. But the bureau has found new habits are hard to change. Harold Henderschot, the FBI's top computer expert, says he often visits companies and finds they have piled their computer security equipment in a corner, uninstalled. The usual explanation is that it makes the computers too cumbersome and slow.[31]

Lowell, a man used to thinking in terms of the whine of gears meshing and the rhythmic stutter of levers working, might have trouble getting his Newtonian mind around electronic technologies, but he would quickly recognize the law that protects them—a law that hasn't changed all that much since his time. Today, it lags far behind the threat. Part of the problem is that victims don't complain. "The only thing a company will protect more than its information is the fact that they've lost it," explains Dan Swartwood, head of a private security consulting company. If there are mute victims, or victims who don't know they are victims, there are no witnesses, no complaints, no cases, no new law, and no actuarial base for insurance underwriters.

A new survey of 325 unnamed American companies done by Swartwood and a colleague, Richard J. Heffernan, shows that this troublesome void is rapidly growing. The companies reported thirty-two cases of theft of intellectual information per month in 1995, more than three times the rate found in a similar survey in 1992. The losses amounted to $5.1 billion. The most common suspect was a former employee, a contractor, supplier, or temporary. Ranked by nationality and frequency of complaints, the top perpetrators were Chinese, Canadian, French, Indian, and Japanese, in that order.[32] The survey's findings roughly track with the experience of the FBI, which is currently investigating eight hundred economic espionage cases involving twenty-three foreign countries. The agency's load of such cases has doubled since 1994.[33]

Then there are pesky definitial problems. If a horse is stolen from the neighbor's barn, that is a serious theft; but if his exotic, proprietary million-dollar software program is surreptitiously removed and zipped away on the

Internet, that may not be a serious theft because the "horse," the original copy, is still in the barn.[34]

Similarly, if a spy comes out of a foreign embassy and snatches a company's secret, that is espionage and automatically brings in the FBI. If a spy comes from a private company or a university and steals the same secret, the FBI may not have a legal basis to intervene.[35] More than a few corporate victims decide to suffer their losses in silence (out of the view of stockholders) and not summon in the FBI. "I know it's a controversial topic . . . there are a whole myriad of problems here, but we need each other," explained Pat Bryant, the FBI's chief of internal security, to a group of corporate executives at a recent OSAC meeting at the State Department. He pleaded with the companies to give the bureau more detail about the nature of their losses, and urged them to use their lobbying clout to help push for more modern laws.

"What we need is more ammunition from you to show how great the threat really is," countered one executive.

Edward Miller is a former president of the National Center for Manufacturing Sciences, a government-industry consortium founded in 1984 to help renew U.S. high technology and promote it abroad. He often hears the same kind of death-spiral, chicken-or-egg logic. Without dramatic proof of theft and damage, he says, U.S. companies simply won't change their ways. But without changing their ways, many companies will never be able to generate dramatic proof. Miller worries that America's feeble defenses against economic espionage from the sixties to the eighties have now put the scent of U.S. blood in the air. It creates a hunger for more. He recalls a barrel-shaped Czech engineer yawning during a technical meeting in Prague some months ago. Miller, also an engineer, had been talking about the promise of new U.S. machines. The Czech shrugged; that wasn't the need in his factory.

Miller challenged him. "I said, if I went into your facility, would I find the latest design capabilities, the latest computer-controlled machines? He says, 'Yeah.'"

During the Cold War anything the Czech government factory needed, the engineer explained, was quickly stolen by the KGB from the United States or developed from stolen blueprints. The process took a few months. The upshot of the KGB connection—now ended—is that Czech plants are relatively modern. "What we need are management skills, marketing, and accounting," said the engineer.

"I had one U.S. government representative there whose jaw hit the floor," recalls Miller. "What they were essentially telling us was that their espionage defeated us. If they defeated us when our guard was up, do you honestly think they would stop?"

To Miller, understanding the problem of economic espionage is simple; the matter of dealing with it, though, is formidable. "We are an open society. What we have to learn is how to get as much as we give away."[36] It will be a strange, daunting challenge for some, but one that would make Mr. Lowell feel quite at home.

TWO

Little Fish

Now the reason the enlightened prince and the wise general conquer the enemy whenever they move and their achievements surpass those of ordinary men is foreknowledge. . . . What is called "foreknowledge" cannot be elicited from spirits, nor from gods, nor by analogy with past events, nor from calculations. It must be obtained from men who know the enemy situation.
—Sun Tzu, 483–402 B.C.

On a hot summer day in 1989, Bin Wu, a thin, boyish-looking college philosophy instructor, hurried into the ornate interior of the Old Cadres' Club, the top hotel in Nanjing, China.

It was a rare oasis of quiet amid the bustle of Nanjing, a large manufacturing center. The fine thick carpets muffled the sound of Wu's steps; the low *whoosh* of its air conditioners all but masked the distant *pok-pok-pok* from the hotel's carefully tended tennis courts. The Old Cadres' Club was a kind of never-never-land for young people like Wu. It was a political officers' club, membership restricted to senior party officials—a dividend for Mao Tse-tung's old warriors who had long since paid their dues to China and its Communist Party.

Fidgeting and chain-smoking, Wu, twenty-three, was about to pay his dues in another way. He was about to become a warrior, but not in the sense that most westerners would understand. Our notion of war is head-on: Gettysburg, the Somme, Normandy, Stalingrad, Okinawa, Hamburger Hill, Khesan, Kuwait. Many of us are taught a history that is punctuated and defined by battles. We understand games of combat: the quick hits of football, the stirring attacks of soccer. There are lines, rules, swaggering winners, limping, dejected losers.

Wu was ushered into one of the hotel rooms where he found several older men waiting for him. Their notion of war was quite different because Sun Tzu, a Chinese warrior-philosopher who is believed to have written some

450 years before Christ, still casts a long shadow in the Far East. He wrote: "For to win one hundred victories in one hundred battles is not the acme of skill. To subdue the enemy without fighting is the acme of skill." War to the Chinese is a matter of guile, feints, endless patience, and above all spies, whose intelligence often reveals the enemy's weak point that, when struck, makes the battle shortlived or unnecessary. Brute strength counts for little. "If ignorant both of your enemy and of yourself, you are certain in every battle to be in peril." But the matter of dealing with agents who carry knowledge of an enemy counts for everything. "It is essential to seek out enemy agents who have come to conduct espionage against you and to bribe them to serve you. Give them instructions and care for them. Thus doubled agents are recruited and used."[1]

The most familiar to Wu among the older men in the room was Zhao Zi-Heng, a Ministry of State Security (MSS) man who had befriended the young instructor during his endless interrogations after the anti-Western crackdown at He Hai University in Nanjing, where Wu taught. Zi-Heng liked to be called "Mr. Shen." Then there was Zi-Heng's boss, and an old man with white hair sitting behind a dim lamp in the corner. The old man was described deferentially as "Mr. Top," the big MSS boss from Beijing. The three continued drinking tea and smoking after Wu entered. As they exchanged pleasantries, Wu peered at the old man through his thick, black-rimmed glasses. Because the curtains on the windows were tightly drawn, all the young teacher could see in the dim light was the glow of Mr. Top's cigarette and his snow white hair. It seemed to radiate toward him in the darkness. The old man nodded occasionally during the conversation, as the other two discussed how Mr. Wu would become a "sleeper," a long-term spy for China in the United States. Throughout, the white head kept nodding. The old man said nothing, but Wu felt he had won his approval.

The other two outlined the rationale for Wu's mission: Since the United States was one of the major enemies of the China, China was preparing for a "long battle." Wu had been carefully selected to be a special player. He would collect critical economic information and technology from the United States in much the same way Japanese businessmen did for their country. Wu would become a successful businessman, they explained. He would patiently, steadily work his way up into the U.S. power structure. He would come to know congressmen and senators and perhaps, one day, even be able to report information from the White House. He would never be alone. "Someone will always be worrying about you."[2]

Wu mostly agreed with the older men. Although the tone of the talk was friendly, it was quietly understood in the dark, smoky room that the MSS had put Wu in a vise that could squeeze him quite painfully if ever he attempted to resist the mission. The young man, who says he had never intended to leave China, was quietly resigned to his fate.

Bin Wu is an avid reader of Ernest Hemingway's novels and he has found that the simplest way to convey his situation to Americans is to describe himself as one of China's "Lost Generation." Hemingway's generation lost its innocence in the Great War. Wu's had watched their parents become inexorably sucked into the strange, crazy, quicksand politics of Mao Tse-tung's Great Cultural Revolution. In the eighties, when Wu came to college, the pendulum had shifted: China had begun to recollect itself and open its borders to foreigners and foreign ideas. "We slowly built our faith, our values up on Western sources, on Western freedoms." In 1986, after he became a philosophy instructor at He Hai University in Nanjing, Wu kept a short-wave radio in his room. He often invited students in after class to listen to the Voice of America. He gave pro-Western speeches.

There were others in China who were also rapidly adapting to Western ways, only they were not focusing on freedom. In June 1983, for example, the MSS was formed by combining the espionage, intelligence, and security functions of the former Ministry of Public Security with the investigations branch of the Communist Party's Central Committee. What had been largely an internal instrument used to hunt down and annihilate political dissidents was now going to do some hunting abroad, like its model, Russia's huge, far-flung KGB. And China's People's Liberation Army, once known for its rigid, antiquated human-wave attacks, was busy forming *quantou*, or "Fist Units": highly mobile, well-equipped 6,000- to 10,000-man outfits that appeared to be modeled after the U.S. Army's 82nd Airborne Division. They were training to react quickly and decisively to crises. And when one of them did just that, crushing a huge student demonstration in Tiananmen Square on June 4, 1989, Bin Wu's life was changed forever.

At He Hai, a second-level university, teachers who had expressed pro-Western sentiments were put on a list. One of Wu's colleagues was beaten senseless by local police. Wu saw that his own name was second from the top of the list. "In that summer vacation, I couldn't leave my university. They brought a special case against me." Over a hundred students and teachers went to jail, but Wu found himself being grilled at the university every day, six or seven hours a day, by three or four stern-faced internal security policemen. They always demanded to know more about his politics and acquaintances. This went on, he says, from July through October. Then he met a very different sort of interrogator, "Mr. Shen," the MSS man. "He didn't question me. He said, we've got something to talk over. He was very friendly." But at first the MSS man's motives seemed obscure. "What they wanted exactly I didn't know. Chinese, they don't say things straight out like Americans."

Over the winter and into the spring of 1990, the MSS laid out a series of choices for Wu. He could, like the other faculty members, end up in prison. Or he could go to the United States for the MSS, which would then promise to take care of his mother and father and younger brother. The MSS even agreed to let Jie Ying Wang, Wu's college sweetheart, have the necessary papers to join Wu in the United States once he had proven himself there.

Wu, deeply in love, wanted that very badly. Now that his economic future seemed secure, he proposed to her and they were married in August 1990.

It was a classic spy recruitment, a process that is known in the intelligence trade as putting an agent "under discipline." Wu's handlers had determined he could be trusted; their "little fish" was judged to be hooked through a combination of fear, concern for his family, and the other baits they had dangled before him. Although many other nations recruit spies in this process, China's operations are different because the MSS recruits armies while other nations recruit platoons. "A lot of people are using their intelligence agents to collect from us in the economic area," says Henry "Skip" Brandon, who recently retired as deputy chief of the FBI's counter-intelligence division. "But the Chinese are a giant vacuum cleaner."[3]

There may a thousand Bin Wu's. Nicholas Eftimiades, the U.S. Defense Intelligence Agency analyst, who has written the first coherent book about MSS spy operations, says the term within the agency is *cheng di yu*, or "fish at the bottom of the ocean." The little fish are sent to the United States to grow, to be activated years, maybe decades later. Because China currently floods the United States with fifteen thousand students a year and recruits its agents from among the candidates being considered for student visas, Eftimiades estimates there could be "a minimum of several hundred long-term agents operating here."[4]

During his meeting at the Old Cadres' Club, Wu was handed a three-page list of U.S. high-tech items and told to memorize it and give it back. "I told them my major was philosophy. I don't know technology. They said, that's okay, we want you for the long term, learn their economics, have a longtime stay in the U.S. Be successful. Be a VIP and have your connections." Wu was so nervous and anxious to get out of that room that he could recall only two items from the list: a piece of computer interface software and a radar system.

The list of items to be stolen was probably mid-level technology, items sometimes as much as fifteen years old. The thefts would be of great help to China, whose economy and military are still emerging out of an almost feudal era of corruption and repression, but they were carefully selected to be just below the political threshold of pain in the United States. From the point of view of the Pentagon, much of what China seeks is outmoded. From the point of view of most U.S. prosecutors, according to Eftimiades, China cases are little more than legal nuisances. "How do you convince a district attorney that this is damaging to national security? Does he do this case or does he prosecute a case involving three kilos of smack [heroin]. The answer is always going to be three kilos of smack."[5]

Little fish also come very cheap. U.S. intelligence agencies have discovered that one of the MSS's many skills is getting the United States to pay most of the costs of their espionage. China and other Far East countries are believed deliberately to form consulting firms to help U.S. companies create business ties abroad. Some of that money is then used to finance espionage in the United States. "We tell U.S. businesses this activity is going on," says Robert A. Messemer, an FBI counterintelligence expert in Los Angeles. "Many of these efforts are directed at the very same companies that they are cooperating with overseas . . . they're funding the operations that are being run against them."[6]

In the case of Bin Wu, the MSS had discovered he had a cousin who ran a computer business in Norfolk, Virginia. "They talked a lot about my cousin," recalls Wu. Approached by Bin Wu's mother, who was distraught at the thought of her son the bookish philosophy professor spending the rest of his life rotting in a Chinese prison, the cousin agreed to receive Wu and give him a job. Suddenly the threat of prosecution for Wu's pro-Western activities, the subject of four months of almost daily interrogation at his university, evaporated. The precious passport with the U.S. visa stamp, which had been denied because Wu had flunked the government's required English test, materialized.

The shock of his sudden plunge into the world of freedom he knew only from books gave Wu second thoughts. In November 1990, on the flight over,

Wu decided that he might not follow all of the MSS's orders. Once settled in America, he thought, he would try to ignore the MSS. That wasn't easy. Mr. Shen, his MSS handler, sent him a Christmas card, then a letter and a fax. "They all said, 'Don't worry. We are old friends and we will take care of your wife and your family.' That was blackmail; they wanted a response," Wu recalls. Late that winter, feeling homesick, Wu confided his problem over a few drinks to another Chinese immigrant, Jing Ping Li, who was also working at his cousin's business. Mr. Li said he had a friend who might just be able to help Wu.

On April 17, 1991, Li took Wu to the parking lot of a suburban mall. There, in front of the Sears store, Li introduced Wu to two FBI agents. One was Blake Lewis, forty-eight, a twenty-four-year veteran of the FBI. He had recently been switched from tracking bank embezzlements to the job of ferreting out potential spies in Norfolk's rapidly growing community of several thousand immigrants from China and Taiwan. The other was Bruce Carlson, an agent from Washington who spoke to Wu in fluent Chinese. They went to a beachfront hotel where the FBI had rented a room for the day. As the surf rhythmically washed the beach, Wu recalls the four men discussed many things. At one point, "Mr. Carlson said they [the FBI] don't have much money to follow every Chinese. I said, I understand the situation."

But the FBI had enough to pay Wu to become a double agent, or as Lewis later wrote in a memo to Washington, "a window" on the workings of the MSS. Li pocketed $800 for introducing Wu to the FBI. For Wu's cooperation, the FBI promised $700 a month, a fax machine, and rent money for an office. If things worked out, they said, the government would let him stay in the United States.

And so, in the annals of the FBI, Wu became known as "Succor Delight" or "Source 422." As a team, Wu and his new handler were something of a mismatch. Wu was a graduate of Fudan University in Shanghai, China's equivalent of Harvard. Agent Lewis had an accounting degree from Strayer College, an obscure business school in Washington, D.C. Wu, a quick study, was rapidly getting up to speed in English and U.S. business methods. Lewis had had a two-week course in general counterintelligence methods and was fumbling around with a "pictionary," a handheld computer that turned English words into their Chinese symbols.

Nonetheless, the two managed to develop a close relationship. Wu gave Blake silk robes and delicate Chinese tile paintings. Blake began to worry about Wu the way one would about a second son. He soon began to let Source 422 do the translations of the messages he was receiving from his other handler, Mr. Shen, in China.[7]

All this gave Wu a busy summer in 1991. Blake wanted to meet with him five times a week. He sent a wire to Washington telling his FBI chiefs that Wu's information was "exceptionally valuable" and had Wu promoted to the status of "operating asset."

Then, one day in August, Wu got word from Mr. Shen: The MSS wanted to see him in Washington. Wu recalls driving to a suburban town house where a short man, puffing nervously on a cigarette, took him to an upstairs room, turned up the volume on a radio, then reached under a bed and extracted $2,000 in fresh new bills from a valise. As the man handed him the cash, carefully keeping the wad below the sill of a nearby window, "he said, 'Very good, you're beginning much more quickly than we expected,'" recalls Wu. Wu took the money back to Agent Lewis, who put it in a special fund he used to finance Wu's counterintelligence operations.

Operating out of one room in a small white office building next to a McDonalds in the vast sprawl of Virginia Beach, Wu and Li set up two export companies that took orders from his MSS contacts in Hong Kong and tried to fill them with U.S. companies. Using Li as a front man, because of his superior English, Wu soon had contracts to export an underwater camera and a power amplifier for satellite communications. The items were legally exportable and the two Chinese extracted a fat profit by marking up the prices they charged the MSS. According to Nicholas Eftimiades, the markups are another hallmark of the way the MSS network functions: "From a Chinese perspective, many of them [the spies] look at this as just doing business." Many China cases, he says, are characterized by people floating in and out of deals at different levels. While it might appear sloppy or "poor tradecraft" to a KGB or a CIA agent, the complexity makes the overall pattern of China's operations a puzzle for U.S. counterintelligence agents that is very difficult to piece together. Eftimiades says that China's agents have set up a maze of some 795 companies in the United States. Many are one- and two-man operations like Li and Wu's. Others are tentacles of the People's Liberation Army.

In the fall of 1991 came the dream deal. Mr. Shen, Wu's Chinese handler, wired that the People's Liberation Army wanted one thousand night-vision scopes. Wu found he could get them from a Garland, Texas, company, Varo Inc., for $1,500 a pop. MSS contacts in Hong Kong agreed to pay

$2,105 each. That promised a tidy $500,000 profit. As a further sweetener, Wu's wife Jie Ying Wang had been given her passport and was arriving in New York in November.

The MSS had pegged one thing about Wu that was right: He was a careful collector of what seemed most valuable. In China, it had been books; he had assembled a library of fifteen hundred volumes. In the United States, Wu had found another coinage: symbols of wealth. Wu and Li met Jie at the airport in Wu's newly purchased 1987 Mercedes with vanity plates that said "BINJAIN" a combination of his and his wife's name in English. His wife handed him a further gift from the MSS, $630 in cash—the equivalent of her annual salary—and Wu explained his new business to her on the way back to Norfolk. As she recalled it later, Wu's philosophy of his new business was based on what he termed the "unharmful principle." If Wu could help his country and not harm his family or his business associates, he would do it.

Ultimately, night-vision devices are harmful. They magnify the available light at night into a kind of greenish daylight, revealing targets unseen by the naked eye. The tubes the MSS wanted were the same ones the U.S. Army used on its M-1 tanks as they blew their way through Iraq's elite Republican Guard divisions in the Gulf War. China's army had used them before, but since the United States cracked down on China in the wake of the violence at Tiananmen Square in 1989, they were deemed illegal for export to China. As a Varo expert later testified, what Mr. Wu had ordered was state-of-the-art U.S. technology, made of fiber optics and exotic ceramics. The tubes had a limited shelflife since their batteries and other components eventually wore out. Both Japanese and German scientists had tried to copy the device and failed. The United States had put the night-vision scopes on the same non-proliferation lists that they put nuclear weapons and missile guidance systems. Whoever got them could almost instantly double the fighting power of an army because it could conduct large scale maneuvers and attacks at night. The CIA tries to keep careful track of potential enemies and such capabilities. As Sun Tzu put it, in war, "foreknowledge" is everything.

But nobody seemed to know or care about Bin Wu. Mr. Wu sent an order to Varo for a first batch of forty-four image-intensifier tubes, the key piece in night-vision scopes, assuring the company they were for domestic purposes. Then he shipped them off to an MSS contact company in Hong Kong in a box labeled "OPTIC TUBES." He listed the cost as $7,900. Wu later insisted that Blake Lewis, his FBI handler, knew and encouraged the scheme.

The FBI denied that, saying Wu had become progressively less communicative as the night-vision deal progressed.

As he began to prosper, Wu attracted some strange friends. First there was Mr. Li, then forty, who had come to the United States as a visiting scholar at Old Dominion University. As Li later explained it, he wanted to "learn about American business" and help China enter the world market. Li refused to return to China, insisting on remaining in America. At times he seemed to verge on superpatriotism—he named his son Robert E. Li. But U.S. investigators were skeptical. Li had arrived with two Chinese passports, one with a Russian visa, another with a Canadian visa—usually a mark of high political connections. Then in the United States he acquired two wives. He seemed to have a knack for breaking rules. An assistant U.S. attorney for Norfolk, James A. Metcalfe, later described him "as a person who apparently cannot cross the street without looking for a red light."

When Wu and Li had a falling out over money, Wu bought out Li's share of their joint enterprise and brought in Pinzhe Zhang, then thirty-five. Zhang had worked for China's Foreign Ministry, and because of his fluent English, happened to be the first Chinese national employed by the U.S. Embassy in Beijing. Now he was working his way through graduate school at Old Dominion University by waiting on tables and moonlighting as a security guard. Zhang, too, had also arrived with two passports. Zhang used his superior English to help Wu draft his contracts with Varo and place orders over the phone. Wu also had a letter from a Chinese man who owned a company in Texas. He wrote that he heard Wu was involved in a prosperous business deal and wanted an introduction.

By October 1992, Wu, Li, and Zhang had exported 144 tubes and the MSS contacts in Hong Kong were eager for more. The Little Fish had taken the plunge, ordering another four hundred. Meanwhile, Blake Lewis had become increasingly worried about his charge's lifestyle. He focused on the Mercedes. It had to go. "Blake Lewis mentioned it to me many, many times," recalled Wu. "He said, it's too flash for you, for young Chinese people here." Wu traded it for a Dodge.

Then, on October 7, something very strange happened. As he walked into his office that morning, bearing a carryout breakfast from the neighboring McDonalds, Wu was arrested by a team of U.S. Customs agents, including a man with a video camera that recorded the event. There are several different kinds of intelligence practiced by the U.S. government. SIGINT in spy agency lingo is signals intelligence that comes from peeping down through satellites or eavesdropping on conversations. HUMINT is the "foreknowledge" gleaned from human agents. Then there is TRASHINT, which was what Customs had been doing. Acting on a tip from Varo, Customs agents had been sifting through Wu's trash. They had found the damning evidence of overseas shipments without an export license and stopped the last batch of tubes before they left the United States.

FBI Agent Lewis, was dumbfounded. He dropped in later that morning for a chat and found his "window" on the MSS had just been arrested. Tom Rademacher, the Customs agent who had taken Wu into custody, remembers the stunned FBI agent showing up at his office. "It was like, well, what are you doing here. And he [Lewis] said, 'What are you doing here?' It was not a great way to start your day."[8]

Was Wu a double or a triple agent? Had the FBI been bamboozled? Didn't the two key agencies protecting U.S. high technology talk to each other? The Bin Wu case raised all sorts of embarrassing questions, and for that reason, Wu was a prime candidate for summary deportation back to China. It was the way many post–Cold War espionage cases end—tidy, simple, and quiet. Only the man who refers to himself as the "Little Fish" would not go back quietly, or at all, if he could help it. Before his trial, two first secretaries from the Chinese Embassy in Washington visited Wu in the Norfolk jail. Wu says they ordered him to return to China. There would be no trial. "They stared at me. I stared at them."

Wu sorted out his problems. It was in the FBI's interest to have the case end quietly with a deportation. It was in the MSS's interest to lure Wu back to China, where he was sure he would face the agency's preferred discipline for spies who displeased it: a firing squad. Undergoing the publicity of a trial, Wu reasoned, was the only way he could save his life.

The star witness against Wu at his trial was none other than Jie Ying Wang, his wife. She had been arrested after trying to remove $50,000 from one of Wu's bank accounts, supposedly frozen by the government. She then decided to cooperate with the prosecution, explaining during the trial that among the more objectionable things she found in her husband's new lifestyle was a girlfriend. She told the jury that Wu knew that shipping the night-vision tubes to China was illegal and that he had warned her not to tell Lewis.

Wu did his best to dispel the impact she had made on the jury. He reminded them that now he stood alone. His wife, his old country, his new country, all had turned against him. He would never see his family again.

He was utterly alone. "Somebody told me that God always has been watching, listening, and knows all that is happening down here. But in fact I only see the blue sky and no truth. It is sorry for me to know that there is no justice or balance to things, and that the world is topsy-turvy and jumbled and confused, which nature wasn't meant to be. I got a cold feeling to know the sky is empty and nobody is there watching."

On September 17, 1993, the former philosophy instructor received ten years for making an illegal export. His helpers, Li and Zhang, got less than half that. Eftimiades, the DIA's China analyst, says that the Little Fish's sentence is "severe." A study of ten years' worth of export cases—some three hundred of them—shows that the average sentence is less than two years, and the usual result is a fine and no jail time. But some punishments meted out to spies are more severe than ten years. After the trial, the two Chinese diplomats appeared at Wu's jail again. Everything was set, they explained. Wu could come back to China.

Wu opted instead for the Federal Correctional Institution at Loretto, Pennsylvania, where, dressed in tan chinos and a gray sweatshirt, he spends his days as a model prisoner at the low-security prison, a former Catholic seminary. Life, he explains, has been a continuing series of traps. First the MSS trapped him. Then the United States trapped him. Lately Wu has been teaching himself French, hoping maybe to live in Paris after his long sentence is done. A U.S. Immigration and Naturalization officer explained to Wu that the door is still open for him to go back to China. Wu shook his head. What if the political system in China changed? the officer asked. "I said the government system can change, but the intelligence system is going to be always the same. Look at the [Aldrich] Ames case," Wu recalls saying, referring to the KGB's top Cold War spy, whom Russia kept operating in the CIA for years after the KGB disappeared.

Still, the Little Fish expresses an odd admiration for China's spy agency because, as he explains, its professionals are almost never caught. "I feel somehow they are very successful because you don't hear very much trouble about the MSS all over the world. That means they use very good ways."[9]

THREE

Big Fish

The beginning of the end of the aerospace industry in Columbus, Ohio, came on a hot day in August 1993 when a dozen visitors wearing business suits walked into the cavernous interior of Plant 85.

If there was a symbol of the power, paternalism, high wages, and technological sophistication of the U.S. aerospace industry, McDonnell Douglas Corporation's Plant 85 was it. The plant's array of over one hundred giant computer-controlled machines, some of which took up almost the width of a football field, made it the largest machine shop east of the Mississippi. The machines had performed the exotic cutting, drilling, and bending required to assemble the Titan and MX missiles.

The plant's four thousand workers were among the nation's most skilled. Machinists made $18 an hour; toolmakers a little more, assemblers slightly less. As a labor force, they shared considerable pride. Over the last two decades they had built the B-1 bomber and the space shuttle. Now, large, silvery pieces of the world's most technologically advanced transport plane, the Air Force's C-17, floated majestically overhead as cranes carried them to the next assembly point. It was part of the daily adagio of their big machines, a rhythm that had long been part of their lives.

Most of the visitors were Chinese. One carried a video camera and slowly panned down the length of some of the biggest machines. They were from a subsidiary of China's National Aero-Technology Import and Export Corporation (CATIC), which deals in both military and civilian equipment.

A rumor quickly buzzed from one end of Plant 85 to the other: The visitors were going to buy the big machines and ship them to China.

Blue-collar workers in America are not shy. Some began yelling insults at the Chinese. According to one account, machinists overturned tables and cabinets to prevent the visitors from getting close to their control panels. Fred Lassahn, who was head of Local 2927 of the United Autoworkers, one of the main unions at the plant, hurried over to the managers' offices. Were the rumors true? Lassahn recalls that the managers told him the rumors were preposterous. There was no way McDonnell Douglas was going to sell Plant 85's sophisticated machinery to the Chinese.

For China, already being investigated by the FBI for wide-scale espionage in the United States and accused by the U.S. intelligence community of proliferating weapons of mass destruction in the Middle East, it was a very bold move. The machinery that CATIC's team was eyeing amounted to an entire military aircraft plant. It would be impossible to steal it and smuggle it out. It would be illegal and impolitic for China to try to buy it and ship it out. Some of the equipment could machine to tolerances that were so precise they were on the U.S. State Department's list of "very sensitive" technology. Whoever had them had the capability of machining state-of-the-art nuclear warheads.

But CATIC had found another way: It was trolling an enormous bait, a $1 billion aircraft order, in front of McDonnell Douglas. The hook was that, to get the order, the U.S. company would have to make the political case in Washington to get the export licenses that were necessary to ship the machines to China.

CATIC knew that McDonnell Douglas was more than just a little hungry. Some U.S. aerospace companies had adjusted to the enormous economic shocks that came with the end of the Cold War, but McDonnell was still struggling to find its balance. The Air Force, McDonnell's most reliable and richest customer during its sixty-year history, was cutting its procurement budget.

Meanwhile, its other customers, the airlines, had grown increasingly demanding and fickle. During the 1950s, McDonnell's predecessor, Douglas Aircraft Company, had ruled the airways. Ninety percent of the world's passenger traffic flew on the company's DC-3. Now Boeing and the European consortium that builds the Airbus ruled the market.[1] McDonnell Douglas's share of sales of new aircraft had dwindled to 10 percent, an all-time low.[2]

Increasingly, McDonnell—the nation's largest defense contractor—had bet its future in the aircraft business on China. China's economy was exploding. "We're in the business of making money for our shareholders," McDonnell's president, Peter K. Chapman, once explained. "If we have to put jobs and technology in other countries, then we go ahead and do it."[3]

The pull exerted by China on U.S. companies during the mid-1990s was enormous. For many of them, China was the moon, and they hoped to ride on the tides created by a market of 1.2 billion people. Some major companies went to China knowing full well that business there poses enormous risks. It is a place where business, military, and criminal deals often intermingle. By some measures, China is one of the most corrupt places on the planet.[4] "The only thing worse than being in China is not being in China," Edgar S. Woolard, Jr., the chief executive officer of DuPont, reasons. "If your competitor catches on there, they're going to come after you with this enormous base."[5]

The big companies created a kind of vortex that drew in smaller companies, firms like Ross Engineering Inc., a small Fort Lauderdale business that had no experience in China. Ross was recruited by McDonnell in the mid-1980s to consider setting up a business in China. Part of the business of selling airplanes to governments involves "offsets," or side deals to sweeten the pot. One of McDonnell's commitments was to encourage other companies to buy goods from China.

Bob Aronson, the president of Ross, liked the business climate in Shanghai and set up a company there to make industrial batteries, the kind that power forklifts. After committing almost $5 million and giving the Chinese company Ross's technology, Aronson discovered the company would only sell him batteries at a markup that was 40 percent higher than the agreed-upon price schedule. He took the case to international arbitration and received a $4.9 million arbitration award, but Chinese courts refused to honor it.

"Now they own it. They got it free of charge from us," complains Aronson. "The Chinese have ways of sucking you in, taking everything away from you, and then kicking you out." Tom Williams, a spokesman for McDonnell, admits his company recruited Ross, but asserts McDonnell had nothing to do with the arrangement Ross made. "We made an evaluation and felt we didn't want to be involved with that."[6]

Yet McDonnell was involved in a major way with China, where officials talked blithely of a need for as many as eight hundred passenger jets over the next two decades. Such huge numbers had aircraft makers salivating over their order books, but none quite so much as McDonnell. It had become the leader in making offset deals to sell aircraft.[7]

China's commercial aircraft industry literally grew up on Western companies' offsets. Starting with a 1979 McDonnell deal to build the little doors that enclose landing gear when they fold up, China had demanded the technology and the right to produce increasingly larger pieces of the planes it purchased in its own factories. Now entire sections of the Boeing 737 and the French Airbus were being built in places like Shenyan, Xian, Chendu, and Shanghai. By being aggressive and generous in this scramble for a new market, McDonnell had emerged with a plum: a $1 billion order for forty of its newest planes, the MD-80 and MD-90. Under the agreement, half of them will be assembled in China.[8]

Much of the technology that McDonnell and Boeing were selling had "spun off" U.S. military technology. In China, U.S. military experts had begun to notice something they call "spin-on." As the Chinese learned how to make fuselages and nose cones for McDonnell airliners, for example, emerging versions of Chinese fighter planes were suddenly improving: their fuselages were better made and their aluminum skins were smoother.[9]

China was persistent. There were always more side deals kicking around. The team from CATIC had made a bargain-basement offer for Plant 85's best machines—roughly 10 cents on the dollar. At first, McDonnell didn't seem to take the demand seriously. The Chinese were always brandishing long wish lists.

When CATIC's purchasing team arrived in August 1993 for a close inspection, the workers at Plant 85 were already in a funereal mood. The C-17 program was coming to an end, and as part of a billion-dollar corporate belt-tightening process, McDonnell was about to shift the remaining work to its other plants. Within a year, Plant 85 would close and their jobs, maybe their careers, would end. Coming on top of that, the visitation from China was like putting salt in a wound.

"It was just the fact that they knew what these machines were capable of," explains Fred Lassahn, who spent the next few months as a kind of human shuttlecock, being banged back and forth between his union and the management. "Basically they [the workers] were worried that the Chinese were getting a military aircraft plant. It wasn't like they was selling them a factory to build wheels or automobiles or something like that."

There is nothing in the Western world quite like CATIC, which is part of China's Aviation Ministry. It can apply the leverage of a government agency, which is what it is. It has the technological know-how of a big defense contractor that develops fighters and missiles for China's air force. It is developing a keen sense of the world's commercial markets: CATIC runs some sixty-six commercial companies, whose profit-making businesses range from making airliners to running luxury hotels and shopping centers to producing fashionable watches.[10]

CATIC's sister agency, the People's Liberation Army, runs over ten thousand private businesses. They export a wide spectrum of commercial products, from Teddy bears to forklifts, many of which are sold in the United States. Part of the money is then used to modernize China's sprawling military—the largest in the world. Just how much money flows from the commercial businesses of China's government into the business of developing new weapons is a mystery, but it is probably a substantial sum. U.S. analysts believe that as much as two-thirds of China's defense budget is hidden.[11]

By September 1993, the sense on the factory floor was that Plant 85 had become a high-tech shopping mall for a Communist state. It was a very touchy issue. So McDonnell officials began escorting the CATIC team in on weekends and evenings when most workers were gone. The company told Craig M. Ziegler, an investigating U.S. Customs agent, that the plant's most sophisticated machines, called "five-axis profilers" were not being offered to CATIC.[12] Meanwhile, the company tried to dampen CATIC's growing interest in the machines.

On September 29, Zhang Juen Lee, one of CATIC's negotiators, sent a fax to Beijing describing McDonnell's attitude on selling the machines as "bricklike." His next move, Lee said, would be to jolt McDonnell by putting "all the cards on the table." The following day, Robert H. Hood, Jr., McDonnell's top official on the deal, received a fax from CATIC's counterpart in Beijing. It stated that a failure to sell the machines in Plant 85 would have a "big influence" on the billion-dollar plane deal and future deals with China.[13]

After CATIC's team showed all of its cards, it appears that McDonnell's players folded. Corporate history was hastily revised. "We always wanted to sell them [China] the machines," explains Tom Williams, the spokesman for McDonnell. As for the peculiar back-and-forth in the negotiations and the threat imperiling the billion-dollar plane deal, Williams dismissed it as "normal." "If you have ever bargained with the Chinese, they are always picking up and leaving the room."[14]

Lassahn and some of his union members were determined not to give up the machines without a fight. A stocky man approaching his forties, Lassahn had spent sixteen years at the plant. First he had stood on the control platform of a five-axis profiler, watching a computer terminal as the software told his 120-foot-long machine how to perform the precise, surgerylike work needed to prepare the metal skin for an intercontinental ballistic missile.

Next he had mastered his union's machinery, eventually becoming his local's bargaining chairman. Plant 85, a three-building complex that could house several good-sized football stadiums, was part of a breed that dated from World War II. It was a so-called GOCO plant, which meant it was U.S. government-owned but company-operated. In 1988, when McDonnell took over the management of the plant, it promised Lassahn and other workers "long-term, stable" jobs. Japanese management techniques were introduced. Wage scales were simplified. Efficiency increased. Lassahn would brag: "this plant is the lowest cost producer with the lowest scrap rate of any McDonnell plant."

Efficiency has been one of the hallmarks of U.S. commercial aerospace. It is among the nation's most efficient and most globally competitive U.S. industries. In 1994, its net exports brought in over $18 billion. Meanwhile, in the previous five years, it had shed almost 500,000 jobs. But there was more bloodletting to come.[15]

Mere efficiency didn't cut it with the cold-eyed customers that McDonnell, Boeing, and Airbus were dealing with. All three had sold planes by signing contracts that exported Western jobs and technology to China. The workers at Plant 85 were seeing only a small slice of what was happening all over the United States. Engineers from China's four main aircraft plants were crawling over other McDonnell and Boeing facilities. The Chinese press talked openly about deals that were targeted on bringing U.S. technology home to China. In theory, such targeting had been outlawed by a 1992 agreement China had signed with the Bush administration. In reality, however, the companies did not complain.

And the Clinton administration appeared to be paralyzed. President Bill Clinton had campaigned among aerospace workers vowing to preserve their jobs, but it was a promise that proved very difficult to carry out. If the deals with U.S. companies broke down over technology transfer, China would find other sellers who were more willing: in France, or maybe Japan. As Jeffrey Garten, then the U.S. Commerce Department's undersecretary for international trade, later put it: "We have virtually no leverage because it's a buyers' market, and there's plenty of tough competition."[16]

As far as Plant 85's machines were concerned, though, it wasn't quite a buyer's market. Other McDonnell factories wanted the machines. Lassahn's local created another buyer—it was called Team Columbus Buyout Association. Over seven hundred members from the union put up their savings, and Lassahn hired a Washington lawyer and visited a number of banks. Team Columbus offered $10 million and cash and commitments worth another $40 million to buy the machinery.

McDonnell rejected the union's offer. There was a $1 billion deal at risk and McDonnell's sales staff was then absorbed in making a pitch that would get Washington to sign the export licenses that would make CATIC happy. John Bruns, head of the company's China program office, put together a slide presentation to tout the deal's advantages. It mentioned "surplus used" equipment that was "not state-of-the-art technology." Thirteen of the plant's sensitive five-axis machines were involved in the sale, but CATIC was promising only to use them to make parts for the McDonnell-designed airlines, Bruns noted.[17]

Moreover, he emphasized, there was a billion-dollar export deal at stake. That, too, touched a sensitive issue. American consumers, attracted by a huge influx of cheap imported goods from China, had run up a $30 billion trade deficit with Beijing.[18] Although many items in this avalanche of imports were produced in Chinese military factories, Clinton administration economists ignored that. They were heavily focused on the bottom line. A $1 billion sale to China would help reduce an embarassing trade deficit.

While the blurry, intimate mix of business and military motives was peculiar, the strategy China was using was not. The Chinese were carefully following a game plan used by the Japanese some thirty years earlier. Like China, Japan had put a great deal of effort into acquiring toolmaking capability because it is the key to becoming an industrial nation. While the machine tool industry is relatively small, it is the stepping stone to much bigger things, such as the aerospace business. In the 1960s, when the Japanese began shopping, U.S. machines were the envy of the industrial world.

The machines in Plant 85 were the offspring of a marriage between the U.S. Air Force and the Massachusetts Institute of Technology (MIT) in 1949. The Air Force wanted bombers that exceeded the skills of U.S. manufacturers. MIT was tinkering with an exotic new device called a computer. It had the potential of making industrial machines operate with levels of control and accuracy that went far beyond human capabilities.

By 1959, the Air Force had poured $273 million into the effort and had, in the process, created an entire new industry.[19] By the early sixties, the Japanese government had become strongly interested in the new U.S. computer-controlled machines. Japan sent teams of buyers around the world. They bought samples of the simpler machines and then took them apart to see how they might be built in Japan, a process called "reverse engineering." Later, Japanese companies persuaded the U.S. companies that made the machines to sell them licenses to use the technology. Some of the companies felt that, by then, the Japanese had learned enough about the technology from reverse engineering to steal it, if they couldn't buy it. Others didn't seem to care.[20]

In the late 1970s, Ira Magaziner, a young business consultant who would later become President Clinton's domestic policy adviser, sat down with the manufacturers of eight U.S. machine-tool companies. He warned them that Japan was about to enter their market. "Only one knew the names of the new Japanese competitor, and even he wasn't worried," Magaziner later recalled. Japan was still considered an industrial backwater that made cheap copies of U.S. products.[21]

The new Japanese company's name was FANUC. Ten years later, it was the biggest computer-controlled machine-tool maker in the world. Dr. Seiuemon Inaba, FANUC's founder, had blindsided and then devastated the U.S. machine-tool industry, which saw many of its customers go over to better-built, cheaper FANUC machines. "For development of a given product, a thorough investigation of the world market must be made first," Inaba later wrote in his autobiography. "And then the price must be set low enough that the product will remain unbeatable for at least five years."[22]

FANUC's impact on the U.S. machine-tool industry was the economic equivalent of an attack by precision-guided missiles. In 1980, America's industry led the world. By 1990, it was a fourth-rank player that had lost over half its market to companies in Japan and Germany. The impact was most severe on smaller U.S. machine shops, often the most creative. In 1982, there were nine hundred of them; five years later, there were three hundred. Overall, the U.S. machine-tool industry lost 55,000 jobs.[23]

By the late 1980s it became clear that China was working on its own version of Inaba's plan. Norman Levy, president of a company that handles auction sales at large industrial plant closings, recalls that Chinese teams became frequent bidders at his sales. He remembers them buying tool-making machines at a Rhode Island plant closing in 1991. "They told me, 'We're not going to use these machines, we're going to take them apart.'"[24]

As for the biggest computer-controlled machines, they were not destined to be taken apart. For reverse engineering, you only need one machine. China's buyers were collecting dozens of them as Cold War–era controls relaxed. By the winter of 1993, U.S. intelligence agencies estimated that China was in the process of importing some forty of the big machines, counting the ones in the McDonnell deal. It was an amount that seemed far beyond the commercial needs of China's fledgling aircraft industry, or any other industrial country in the world, according to one U.S. official. What was going on?

One theory was that China was gearing up to export a large number of airliners—sales that would compete directly with Boeing and McDonnell. Another was that China was preparing what U.S. defense planners call "surge capability," the capacity to produce a large number of high-technology military planes and precision-guided missiles in a hurry. What was worrisome to experts in the Pentagon was that, when it came to China, the two goals are not incompatible. There is plenty of evidence that China wants to deal in both guns and butter.

China is investing in weapons systems that would bring it up to super-power level in several categories, including new jet fighters and submarines from Russia. It is tinkering with globe-spanning cruise missiles that draw precision guidance from U.S. navigation satellites. China is also testing rockets and nuclear warheads that lead U.S. experts to conclude that ballistic missile submarines and MX-like missiles carrying multiple, independently targeted nuclear warheads are on China's order books.[25]

F. Michael Maloof, the Pentagon's director of Technology Security Operations, opposed McDonnell's bid to export the machines from Plant 85 during a midwinter meeting at the Commerce Department. The deal, he argued, meant a direct loss of ten thousand U.S. jobs. He presented an analysis from his staff that drew a parallel between "the manner in which we are catapulting the Chinese into the airplane business and the disastrous way the U.S. rebuilt and modernized the Japanese steel industry after World War II." Once it was rebuilt, the analyst noted, Japanese steel put American companies out of business.[26]

Maloof trotted out evidence which showed that, as far as high-technology military equipment is concerned, China is a sieve that steadily leaks into the Third World. It was selling missile systems produced in factories with U.S.-made machine tools to Iran, and missiles and a jet trainer powered by a U.S.-designed engine to Pakistan. Once Plant 85 machines arrived in China, Maloof asserted, the United States had no way to keep them from being put to military use.[27]

McDonnell's case for the export licenses weighed heavily on economics and geopolitics. The licenses were needed to carry out a billion-dollar deal which also had great symbolic value because it was "one of the largest U.S.-China agreements." The Plant 85 machines would be installed in a brand-new subsidiary of CATIC's in Beijing, a machining center that all four of China's big aircraft companies would use. McDonnell noted that it "has been assured by CATIC that this factory will only produce parts for civil aircraft."[28]

In the end, China's billion-dollar lure hooked the Clinton administration. Commerce and State voted for the export licenses. The Defense Department, guided by Secretary William J. Perry—a longtime China enthusiast—and heavily lobbied by McDonnell Douglas, voted against its own experts.

In March 1994, Plant 85 shut down and some four thousand American aerospace workers were out on the street. For most, according to Fred Lassahn, their union leader, the job search was a dismal experience. Those able to travel found similar layoffs under way at other aerospace companies. "A lot of them stayed in the area and took lesser-paying jobs," explains Lassahn.

That meant working in a glass factory, a bottle-cap factory, or, "for those who were lucky," running relatively high-tech machines at a factory that makes truck axles. For many of the machinists, it meant sinking from a wage of $18 an hour to between $8 and $11 an hour. Mortgages went unpaid. There were wrenching shifts in lifestyles. There were reports of a number of suicides; Lassahn says he has been able to verify three.

In the summer, Norman Levy arrived to auction off Plant 85's machinery. It was an odd auction, he thought, because the U.S. buyers watched most of the best equipment, the computer-controlled machines, being carefully disassembled and packed in crates by a team of thirty Chinese workers in identical blue jumpsuits. They were exempt from the sale because they had already been purchased by CATIC.

Lassahn and a couple of his former co-workers listened as Levy went into his spiel. "It took our breath away to see how much the Chinese had taken," Lassahn said. They watched as heavy trucks loaded up the crates and headed toward the West Coast, where they would be loaded on a Chinese freighter. The machines were so big, the shipment required 275 truckloads. "Now they can build military aircraft, missiles, whatever they want," sighs Lassahn. "We'd better duck. I can't believe our government let this happen."

The move was not without some hitches. Under the terms of its agreement with the U.S. government, McDonnell promised to take an inventory of the machines every three months. When it did so, it found two of them had wound up in Nanchang at an aircraft facility not covered by the agreement. The Nanchang factory makes cruise and ballistic missiles. "That was not a proper end use, so that was rectified," explains Williams, the company's spokesman. According to one government official, McDonnell's way of rectifying matters was to ask the U.S. Commerce Department to suspend the export license it had granted for the machines—a move of dubious value since the machines were already in China, somewhere.

In the summer of 1995, Barbara Shailor, an official of the International Association of Machinists and Aerospace Workers (IAM), watched two U.S.-built five-axis machines—which, she was told, also came from the batch shipped from Plant 85—being installed at a plant in Xian, in China's heartland. The plant's workers, who make approximately $50 a month, were working simultaneously on the B-6D, a medium-range, nuclear weapons–carrying bomber; making tail sections for the Boeing 737; and planning for a new airliner, which could be largely indigenous. She asked a technician for an American company working at the plant whether the two-headed nature of the plant bothered him. "Everything around here is dual-use," he shrugged.

"From the [U.S.] companies' perspective, no one wants to complain about this," asserts Shailor. "From their perspective, as long as they're selling aircraft, there's no damage. The larger question is that if you're losing American jobs and American technology while simultaneously building an industrial base in China that will compete with you, there is in fact great damage going on."[29]

By the fall of 1995, Aviation Industries of China (AVIC), CATIC's parent, announced that the new airliner would be a hundred-seat plane that would be built in China with the help of a consortium from South Korea. Western companies were invited to participate, but China appeared ready to launch the project by itself. In the Chinese press, it was called "Asia's

Airbus."[30] Meanwhile, back in the United States, there were strikes at three Boeing plants, where workers were asked to begin paying part of their health insurance premiums.

Questioned about the U.S. worker unrest, part of which was aimed at recent deals both Boeing and McDonnell had made with China, Lu Zhanjun, an official of AVIC, said: "I know about this, some of us know about this. But it isn't our problem. It's because Boeing and McDonnell Douglas want to make money."[31]

George Kourpias, president of the 750,000-member IAM, confronted President Clinton. During his 1992 campaign, Clinton had promised Boeing workers in Seattle that he would preserve U.S. aerospace jobs. Since then, eighteen thousand more jobs had been lost at Boeing alone, Kourpias argued. Kourpias pressed for technology transfer deals to stop, a move that appeared to intrigue the president. In September 1995, Clinton assigned an interagency panel to reexamine U.S. trade policy. It was the beginning of a renewed political debate over the merits of free trade and the absence of a U.S. industrial policy—a debate that will likely resonate for a long time in Washington and within the ranks of the Democratic Party.

As for Plant 85, once filled with the shrill sounds of cutting, grinding, and drilling, it no longer resonates at all. Its big computer-driven machines are being reassembled and introduced to a new labor force in Beijing. Fred Lassahn, who once tried to buy them for his union, has had to scale down his dreams like most workers in his industry. He and a few former colleagues have started a small machine shop called Team Columbus Aerospace. With ten men working on a few small machines, it is the last survivor of the once-thriving aerospace business in Columbus. "We do a little work for General Electric," says Lassahn. He adds, somewhat wistfully, "and we're trying to get in at Boeing."[32]

FOUR

A Yen to Know

Cecil Haga's first encounter with the Japanese came on a bright summer day in 1945 when he was a twenty-year-old Navy enlisted man standing on the flight deck of the U.S. carrier *Wasp*. It was an experience that will live forever in his mind.

A kamikaze dive bomber peeled down out of a bright blue sky. First it was just a dot, but the dot grew larger and larger as the eerie scream from the pilot's death dive focused the attention of every gunner on the carrier. *Pow-pow-pow-pow-pow-pow!* Tracers crisscrossed, making a fiery latticework in front of the kamikaze. "It was so close I could see the 20-mm. rounds going into the engine," recalls Haga. "It kept coming."

Suddenly there was a small explosion in the kamikaze's cockpit. The bomber veered, missing the island in the middle of the carrier—its command center—by about twenty feet. As the riddled plane splashed into the Pacific, pieces of the map the pilot had used to find the *Wasp* floated down on Haga like so much confetti.

Haga's second encounter with Japan was a bit more subtle, but equally memorable. In 1987, he received a call from his brother-in-law, who told him: "I've got a Japanese client. He has some money to spend."

After almost fifty years in the U.S. aerospace industry, Haga had something to sell. A thin, wiry man, a chain smoker who has no patience with textbooks, Haga prides himself on being a "Florsheim engineer." He is among the last of the breed of self-taught men who pioneered the industry.

Modern engineers use computers and wind tunnels to design airfoils, or the leading edge of wings. Old-timers like Haga would simply bend a piece of metal around his shoe; hence the nickname.

Haga had a flair for building models and generating concepts from scratch. One of his dreams was to build a commercial variant of a plane the U.S. military had rejected in the 1970s. It was a tilt-wing airplane, which took off like a helicopter and then tilted its wings back and flew like a plane.

Haga's idea was attractive to the big Japanese investor, who turned out to be Taiichi Ishida, grandson of Taizo Ishida, the man who changed Toyota from a garage-sized operation into an automaker that took on the world. The younger Ishida, a plumpish man in his early forties, had a piece of his grandfather's fortune, but fame had eluded him, and so had his grandfather's management skills. Taiichi Ishida was a dreamer. He wanted to become one of Japan's best-connected industrialists. He used to doodle names of his companies, hooking them up in fanciful organizational charts with big U.S. and Japanese companies. After money-losing ventures in real estate and a chain of fashion boutiques, Ishida had decided on aerospace. He would become one of Japan's great airplane manufacturers. And like Haga, he was a man used to flying by the seat of his pants. They hit it off. "I had a great time with Ishida. He liked my brand of bourbon," recalls Haga.

What followed was a kind of high-tech *Rashomon*, a variant on the riveting Japanese murder mystery in which the events meant widely differing things to different people.[1] Ishida's Texas-based venture, called Ishida Aerospace Research Inc., eventually attracted the attention of the FBI, the U.S. Customs Service, the Marine Corps, the National Aeronautics and Space Administration (NASA), and Bell Helicopter, Haga's former employer.

Haga still chuckles over the fact that Ishida and his Japanese backers plowed as much as $25 million into a venture to build the TW-68, a sixteen-passenger tilt-wing aircraft. He believes they wound up with little more than a large stack of paper buried somewhere in a Dallas office. "It was a comedy of errors, total, and complete with standing ovations."

John Zuk, a technical manager at NASA's Ames Laboratory at Moffet Field, California, sees it much differently. He thinks Ishida's aborted effort to build the TW-68 was a "classic" tunneling operation, a ruse used by the Japanese to raid $3.5 billion worth of U.S. government technology and forty years' worth of research behind Bell's much bigger venture, the development of the V-22 Osprey for the Marine Corps. The V-22 is a stubby-winged aircraft whose engines tilt, allowing it to take off like a helicopter and fly at 300 mph, almost twice as fast as a chopper. For the Marines, the V-22 will be a more potent, longer-ranged successor to the aging helicopters it uses for amphibious landings.

Airplane manufacture is becoming a high-stakes gamble. The global market for aircraft will generate somewhere between $800 billion and $1 trillion worth of income and hundreds of thousands of high-paying jobs over the next two decades.[2] For nations that win a piece of this pot, it will mean exports and hundreds of thousands of high-paying jobs. For losers, it will mean mothballed factories, high unemployment, and trade deficits. It is a game that the United States has steadily won for the last fifty years, partly because three-quarters of the nation's aircraft research and development base has been paid for by the federal government.[3]

But the future looks less secure as the Pentagon's spending tapers off and aggressive new competitors in Europe, Japan, and China acquire some of the cutting-edge technology. Partly by studying and helping to build U.S. military aircraft, Japan is entering into the big leagues. It has launched an understated, partially concealed effort to build an industrial base in aerospace, driven by what Richard J. Samuels, an MIT political scientist and expert on Japan, calls "technology lust."[4]

While the U.S. focus has been largely defense-related, Japan's drive has been to make money. That meant that during the seventies and eighties, while U.S. engineers were focused on invisible bombers and 2,000-mph fighters, Japan's industry—which was revived to maintain and repair U.S. planes during the Korean War—was figuring out how to apply U.S. military technology to the commercial sector. "Learning mattered enormously," says Samuels, who notes that the disc brakes used on the runway in U.S. F-104 fighters were quickly studied, modified, and then rolled out as better automobile brakes for new cars being sold to the United States.[5]

But the matter of how Japan has quickly climbed out on the cutting edge of commercial aerospace, moving past current technology and drawing on hidden work in U.S. research labs, has long baffled U.S. intelligence analysts. Unlike the United States, Japan employs no large government intelligence bureaucracy, a fact that sometimes causes embarrassing gaps. In May 1993, for example, Tokyo remained ignorant that North Korea had just tested a ballistic missile by firing it toward the Japanese mainland. The United States informed Tokyo of the event about a week later.[6]

Still Japan's commercial sector has eyes that look out in all directions.

American companies don't often talk to each other; Japanese corporations sometimes function as one large national spy agency. "We have seen faxes go over there, ostensibly to one group of large companies, and within twenty-four hours they get turned around and disseminated to rival groups," says one U.S. official. "And they [the Japanese] are not shy. For years they have been studying how you can go right up to the edge of the law."[7]

Japan has institutions that feed on commercial intelligence that are unlike anything in the West. The Japan External Trade Organization (JETRO), an elite bureaucracy, partly funded by the government, sometimes uses Japanese businessmen to train its people on where and how to look for new technology; it runs seven offices in the United States.[8] Then there are the *sogo shoshas*, twenty major Japanese trading companies that orchestrate business deals across hundreds of different industries around the globe.[9] They are huge, savvy players who collect commercial intelligence. It pays. In 1990, for example, Japanese trading companies earned about as much as major U.S. oil companies.[10]

Japanese businessmen come from a culture where knowledge is gold. They are often shocked to find that, in the United States it's considered dross. In 1992, Michio Hamaji opened a New York office for Teikoku Databank Ltd., which has the largest database on businesses in Japan. American companies, he assumed, would flock to his door, but they didn't. He went out to sell them on the value of Teikoku's data. For the most part, they weren't interested. "It's sad to me," he says. "People say that Japan is too tough as a market, too closed. So Americans say, let's go to an easier market, to Vietnam or Hong Kong or Taiwan. Well, there they will find another competitor—Japan. They'll meet them again over there."[11]

Finally, there are Japanese philanthropies with pots of money. They, too, have a keen interest in U.S. technology. Ishida's company was one of these. By 1991, it had built a handsome laboratory in an industrial park at Fort Worth's Alliance Airport and hired some forty people. Most of its top staff were people like Haga, engineers who had just left Bell Helicopter, a major defense contractor that operates a half-dozen plants in the Dallas–Fort Worth area. The closest one was only twenty-five miles away.

And, like Haga, they had all worked on the V-22. Ishida hired the V-22's top test pilot, the two engineers who helped design the software for the aircraft's control system, and engineers who had worked on its fuselage and its landing gear. To lead the Ishida Aerospace team they chose Dr. J. David Kocurek, who formerly led the group at Bell that perfected the V-22's aerodynamics. When they arrived, the engineers brought with them a sizable library of information about the V-22 and related aircraft. Some of it was stamped "NORFORN," meaning the information could not be shared with non-U.S. citizens.

Many U.S. commercial aircraft are derived from government defense projects. Boeing's 707 started out as a tanker for the U.S. strategic bomber fleet, and Boeing's 747 was cloned from the C-5, the Air Force's tank-carrying transport.[12] Because commercialization of the V-22 hasn't happened yet, U.S. taxpayers have paid almost all the bills during its long, difficult, and expensive birth, which dates back to the 1960s.

The U.S. Army tried a variety of ways to get soldiers and gear into the air. It tried flying saucers, backpack rockets, and all sorts of bizarre-looking hybrids between a plane and a helicopter. Tilt-wing planes were in vogue in the sixties, only to be replaced by tilt-rotor planes in the seventies. Both aircraft had a lot in common, including complex gearboxes, drive systems, and control systems that had to handle two modes of flight. No one knows more about the tilt-wing/tilt-rotor tests than Charles Crawford, an engineer who had spent thirty-four years working in the Army's technical aviation program. Ishida hired him, too.

"Tunneling" is a practice long used in Japan to steal a rival's secrets. Company A can avoid expensive research and development by starting up a small, anonymous-looking R&D effort near Company B and hiring its disgruntled employes.[13] From the outset, Ishida made it clear to Dr. Kocurek and his other ex-Bell employees that he understood the legal problems involved with military-derived technologies. The TW-68 would be a wholly independent creation, built and produced first in the United States, he promised his staff.

Ishida ran the Fort Worth operation from the headquarters of his Ishida Foundation in Nagoya, Japan. Almost every month he would visit, bringing with him a growing entourage of engineers and others. If there was a motto for the early stage of the company, it was "Gung-ho": A prototype had to be ready to fly by 1994.[14]

In September 1990, just six months after his research efforts started, Ishida took a mockup of the TW-68 to the aerospace industry's air show at Farnborough, England. That baffled Haga. "I talked to Ishida about that. We didn't have anything, no design or pricing information. You just don't do that kind of thing."

Nonetheless, the TW-68 mockup got some U.S. subcontractors excited.

There was Fred Dickens, the head of business development for LHTEC, a company then developing the T-800, a radically new lightweight engine for the Army's next-generation helicopter. He called Ishida and sold him on the idea that the T-800 was perfect for Ishida's plane. "As soon as you hear 'Japanese-funded,' you assume it's going to go," recalls Dickens. "I just wanted to get our hat in the ring." To further its chances, LHTEC added some documents on the T-800 to Ishida Aerospace's growing library, including more that were stamped "NOFORN."[15]

Haga began to notice something odd about the visitors from Japan and the four Japanese who worked at Fort Worth. "They were reporting everything they saw and heard back to Nagoya. They were running around and Xeroxing stuff, copying even the scraps out of the trash can and faxing them back to Nagoya."

After working at length with several of the Japanese engineers, Haga concluded that they knew almost nothing about building a real aircraft. "I saw them doing things on the drawing board and on the computers that . . . why they would have been sat in a corner with a dunce cap on in Aerospace 101 if they ever suggested such a thing." So he ignored the copying that was going on. "I just laughed at it."

But Kocurek, who was responsible for the company's information, didn't think it was so funny. "There was always a problem keeping information that they [the Japanese] didn't need to have away from them. They were collectors. I had problems at night. Sometimes the security company would call to say the doors had been left open. People were complaining that their computers were tampered with."

When Kocurek drew the line, though, he would get demands from Ishida in Nagoya for more information. He refused. Ishida got angry. So, one day in September 1991, Toru Shinohara, an engineer from Nagoya, walked into the Fort Worth facility and announced he was taking over. Ishida Aerospace would respond to him, or Mr. Ishida would shut it down and take everything back to Japan, he said.

Words were exchanged. Kocurek, a linebacker-sized man who favors tweed jackets, jeans, and cowboy boots, escorted the red-faced Shinohara to the door. The next day, a Saturday, Kocurek had the locks changed so that neither Shinohara nor the other Japanese at the plant could get in. Then Kocurek stepped on a plane for a prearranged meeting with Ishida in Nagoya. The following Monday, the locked-out Japanese called from Fort Worth just as Kocurek was sitting with Ishida in Nagoya. Listening to the angry screaming from Fort Worth, Ishida maintained a poker face. It was eerie, the Texan recalled. "Ishida never said a word."

Kocurek's concerns were shared by John Zuk of NASA, who was aware of the strange goings on at Fort Worth. "My concern and our concern at NASA from day one was that this was a potential technology drain operation," Zuk says. "We were concerned about protecting critical U.S. technology from going overseas."

The problem was there wasn't much U.S. law to back Zuk up. There are, he says, a lot of "gray areas" when it comes to protecting technology that is not strictly military. Because Ishida Aerospace was a U.S. corporation run by U.S. employees, a good deal of the old NASA tilt-wing/tilt-rotor research was available to it. Moreover, as a U.S. company, it was entitled to use a sophisticated, computerized flight simulator at Ames Laboratory. When the request came in from Ishida to use the facility, Zuk wasn't sure if or how he could stop it. He knew that the information derived from simulating flights, testing the TW-68's software, would be crucial. "You basically replicate what the flying qualities of the aircraft will be."

Ishida Aerospace didn't go to Ames, it turned out, because it found it could use a closer simulation facility then operated by the McDonnell Douglas Corporation at Mesa, Arizona. It had been used to develop the Army's Apache helicopter. On his trips with Japanese visitors to simulation tests, Cecil Haga continued to be amused by their antics. "One asked me if I could drive them to an aircraft parts store. They believed you could come to the U.S., buy aircraft parts, and then bolt it all together. That's how informed they were of the airplane business."

Up to this point, U.S. industry had shown very little commercial interest in tilt-wing/tilt-rotor technology—despite the government's huge investment in it. But others were keenly interested. In an espionage target list that was later leaked to the United States, the French intelligence service had made the V-22 a top priority.[16] Japan's Ministry of International Trade and Industry (MITI) had targeted U.S. aerospace, particularly helicopter-derived techology. Japan had an ambitious plan to build some six hundred regional heliports to overcome crowded roads and a shortage of land for conventional airports.[17]

Hiraku Matsunaga, the minister of MITI, dropped more than a hint of interest when he visited Bell's V-22 plant at Fort Worth in January 1990. If the United States didn't build this, Japan would, and then sell it back to the Americans, he told reporters.[18]

Unlike commercial ideas, U.S. military technology must often endure a strange and time-consuming political dance. In the case of the V-22, it was marathon dancing. After giving it quite a whirl, the U.S. Army, the aircraft's original partner, dropped out. Then, when the Marine Corps took over the lead, the Bush administration stopped the music, terminating the V-22 as a budget-cutting gesture in 1989. Congress objected, but White House opposition made the V-22 a fiscal wallflower until late 1992. Finally, in a gallant pre-election maneuver aimed at winning the Texas vote, Vice President Dan Quayle steered the V-22 back out on the floor. Its budget was suddenly restored.

The shift was a little late for aerospace workers in the Dallas–Fort Worth area. During the 1980s, Bell had been enticed by the Canadian government to build a helicopter plant in Canada. To make way for the V-22, Bell had begun shifting its commercial helicopter production to the Canadian plant. Then, when the V-22's funding got hung up in Washington, the layoffs and attrition had to take place in Texas, according to a spokesman for Bell.

While all this was going on, there was also some strange maneuvering at Ishida Aerospace in Fort Worth. "We were told by the secretaries that we were using a tremendous amount of copy paper," recalls William A. Jones, a mechanical engineer who was working on the wind-tunnel tests for the TW-68. He remembers the company's bookkeeper giving weekly harangues about the cost of all that copy paper. "And we were all saying, 'Where's it being used?' because we weren't copying anything."[19] One of Ishida's Japanese staff, an engineer who habitually swept interesting documents into his briefcase, became known as "the spy."

Kocurek and the other American workers began taking sensitive documents home at night in their briefcases for safekeeping. There was a kind of earnestness, a sense of mission about his Japanese co-workers that puzzled and annoyed Haga. Every design detail had to be flawless, ready for mass production. Haga wanted to get a prototype up in the air. "Everything you do is for future generations. You don't do anything for yourself in Japan, you do it for future generations, you know, for some poor student seven thousand years from now. That's not Texas logic. I was trying to use Texas-Oklahoma logic with those people and it just didn't fit."

Kocurek was pushing the staff to move faster toward production. Ishida's people kept calling for more research and tests. The dispute caused a lot of bitter talk among Jones and the younger staff engineers during their lunchtime games of dominoes. They were eager to see something fly. It ended at the company's Christmas party in December 1991, when Kocurek announced that Ishida was giving him other duties for six months.

Ishida himself took charge of the project, appointing John Stowe, another Bell alumnus, second in command. Over the next six months, Stowe began to wonder whether Ishida was seriously interested in producing a plane. "He didn't honor his spoken intentions to me on many occasions. I would have to question his integrity."

Meanwhile, the midnight copying continued. "I don't doubt for a minute that the Japanese copied everything that was left out and available to them that our engineers produced," says Stowe. According to company documents, Ishida signed at least two agreements to share research with Japan. One was with Shinmeiwa Industry Co. Ltd., a Tokyo firm that makes seaplanes. Another was with the Japanese government's National Aerospace Laboratory (NAL). "Interchange of technical information" with NAL would benefit research activity in Fort Worth and Tokyo "simultaneously," the agreement states.

Dr. Kocurek quit in disgust in August 1992. After that, the U.S. Customs Service began getting complaints about the theft of information at Ishida Aerospace. Customs did nothing at first, but began to move toward the end of the year when the Defense Technology Security Administration at the Pentagon prodded it to investigate.

Then the Marine Corps raised a question: If most of the information at Ishida Aerospace was related in one way or another to U.S. defense efforts, Ishida needed export licenses to operate. Why didn't it have any? In early 1993, Ishida's top people were summoned to a meeting in Washington that included representatives from the Departments of State, Defense, and Commerce, and NASA.

U.S. officials were concerned that V-22 technology might be transferred to Japan. Charles Crawford, brought in as Mr. Ishida's technical expert, says he tried to convince the panel that the TW-68 technology Ishida was working on was unrelated. The panel decided to take no action on Ishida's applications for export licenses. The hawking of the TW-68 continued. Stowe was showing off models of the tilt wing at an airshow in June 1993—one of at least a dozen where Ishida Aerospace rolled out its mockups—when a press release arrived in Fort Worth from Nagoya. Taiichi Ishida announced that he was shutting down the TW-68 project, blaming the closing on the project's failure to attract expected support from a "consortium organization of major U.S. manufacturers." Ishida would spend no more money.

Crawford was shocked. "In my personal opinion they grossly misjudged the cost of commercial development," he said later. " . . . I always made clear that it was a large financial endeavor from the very beginning. I initially thought they took it seriously. In fact, they were serious. They just didn't have the money."[20]

Before Ishida Aerospace shut down, however, there was one last chore for the American staff. Ishida wanted complete documentation of every bit of research that had been done on the TW-68. "It was a series of summation documents broken into various disciplines. It represented several million dollars worth of research effort," recalls Stowe, who says the resulting reports made a stack two and a half feet high.

Stowe had deep misgivings about compiling the report. "In my estimation, that shouldn't go out of the country. As an American engineer, I think it was technology that was developed here, and it should stay here. A lot of that information was developed with U.S. tax dollars. I realize that, on the other hand, Mr. Ishida paid people salaries to modernize it, but somebody in federal authority should have the say so as to when something like that goes out of the country."[21]

In June 1993, Ishida Aerospace closed the Fort Worth laboratory and moved its records to a small office in suburban Dallas. Agents from the FBI and Customs began intensive interviews of Jones, Kocurek, Stowe, and other Ishida employes. Meanwhile, lawyers for Ishida were also on the move, promising severance pay to Ishida Aerospace employees if they agreed not to talk about their work.

According to Kocurek, Customs seemed uncertain where to look. "They kept coming back, saying, 'Where's the smoking gun?' I said, 'It's probably already on the plane.'"[22] Eventually, Customs and the FBI couldn't find anything that was really "smoking." The final stacks of reports from Ishida—at least the originals—are believed to be still in Dallas.

The saga of Ishida Aerospace was like a black hole that was in the process of closing up. The federal investigation shut down in December 1994 without reaching a conclusion. The following month, Mr. Ishida's lawyers announced a settlement with David Kocurek, who had sued his former employer for an alleged breach of his employment contract. One aspect of the settlement, according to Kocurek, is that he can't talk about it.

As for Mr. Ishida, he is back at his philanthropy's headquarters in Nagoya. During the investigation, Mr. Ishida asserted through his lawyers: "We have paid careful attention not to raise any problems regarding technology transfer."[23] Since then he has gone on to other things. "I don't think Mr. Ishida wants to have a conference with you," his Dallas attorney, Hugh W. Ferguson III, told a reporter.[24]

As a kind of philanthropic postscript to his American work, Taiichi Ishida had his lawyers state that he "is willing to share the technical data concerning the aircraft with others who are willing to continue its development."[25]

The aerospace business in the United States goes on, but it goes on very slowly with Japan, at least as far as TW-68–related technology is concerned. LHTEC hired a major *sogo shosha*, C. Itoh & Co. Ltd., to try to sell Japan on the merits of the T-800 engine. But the effort has been stymied by recent news that a consortium of Japanese aerospace companies are developing a very similar engine of their own, for use in a light helicopter being developed for Japan's Army.

Both Boeing and Bell have been trying to sell Japan a civilian version of the V-22 for search and rescue operations. Boeing is using C. Itoh & Co., and Bell is working with another *sogo shosha*, Mitsui & Co., to help promote the technical merits of the aircraft. But money that had been earmarked for the purchase seems to have disappeared from Japan's future budget plans.

Meanwhile, Japanese researchers have not exactly been standing still. According to a report by NASA, its sister agency in Japan, NAL, has begun experimenting with software simulating the flight characteristics of the TW-68. "We know they've got it, because we've talked to people who've flown it," says NASA's Zuk.

It's more than just possible that a family of new aircraft that spent forty years germinating in the United States might take off first in Asia, according to the NASA report. Crowded, rapidly developing countries, without the land or the substantial resources required to build major airports, might use tilt-rotor or tilt-wing aircraft instead to "leap into the twenty-first century."

If Japan does become the world leader of this technology, as it has done with many other U.S.-derived ideas, it will be a monumental loss. A panel of experts has told the U.S. Department of Transportation that a civilian version of the V-22 could generate as many as 684,000 man-years worth of American jobs and earn $17.8 billion worth of exports.[26]

As far as Cecil Haga is concerned, a Japan-led industry is not even a remote possibility. He clings to his stereotypes. Japanese engineers, he insists, aren't innovators, and Japan's workers, he believes, won't properly inspect their work. "To find a flaw would be a face-losing thing."[27]

To John Zuk, what happened at Ishida's U.S. company involves questions about a much different contest than the World War II images that still play in Haga's mind. Zuk worries about America's seeming inability to protect the remaining riches in its technology base. For engineers, the matter of tilt-rotor/tilt-wing technology can be an emotional issue. "You know, whole careers are wrapped up in this. We want to see useful results of our work."

Ultimately, the questions go far beyond matters that merely race the pulses of engineers or readers of *Popular Mechanics*. For many Americans with skilled jobs—like those that are fading away in Dallas–Fort Worth—and those who hope someday to land such a job, they are questions of how people will survive.

"The U.S. has to find a way to encourage technology like this that takes a long time to bring in commercial returns," says Zuk. "I'm convinced now you can't sit on these things any more because someone will take it. It's especially true now. You can prevent it for a while; you can delay the dissemination; but you've got to act on it, or others will catch up and get ahead of you."[28]

FIVE

A Yen to Win

*The contest was between small, single product, inexperienced, underfi-
nanced American startups and the heavyweights of Japanese industry.
David did not defeat Goliath.* —MIT Commission on Industrial
Productivity, 1989

Early in 1988, Takeshi Sakurai, president of Mitsubishi Electric America, Inc., ushered a platoon of American lawyers, lobbyists, and public relations men into his office in the nation's capital.

Collectively, the Americans were known as "the Mitsubishi team in
Washington." They had been carefully selected and retained to create a
political presence for Mitsubishi Electric, a branch of the largest industrial group in Japan.

A graying, slender, elegantly dressed man, almost six feet tall, Sakurai
is well steeped in the American culture. As a business strategist, he had
few peers inside his company. But playing the role of field marshal in a big
political battle was new to him. Sakurai settled his team into overstuffed
chairs at one end of his large, somewhat austere office on Connecticut
Avenue.

Speaking in his almost flawless English, Sakurai told them this story:
There was an American entrepreneur, a man named Donald M. Spero. He
was president of a tiny Maryland company that was giving Mitsubishi a
headache in Japan. It was a trivial dispute, a matter of who owned the controlling patents to a device called a microwave lamp. To Mitsubishi, it was
a matter of a few million dollars, mere beer money for an industrial giant
then worth some $20 billion.

But by tirelessly courting the press, by going to the office of the U.S.
Trade Representative (USTR) and to senators on Capitol Hill, this man

Spero had somehow managed to turn his problem—one of thousands of commercial disputes between U.S. and Japanese companies—into a symbol of them all. USTR officials had recently warned Mitsubishi executives that unless they resolved Spero's case, it would become a major issue in trade negotiations between the two countries. Senator John D. Rockefeller IV, chairman of a Senate Commerce subcommittee, was about to hold hearings featuring Spero. Something, Sakurai summed up, had to be done to get rid of this problem.

But what? Japan and its companies had built a formidable political presence in Washington. They had retained over one hundred of the city's top law firms and made generous donations to its major opinion-forming think tanks. But some political problems transcended mere money. Toshiba Corporation had discovered that a year earlier when it admitted it had evaded export restrictions to sell computer-controlled milling machines to the Soviet Union. The machines created submarine propeller blades whose shape made them so quiet-running that the subs evaded U.S. Navy detection systems, including networks of undersea sensors that had cost U.S. taxpayers billions to put in place.[1]

Videotapes of U.S. House members flattening a Toshiba boombox with sledgehammers in front of the Capitol were still being played to shocked audiences in Japan. Toshiba and Japan's Ministry of Trade and Industry had brigades of expensive lawyers running around town putting out the fires. And now this man Spero was lighting some more.

As the team members hashed out the problem, Sakurai sat back and took notes. For him, as for many Asians, direct confrontations—the kind that this Spero was encouraging—are distasteful. What matters enormously is not noisemaking but winning, and winning decisively. And the best ways of winning are often indirect. "Go into emptiness, strike voids, bypass what he defends, hit him where he does not expect you."[2] That was the way Sun Tzu, China's ancient military strategist, counseled his generals. Whereas Asians are brought up on his theories of war, Americans are brought up on sports analogies.

When it comes to the game of peddling and protecting influence in Washington, Sakurai's "Mitsubishi team" was a World Series Contender. Just having the team on retainer probably cost Mitsubishi at least $1,300 a day.[3] There was James H. Lake of Robinson, Lake, Lerer & Montgomery; a talented switch hitter. As a press handler, Lake had scored for President Reagan and Vice President Bush. As a lobbyist, he had done some heavy hitting for companies with trade problems. One of Lake's many power connections was Clayton Yeutter, who then headed the office of the U.S. Trade Representative.

As Lake recalls the conversation, all of the Americans pushed Sakurai to hang tough. "Here was an aggressive guy [Spero] trying to take a commercial dispute into the political arena. We said, don't take this crap." Lake was in favor of finding another senator to counter Senator Rockefeller. "It was to make sure Rockefeller didn't have an open field to do anything he wants, when it comes to Japanese trade policy."

Two lawyers from Baker & McKenzie, the huge international law firm, monitored Spero's patent case for the team. Then there were two more sets of lobbyists: two men from Thompson & Company who did routine legwork for Mitsubishi Electric on the Hill; and Steven R. Saunders, who ran a small Alexandria, Virginia, lobbying boutique. Saunders handled more sensitive matters for a variety of clients, including the Japanese Embassy.

Stories of patent disputes are mind-numbing affairs that rarely get into the mainstream U.S. press, but Spero's story had struck a nerve. "So the advice the team gave to Mr. Sakurai was: Well, there is no real way you can win in any kind of situation like this," Saunders later recalled. "This is a home-grown American entrepreneur fighting this Goliath of a Japanese company." The best move, Saunders felt, was to "dog Spero so that wherever he goes and says Mitsubishi Electric has done this, this, and this, you simply go in and present the facts of what the situation is."[4]

As was his custom, Sakurai remained silent until his team finished. Then he read off from his notes a summary of steps to be taken. Lake, formerly a protégé of Yeutter's at the Agriculture Department, was to get the USTR out of Spero's case. Saunders, formerly an aide to Senator Robert Packwood, was assigned to get the senator involved. The Oregon Republican would be the best man to lead the charge for Mitsubishi on Capitol Hill.

Donald M. Spero loves sports in a way that few Americans do. A tall, lean, balding man, now in his late fifties, he is not a fan but a player. As an undergraduate at Cornell, he was a member of its cup-winning rowing team. Later, as a graduate student in physics at Columbia, he raced single sculls for the New York Athletic Club. His determination earned him a berth on the U.S. Olympic team that went to Tokyo in 1964.

Spero beat the reigning Olympic champion, a Russian, in the preliminary heats, but then lost to him in the final. "It was one of the worst moments of his life," recalls Spero's wife, Nancy Chasen. "Don hates to lose." Two years later, in Yugoslavia, Spero came back, beat the Russian, and took the world championship.

In 1971, when he and four other young scientists decided to develop a microwave lamp, Spero brought the same intensity to business. He left his job as a university researcher and became the first employee of the company, Fusion Systems Corporation. Fusion's first office in Rockville, Maryland, a Washington suburb, was so small that the lanky Spero had to open the door before he could bend over and examine his laboratory equipment.

Fusion invented a high-powered microwave lamp that generated ultraviolet radiation so intense it could instantly dry inks and coatings, such as the ink on a freshly made beer can, at a fraction of the time and expense of the normal curing process. It was also useful for making semiconductor chips that are used in electronics. One of the early goals of Fusion was to market the lamp in Japan, which was rapidly becoming the electronics capital of the world.

Spero arrived in Tokyo in 1975 and found a peculiar process awaiting him. He applied for a patent at Japan's patent office, an affiliate of MITI, the nation's aggressive trade promotion agency. Two years later Mitsubishi bought one of Fusion's devices, took it apart, and then began to file some 257 patents, all on tiny pieces of what amounted to the same basic technology.[5]

To fortify its claim that it invented the lamp, Mitsubishi commissioned three independent legal studies. Then Spero was given a choice: He could either slug it out in Tokyo in 257 patent actions—a loss in any one of which might rob Fusion of its Japanese market—or Fusion could make a deal with Mitsubishi.

Like Spero, Mitsubishi also hates to lose. Founded in 1870, it became a key piece of the military-industrial complex that dragged Japan into World War II. Among many other weapons, it developed the Zero, one of the most innovative and maneuverable fighter planes of the war. Then, one day in 1945, as its factories stood amid the ashes of defeat, Mitsubishi and its eighty-two business affiliates were summarily dissolved by the order of an American colonel.[6]

In the fifties, Mitsubishi, along with many other pieces of Japan's war-shattered industry, clawed back out of the grave. The byword for Japanese businessmen in the sixties and seventies was "Export or die." Mitsubishi men often rolled over their competitors with their determination to win.

General George S. Patton, Jr., the American field commander who rolled over the German Army in the closing days of World War II, once described the art of winning:

"I have studied the German all my life. I have read the memoirs of his generals and political leaders. I have even read his philosophers and listened to his music. I have studied in detail the accounts of every damned one of his battles. I know exactly how he will react under any given set of circumstances. He hasn't the slightest idea what I'm going to do. Therefore, when the day comes, I'm going to whip the hell out of him."[7]

Ten years later, as Americans turned to business, Patton's formula still worked, but it was being applied by Japanese companies to whip the hell out of American competitors. Thomas J. Murrin, a former group vice president for energy and advanced technology at Westinghouse, recalls the mismatch between his company and Mitsubishi, which engaged in a number of joint ventures. When a Mitsubishi team arrived at Westinghouse, it was often a composite drawn from the whole company. "Every night after their visits," Murria says, "even if there had been a lot of drinking and it was late, they'd go back to the hotel rooms and spend maybe a half hour discussing the intelligence they'd learned from us that day. Often they would wire a report back to Japan."

Westinghouse rarely expressed any curiosity about what Mitsubishi was doing. When Murrin returned from an occasional visit to Mitsubishi plants, he says his superiors would usually dismiss his accounts of the Japanese company's growing engineering prowess by saying, "It's all bullshit." Murrin, now dean of business at Duquesne University, believes that "all of their [Mitsubishi's] early successes in energy equipment derived from transferring our know-how back and then adapting it." Later Westinghouse had the experience of seeing its innovations applied in Japanese products before the Westinghouse products hit the market.[8]

By the time Spero squared off against Mitsubishi, Westinghouse had begun to falter. Meanwhile, Mitsubishi Group had become a global colossus with 29 member companies and 250,000 workers.[9] Mitsubishi Electric was a relatively minor member of the group, but it was still six hundred times larger than Fusion.

In the summer of 1985, after investing in a number of lawyers and business consultants in Tokyo, Spero decided to see if the patent mess could be resolved by approaching Mitsubishi directly. He recalls a Mitsubishi official drawing a picture of a pair of scales. On one scale he put a few X marks, signifying Fusion's patents. The other scale was brimming with X marks, signifying patents that Mitsubishi was applying for. "To balance this out, you have to put some money on the table," Spero recalls him explaining.

After six months of negotiations, Mitsubishi agreed to allow Fusion into Japan without a patent fight. But there remained one catch: The Japanese company demanded a free license to use all of Fusion's technology, worldwide, plus a 3 percent royalty on all of Fusion's business in Japan. "They said that's the way we do business in Japan," recalls Spero. Spero walked out in a rage. He was not about give away his little company's competitive edge for the right to do business in Japan. "I said: 'this meeting is over.'"

For a U.S. company, Spero's walkout was a rare moment. Granting cheap licenses *was* the way American companies did business in Japan. According to one estimate, U.S. firms, many faced with the alternative of running Japan's expensive patent gauntlet, sold some 32,000 technology licenses to Japan between 1950 and 1978. While Japanese firms paid $9 billion for the licenses, the technology they received was worth $1 trillion.[10]

The typical deal was struck between small American startups like Fusion and major players like Mitsubishi, but big U.S. companies licensed their technologies as well. Japanese companies got nylon from DuPont, color television from RCA, transistors from Bell Laboratories, and the VCR from Ampex through this route.[11] A panel of engineers from the Massachusetts Institute of Technology that later surveyed the damage found that the once-booming U.S. field of consumer electronics "had taken on the appearance of a war zone." It was ground that most corporate managers ceded to Japan.[12]

After two more years of fruitless discussion, Spero left Tokyo in 1987 with the sound of one of Mitsubishi's negotiators ringing in his ears:

MITSUBISHI: "Mr. Spero, it's not right! You have dominant market share in Japan. It's not fair. We're a small company."
SPERO: "That's ridiculous, you're a $20 billion company."
MITSUBISHI: "In the lamp business we're small."
SPERO: "It may be small to you, but it's 100% of my company."[13]

Fusion won its fight for the first three patents. Then, on appeal, Mitsubishi had the decision overturned. Spero grew tired of battling uphill in Tokyo. He would take his fight to Washington. While his budget for lawyers was running dry, Spero had one left: his wife, Nancy Chasen. She helped plan his lobbying campaign. With help from the U.S. government,

Spero hoped, he could take away Mitsubishi's leverage. He had concluded that Japan's system was designed to force an American company to make cheap licensing deals. It was pay to play, but Fusion wouldn't pay. "Their engine only goes one way," he told his wife. "If you stand in front of it, they don't know what to do."[14]

A few days after the Mitsubishi team's meeting in his office, Sakurai brought the team into La Brasserie, a small, elegant French restaurant on Capitol Hill, tucked just behind the Senate office buildings. There they found Senator Packwood and an aide waiting for them. Steven Saunders, the lawyer who had set up the luncheon, later described to the Senate Ethics Committee what followed:

"I remember Mr. Sakurai started explaining in a very Japanese way, which is to explain things from the beginning of time to the present day. The way I earned my money that day was, as I saw Senator Packwood's eyes sort of closing . . . I intervened and gave a four-and-a-half minute summary of what the problem was. Which was that Fusion was alleging that they were a victim of Mitsubishi Electric, but that the cover they were using was that the Japanese patent system was unfair."[15] Japan's patent system, Saunders explained, was really one of the best in the world.[16]

Senator Packwood introduced that theme at Senator Rockefeller's hearings in June, 1988. While Spero and a number of other witnesses attacked Japan's patent system, Packwood argued that what the subcommittee needed was more information. "I would like to have another hour or two of hearings at some stage" with American companies that had had good experiences with Japan's patent system, he noted, "companies who can say, well, we have gotten along with it."[17]

Saunders also primed Senator Packwood to counter Spero's next Hill move, which was an appearance before a Senate finance subcommittee in November 1989, but first the lobbyist had to overcome a couple of difficulties. Three days before the hearing, Packwood invited Saunders to dinner, where the senator explained to his former aide that he was divorcing his wife. Mrs. Packwood's claims for alimony bothered the senator. They would be lower if she had a job. After many drinks at a Mexican restaurant, Packwood wondered whether Saunders might provide some help.

As it happened, Saunders could. He was planning to set up a small art gallery where Mrs. Packwood might earn $7,500 a year, a figure that made the senator brighten up. The matter of Spero and Fusion, Saunders later explained, never came up at the dinner. "Nobody in his right mind ever talked to Bob Packwood about business when he was drinking, because you'd have to go over it all over again."[18]

But the Spero matter came up three days later, when Saunders in a panic discovered Packwood had a scheduling conflict and couldn't attend the hearing. "If you could stick your head in even for a few minutes and just read some questions into the record, I would appreciate it," Saunders pleaded. He faxed some questions prepared by the Mitsubishi team to the senator's office.[19]

That afternoon Packwood dashed into the hearing, announced he had some questions for Spero, read the Mitsubishi team's questions, and then dashed out again. Spero, sitting in the audience, was baffled. "Why is this man against me?" he wondered.

Later that night, the senator recorded the business of the day in his diary: "At a request of Steve Saunders I stopped in at the Finance Committee to read two questions which I wanted asked of a man named Spero, the President of Fusion something or other." The politics of Senator Rockefeller, who was supporting Spero, in turn baffled Packwood. "It's funny. Fusion is in Maryland. I don't know what the connection is with West Virginia."[20] Meanwhile, the Oregon senator's Tokyo connection was pleased. Mitsubishi raised Saunders' retainer by $1,500 a month in "appreciation" of his relationship with Packwood.[21]

Sakurai had other reasons to be pleased. Using Lake's entree with his former boss, the Mitsubishi team had paid a call on Yeutter. They explained, according to Lake, that the Spero matter was merely commercial. "It didn't have any characteristics that deserve to be considered a public policy dispute between the U.S. and Japan." Yeutter agreed.

This was totally opposite to what Yeutter had been hearing from his staff. "This was really dirty stuff in my view," recalls Ambassador Michael Smith, who chaired negotiations with Japan at the time. "I thought they [Mitsubishi] were trying to intimidate Spero." But after the Mitsubishi team's visit, Yeutter's view changed. "Clearly, Lake just went around me," Smith says. "Yeutter just sort of wiped his hands of the whole thing. He was the boss."[22]

Throughout 1989 and 1990, the climate in Washington remained difficult for Mitsubishi and other Japanese companies learning to pull strings on the U.S. political stage. Clyde V. Prestowitz, Jr., a former Commerce Department lawyer and one of the few U.S. trade experts fluent in Japanese, wrote a book entitled *Trading Places: How We Are Giving Our Future to Japan and How to Reclaim It*. Prestowitz maintained that Japanese companies were using licenses and joint ventures to "siphon" technology out of the United States, and that in Japan, "business is frequently portrayed in terms of war with foreigners."[23]

Then Pat Choate, a Washington-based vice president for policy analysis with TRW Inc., published *Agents of Influence*. Based on an exhaustive search of U.S. records of lobbying and foreign agent registrations, Choate concluded that Japanese companies and government-related firms were spending at least $100 million a year to hire lobbyists and lawyers, and another $300 million a year to shape public opinion. Choate argued that by financing think tanks, university chairs, and even high school courses, Japan was creating grass-roots pressure to fortify its lobby in Washington.

The two books, both best-sellers, roiled public opinion. In 1994, the Japanese Embassy in Washington commissioned an elaborate public opinion survey to see how Americans really feel about Japan. By this time, Japan had a major investment at stake. The survey was done by Robert D. Deutsch, an American clinical psychologist, who says he conducted focus groups involving several thousand Americans for over a two years. What he found almost everywhere, he says, was a five-step sequence:

"People start out by saying the Japanese are only concerned with business. They [the Japanese] are always concerned about the future. They're capable of anything. They always have a hidden agenda. We'd better watch out. That's the mind-set that colors everything," explains Deutsch, who spent three and a half hours probing each small focus group.

He has vivid memories of one woman just throwing up her hands, saying, "That's what they [the Japanese] will do. They'll come to America, take what they want, and leave us barren and dead!" Chinese, on the other hand, were exempt from Americans' fears because they were regarded as coming from a culture that was more exotic and outside the range of commonly held concerns. Along with the deep negative feelings about Japan, Deutsch says he also found widespread feelings of guilt. "People across the country are almost dismayed that they feel this way."

Despite their strong feelings on Japan, Deutsch found that Americans had very little basic knowledge about the country. When he asked the groups to name three well-known Japanese, Deutsch says Yoko Ono, Godzilla, and Bruce Lee were often at the top of the list. "I tell focus groups Bruce Lee is not Japanese."

To Deutsch, America's attitudes about Japan also say something about Americans. "We do live in a dream state. It's a state of hope. It's: 'I can wipe the slate clean and start again and do anything I want, any time.' It means I don't always have to be concerned about the future and I don't always have to be concerned about business."[24]

Deutsch's finding of guilt was no surprise to the Japanese. They've watched it play in the American arena since the early 1980s when Robert C. Angel, an employee of the Japan Economic Institute (JEI), coined the term "Japan-basher." JEI was the forerunner of Japan's big lobby in Washington, and as one of its first hired strategists, Angel was looking for a term that would quickly discredit Japan's critics.

"I looked at the Israeli lobby and found if anybody criticized Israel they were called anti-Semite and with that they shut up." Angel came up with "anti-Japanism." "That didn't sell. I peddled it to anybody I could buy lunch for in Washington and nobody picked it up. I couldn't even get it in the Japanese press." Then one evening Angel was watching a television special about racial prejudice in London and heard the term "Paki-bashing." That was it—Japan-bashing. Angel's new epithet quickly took off, first in Japan, then in the American press. People who opposed Japan's positions were Japan-bashers.

"I'm not terribly proud of this," says Angel, now an associate professor of government at the University of South Carolina. One reason is that in 1983, he had a falling out with his Japanese employers. They wanted a more pro-Japan slant in publications that Angel edited for JEI. When Angel resisted, he was accused of being a Japan-basher and fired.

The term became part of the arsenal of tools that Japan uses to wear down its enemies. While they know little about Japan, Americans are very sensitive when it comes to political correctness. Prestowitz was labeled a "Japan-basher" even before his book was published. He approached a prominent Washington think tank for a place to write the book and was rejected, largely because it felt Prestowitz might imperil its large donations from Japan.

Later, after *Trading Places* hit the bookstores, Prestowitz recalls his adopted Japanese son coming home from school in tears. An American teacher had announced to his class that his father was a Japan-basher. It was one of a number of painful incidents for Prestowitz. "I have had speaking invitations from groups that were later withdrawn. Pressure has been put on people not to invite me."[25]

Choate was fired by his company, TRW, shortly after *Agents of Influence* was published. What apparently did Choate in was a prepublication article calling him "Japan's most-feared Japan basher." As one fearful TRW executive put it in an internal memo: "it is almost a given that the Japanese will also get hung up on perceived bashing—and that alone, aside from the book's actual content or when/where it was written, is bad business for TRW."[26] The company—a major U.S. defense contractor hoping to widen its market in Japan—later issued a statement disavowing any connection with Choate's book, noting that "TRW will continue to strengthen the Japanese relationships that it has come to value so highly."[27]

As for Spero, he has always taken great pains to point out that he admires the Japanese culture and that he values Fusion's customers, employees, and suppliers in Japan. He has been labeled a Japan-basher in the Japanese press, but the racial epithet didn't seem to stick on him in America. He was still David. There were signs, though, that Goliath was gaining on him.

According to Lake, Takeshi Sakurai was being pushed by Tokyo to settle quickly with Spero; but as time went on, Sakurai grew more confident he could win. His team kept pushing him. "We told him if he relented on this one, there would be a next time and a next time and people will see you as a sitting target. This is wrong. The substance is wrong and we can't let them win this," recalls Lake. Tokyo evidently decided to let its man in Washington call the shots. In 1989, after Lake had dampened enthusiasm for Spero's case at USTR, Spero recalls Sakurai telling him over a leisurely lunch, "Your government doesn't represent you any more."

Although it was a hot story for a while, Spero's public relations campaign crested. By 1990, the story of Fusion versus Mitsubishi was old news and editors didn't tumble to it any more. "It sort of died," says Lake, who maintains he still admires Spero for his spunk. "Every time we stopped him at one quarter, he'd find another."[28]

There was one quarter that Spero didn't know about. According to Lake, other stockholders from Fusion had begun talking with Sakurai and the Mitsubishi team behind Spero's back. Some of them felt Spero was standing in the way of a sale of Fusion to Mitsubishi, which, they felt, would have paid top dollar for their stock.

Fights within Fusion over the issue erupted in 1991. Spero wanted to take the company public and keep the technology in U.S. hands. Others wanted to sell it to the highest bidder. The matter ended one summer day a year later, when Fusion's board fired Spero, the company's president, and elected an investor and a board member, Daniel Tessler, as its new leader. By 1993, Fusion had worked out a deal with Mitsubishi that involved making a payment to the Japanese company to settle the patent dispute.

Just what Mitsubishi's settlement terms were remains a secret. "I have no comment on any aspect of it," says Tessler.

With the exception of Mitsubishi Electric, which retains a robust political presence in Washington, most of the players in this David and Goliath saga have gone on to other battles.

In 1995, Takeshi Sakurai, Mitsubishi's patient field general in Washington, returned to company headquarters in Tokyo. Reached two days before he left, he apologized that he had no time to discuss the Fusion matter with a reporter.

Senator Packwood, Mitsubishi's spear carrier on the Hill, resigned from the Senate in 1995 after a bruising fight with the Senate Ethics Committee over charges that he altered his diaries to conceal evidence that might support complaints from seventeen women who had accused Packwood of unwanted sexual attentions. Many of them were from his staff. "I'm aware of the dishonor that has befallen me in the last three years, and I don't want to visit further that dishonor on the Senate," he announced, as he fought back tears on the Senate floor.[29]

James Lake, Mitsubishi's chief tactician, resigned from his lobbying firm in 1995. He admitted to prosecutors investigating financial wrongdoing at the U.S. Department of Agriculture that he had arranged an illegal campaign contribution to a congressman at the request of one of his commercial clients. Lake, a near genius when it comes to explaining complicated matters to the press, had no answer for a *Washington Post* reporter who asked him why he did it. "I've asked myself that a million times. I just can't explain it," he replied.[30]

Steven Saunders, Mitsubishi team's point man on Capitol Hill, was never able to sell Senator Packwood's wife on the idea of working for him. In 1995, he agreed to accept immunity against possible criminal charges in his dealings with Packwood in exchange for his testimony before the Senate Ethics Committee. "I haven't talked to any reporters about this [Fusion matter] from the very beginning and I'm not about to start now," he told this reporter.[31]

As for Don Spero, the man who dared to stand in front of Mitsubishi's moving train, he can be found around dawn most mornings, rowing his scull briskly up the Potomac. Since he's had more time for rowing, he's won a national title for single-scull competitors over fifty years old. Despite losing his company, he remains hopeful and acts as an adviser to a number of high-tech startup companies. Japan, he notes, has recently promised to remove some of the abuses from its patent system. "When it comes to the public policy issue, we won."[32]

SIX

Farewell

The spy of the future is less likely to resemble James Bond, whose chief assets were his fists, than the Line X engineer who lives quietly down the street and never does anything more violent than turn a page of a manual or flick on his microcomputer. —Alvin Toffler, *Power Shift: Knowledge, Wealth and Violence at the Edge of the 21st Century*

Because Rublovsky Chosse meandered through the most exclusive suburb of Moscow, it was a street that had many secrets. It usually hid them very well. Tall green fences shrouded the sprawling, forested estates where the top Soviet officials lived in regal splendor. At the gates, uniformed guards of the militia carefully watched the black limousines as they came and went. And members of an elite unit of the KGB carefully watched the militia.

But the dog-legged street in the hills just west of Moscow had other places: little wooded pockets where the watchers seldom went. In one of them, Vladimir Vetrov, a paunchy, well-dressed man in his late forties, used to park with his mistress, Ludmilla. On evenings after work they would turn up the car radio and sip champagne. It could get quite warm in the little car. As the windows fogged from the contrast with the early winter's numbing cold, they'd make love.

On one such night in November 1982, however, Vetrov's secret almost came out. What was going on behind the steamed windows of his car that night was definitely not foreplay. It was an argument. Ludmilla's voice was rising, sounding shrill, accusatory. Then she was screaming—not in anger, but in terror. Vetrov was trying to kill her, beating her with the champagne bottle. When that didn't work, he groped under the front seat and found a knife.

A man walking nearby heard Ludmilla's screams as Vetrov stabbed her.

He rapped loudly on the car window. Startled and probably a bit drunk, Vetrov leaped out and plunged his knife into the man. As the passer-by slumped to the ground, dying, Vetrov disappeared into the woods. Later, though, he suddenly reemerged, to the astonishment of police who had arrived at the scene. They promptly arrested him. They were shocked to discover their killer was a KGB colonel with a very sensitive job in the spy agency's First Chief Directorate, which handles foreign intelligence matters.[1]

Vetrov's job was even more sensitive than the KGB knew. For at least eighteen months he had been a mole, a double agent, working for French intelligence. He had given the West its first detailed glimpse of the most lucrative spy scheme of the Cold War. Using teams of specially trained scientists and engineers, the Soviet Union had mounted the most systematic economic espionage campaign in history. It was spending roughly $1.4 billion a year in salaries and bribes to obtain the secret details of thousands of NATO weapons systems and related civilian technology. The systems had cost taxpayers hundreds of billions of dollars and taken many years to develop. About 60 percent of the technology was stolen from the United States.[2]

Western leaders had known for years that some thievery was going on, but the scale and phenomenal success of the Soviet effort—as seen from documents supplied by Vetrov—was far beyond anything they'd imagined. "The West is financing two military budgets: their own and that of their adversary," wrote one French official, after studying Vetrov's papers.[3] What was "more absurd," he noted, was that Soviet spies were getting the information largely from open sources. The West, especially the United States, was wide open to people who knew what they were looking for and who could move quickly. Weapons secrets were being stolen and copied before they were deemed secrets.

This was shocking information, and François Mitterand, France's newly elected Socialist president, put it to good use. In July 1981, he was headed for a summit meeting in Ottawa, and needed something shocking to convince President Ronald Reagan that, despite having appointed four Communist ministers to his cabinet, Mitterand would be a staunch anti-Communist ally of the United States.

Vetrov's case—which went under the French code name "Farewell"—was Mitterand's gift to the new American president. It was an instant success. Reagan's people, grappling with a bureaucracy in Washington that had for years dismissed Soviet espionage as inconsequential, now had something to fight with. The Soviet collection effort began right at the top with the unit called VPK, the Military Industrial Commission, which was placed just under the Politburo. It drew up vast "shopping lists" of needed Western items and used at least six different entities to get them. They included the KGB, Russian military intelligence (the GRU), and the spy agencies of various satellites such as Bulgaria, Romania, Czechoslovakia, and East Germany.

Members of Russia's prestigious Academy of Sciences were also tasked for stealing. Alexei Brudno, a mathematician and computer software specialist, remembers that the system was very effective. Usually only scientists who agreed to participate in KGB thievery schemes received permission to travel abroad. Western scientists, eager for the contact, often shared papers with Russian peers that they wouldn't give to their NATO colleagues, especially those who worked for competing nations or companies. Upon returning, a Soviet scientist was carefully debriefed by a panel of KGB experts. Often they didn't bother to introduce themselves; they were only interested in the haul.[4]

Eventually U.S. security people began to catch on. In 1983, a delegation of Soviet scientists invited to tour a Grumman aircraft plant on Long Island were told they could carry no cameras and take no notes. Still, by putting adhesive tape on their shoes, the scientists were able to collect slivers of metal alloys being used for new U.S. fighter planes.[5]

But the most inventive and powerful collection agency was Vetrov's, known as the KGB's "Line X." Because Vetrov was such an enthusiastic mole, in the months that followed the French were able to send to Washington a large roomful of documents showing how the KGB's technology thieves operated in the United States: how they bribed sources in U.S. corporations and pieced together weapons secrets from open files in government agencies such as NASA; and how they developed contacts in major U.S. universities—the most heavily used one being Massachusetts Institute of Technology—to fill in the gaps on the VPK's wish lists.

The "Farewell" material being sent to Washington had to be very closely held, for in the summer of 1981 Vetrov was still producing. It was kept in the CIA library under the code name "KUDO" and only a handful of officials were allowed to read the blue-bordered documents, which signified a compartmental level of secrecy well above "top secret." One official,

Maynard C. Anderson, then director of security plans for the Undersecretary of Defense, found the Vetrov files amazing. Through the magic of economic espionage, as he later put it, parts of U.S. industry had become "a Soviet national asset."

While the United States expected its heavy investments in high-technology weaponry to give it many years' worth of military advantages over the Russians, Anderson found Line X's thefts were cutting that lead by half. "What you had as a result of our slowness [to develop] and the loss of this technology was that American industry was building weapons against a threat that was really no longer valid. By the time we had produced a system, they had already developed countermeasures," he said.[6]

Vetrov's papers also gave the West the names of hundreds of Soviet agents and the spies they were running in dozens of countries, and for the first time, it gave NATO strategists an accurate picture of what the Russians *didn't* have. So Paris and Washington took great pains to give Moscow no sign that they were enjoying such a bonanza until that fateful night in November 1982 when contact with "Farewell" suddenly went dead.

What had happened? No one knew. Not even the Soviets, who hastily investigated the case and prosecuted Vetrov as a common criminal. Ludmilla survived her wounds and testified against him. The KGB was eager to have such an embarrassment removed from their ranks. Vetrov got fifteen years for murder and was sent to a prison labor camp in remote Irkutsk. It took the Russians months to figure out that the man they had locked up for a crime of passion was the Communist equivalent of the CIA's Rick Ames, who singlehandedly rolled up dozens of U.S. espionage operations in the late 1980s.

Like Ames, who had a history of drinking and living beyond his means, Vetrov was an accident waiting to happen. He too had a history of drunken misadventures and always seemed to have more spending money than could be reasonably extracted from his meager salary as a technology gatherer and later an analyst for Line X. While Ames bumbled around in the U.S. spy trade, which consisted mainly of recruiting agents and keeping track of counterspies, Vetrov was a bumbler in one of the KGB's main efforts, which ran more like a conventional business.

Line X, which took shape in the thirties after successful KGB thefts of technology from Germany, had a product: other people's blueprints, research papers, devices, or machinery. Stealing them, the KGB discovered, was one crime that pays. KGB defectors say Line X officials repeatedly boasted that Line X not only covered its own costs; the value of what it brought in sometimes exceeded the annual budget of the entire KGB.[7]

When it couldn't get the right hardware or weapons blueprints in the United States, Line X often found that the same items could be acquired from U.S. allies in Europe or Japan, where small bribes worked wonders. "You pay some engineer maybe $100,000 for something that costs $5 million. It's even more profitable than gambling," recalls Stanislav Levchenko, a KGB officer in Tokyo during the late seventies.

By then, Japan had its own campaign under way to collect technology from the United States, The Russians took pains to cultivate Japanese collectors of U.S. technology and found they cared little about what happened to it once it arrived in Tokyo. While "Japan Inc." functioned as an enormous intelligence machine, it had almost nothing in the way of counterintelligence, so Line X flourished in Tokyo. Levchenko recalls that the twenty-five Line X operators in Japan produced a ton of samples and documents that was assembled and flown to Moscow every two weeks.[8]

The result was that years of American sweat, money, and scientific frustration were deftly bypassed when the U.S. plans reached the Soviet laboratory. Soviet scientists often joked that much of what they did amounted to "translations from the American."

The list of items "translated" was enormous. Russian documents stolen or photocopied by Vetrov estimated that five thousand Soviet military systems benefited from stolen Western research each year. The CIA later toted up a list that ran the gamut from the space shuttle to cruise missile guidance systems, to components from all of the later U.S. fighters, nuclear submarines, laser-guided artillery, and high-speed computers. Soviet engineers didn't even bother to research such mundane but useful things as cold-rolled steel armor for their ships; they had the U.S. formulas.[9] There were many willing hands to do the work. It has been estimated that at any given time during the 1980s at least 1,000 of the 2,800 registered diplomats for the Eastern Bloc were intelligence agents, and the bulk of them were involved with science and technology.[10]

Equipment from General Electric, Boeing, Lockheed, Rockwell International, and McDonnell Douglas made up the top of Line X's shopping list, while MIT, Harvard, the University of Michigan, California Institute of Technology, and Princeton were the Soviet scientists' favorite hunting ground for ideas.

Like the CIA, the KGB tried to recruit its agents from the best universities. While the CIA drew heavily on liberal arts graduates like Ames—who would have a hard time telling the difference between a capacitor and a thermocouple—Line X fed on the cream of gruaduating scientists and engineers, men like Vetrov, who had initially set out on a career designing automobiles.

Automobiles always seemed to play a part in Vetrov's meandering career. He wrecked one of the KGB's cars during a tipsy escapade while serving as a "diplomat" in the Soviet Embassy in Paris during the late sixties. Because KGB budgets were closely watched, that alone might have ended his career, but an obliging Frenchman arranged to fix up Vetrov's car at no cost.

Russian investigators later suspected that French intelligence got its hooks into Vetrov right there; but French accounts insist that Vetrov remained untainted until 1981, when he sent a letter to a French businessman friend, offering to volunteer as a spy. French descriptions of "Farewell" depict him as a closet Francophile. One says he "never asked anything" in exchange for his secrets.[11] Another sums up the case as a matter of "cool nerves and Gallic panache."[12]

Certainly, dealing with Vetrov required more than a little of each. His last "diplomatic" post was Canada, where he was expelled in 1979 after continued bouts of heavy drinking and involvement in some scandal involving diamond dealing. KGB investigators later concluded that both Canadian and French intelligence operatives cultivated the hard-drinking, free-spending Vetrov in Canada.

Back in Moscow, as an unmistakable sign that his career was not exactly flourishing, Vetrov was assigned to a lower-level slot in Directorate T. As the CIA learned with Ames, lower-level positions in an intelligence agency can be very fertile places for moles. Directorate T happened to be the coordinating and analysis center for orders sent down from VPK to the Line X units in various embassies, which worked under the directorate.

In 1972, Directorate T, along with the rest of the KGB's First Chief Directorate, was moved from Lubyanka—the spy agency's forbidding, soot-encrusted fortress on Dzerzhinsky Square near the Kremlin—to a cluster of buildings in a forest in the suburbs. Its buildings are said to resemble the CIA's campuslike facility at Langley, Virginia. And Vetrov, probably smarting from his downgrading, found still another resemblance to Langley. Like Ames, he found he could leave his building with bags filled with documents and other items and no questions asked.

The sheer volume of material offered by Vetrov presented another problem for the French, who already had great trouble figuring out how to handle their mole. In theory, Vetrov should have been managed by the SDECE (Service du Documentation Extérieur et de Contre-Espionage), France's equivalent of the CIA; but Mitterand's government had concluded that the SDECE had been so thoroughly penetrated by the KGB that it was "a nest of spies." Even telling the agency about Vetrov would be dangerous. So the job was given instead to the Direction de la Surveillance du Territoire (DST), the equivalent of the FBI.

DST's problem was that it didn't have many agents outside of France, but Mitterand's people fixed that by picking an obscure army captain in the French Embassy in Moscow for the mission. As far as the French professionals were concerned, it was terrible "tradecraft" to give such a mission to a novice.[13]

But it was a strategy of such Gallic panache that it completely threw off the KGB's watchdogs, especially when the captain commissioned his wife to handle some of the more dicey meetings with Vetrov. It was she who exhibited the "cool nerves" one evening when Vetrov unloaded a sack of documents in her car on six-lane Kutuzovski Prospekt, one of the busiest streets in Moscow. Included in the bag were two live shells, newly designed ammunition stolen from Western arsenals. The shells rattled around on the floor of her car as she and Vetrov swerved through the fast-moving traffic.[14] After weeks of Xeroxing Vetrov's documents in their embassy, the French gave the spy a special mini-camera that allowed him to photocopy Line X's personnel files.

But the activity suddenly stopped that fateful day in November. Two nerve-wracking months followed as the captain worried that Vetrov had been arrested and that he might be next. As the ominous silence wore on, officials in Paris and Washington faced a tough decision. To protect Vetrov, they had not taken any action against hundreds of Russian agents he had identified, but now it appeared that their mole might be dead. If that was the case, then the agents had to be stopped. NATO could not simply stand still while legions of rodents nibbled away at its secrets.

By spring 1983, a few Russian agents had begun to disappear. Later, hundreds more were either arrested or expelled as France began to make moves and the Reagan administration sent a secret diplomatic mission to its other allies in Europe to give them the specifics of Line X's many penetrations. While Line X's operatives in the West were being sent home, the

Reagan administration cranked up the volume on its Strategic Defense Initiative or "Star Wars," the somewhat exaggerated plan for a high-tech "shield" against enemy missiles. Vetrov had set the stage for one of the more interesting moves in the arms race. Where were the bright techno-thieves of Line X when the Kremlin really needed them?

The early removal of Soviet agents lit up warning lights in the KGB's counterintelligence section in the summer of 1983. "Some agents disappeared in France, Germany, and India," recalls Victor Budanov, then a KGB lieutenant colonel and the assistant chief of the section. Budanov's boss, Vitaly Yurchenko, had led the investigation that packed off "Farewell" to Irkutsk as a murderer.

Now Yurchenko was busy with other matters, so Budanov was handed the puzzle of the disappearing agents. Yurchenko had been a nervous, peripatetic investigator, a classic apparatchik eager to find quick, artful solutions that would please his superiors, whatever the results.

Budanov was different, a plodder—a gruff, fullback-sized man who had the patience and penchant for small detail of a fly fisherman, which was what he liked to do when he wasn't hunting spies. Temporary fixes that merely appeased superiors wouldn't do. Budanov liked to bag "traitors." Having Budanov on your trail was not a pleasant experience. Oleg Gordievsky, a former KGB station chief in London who had been recruited as a double agent by the British, was once treated to a grilling by Budanov. He called him "one of the most sinister" officers in the KGB.[15]

The first piece of the puzzle, the agents who initially disappeared, were specialists in collecting technology in space and aircraft industries. This happened to coincide with the checkered career of Vetrov, whose last responsibility was assigning such tasks. Budanov knew Vetrov slightly, having seen him once or twice at his office. He summoned up the mental picture of a man who rarely exercised and had the puffy pallor of a heavy drinker. This profile was not all that unusual in the KGB, but Budanov sensed there was more.

Budanov ordered up all the files on Vetrov, including the evidence presented at his murder trial. The records showed that Vetrov had developed a pronounced taste for luxury goods. Again, that was not unusual for KGB agents overseas, but for the last three years Vetrov had been a relatively low-paid analyst in Moscow, where the goods—and the hard currency to buy them—were very hard to come by.

Budanov paid a call on Ludmilla, a clever, attractive woman in her middle forties, who worked as a translator in Vetrov's office. She showed Budanov diamond bracelets. In her closets he found French-designed fur coats. Gifts from her lover, she said. They were so expensive that they had triggered the last argument between her and Vetrov. While she had developed a taste for his champagne and his furs, she had always felt that it was somehow wrong for a man in Vetrov's position to have so much money. Vetrov was upset, she said, because he knew that she was suspicious. He was afraid she'd turn him in.

Vetrov, as it turned out, had been attentive to other women in his office. By outward appearances he was not cut out to be a ladies' man, but he had found other ways to attract them. "Quite often he would take them to bars and restaurants, which was quite unusual for us. It was very expensive," recalls Budanov. "Once he said, 'Okay, let's go somewhere for a drink.' And they scoffed at him: 'You are as poor as a church mouse.' He says, 'You think so?' and he took them out to his car. He took up the rubber cover of the floor-mat and showed large quantities of bank notes. At that point in time, that was unexplainable."

Budanov sent for Vetrov. In the fall of 1983 he was brought back from Irkutsk and placed in an isolation cell in the KGB's Lefortovo Prison in Moscow. After interrogation, Vetrov signed a confession to having spied for the French. He was probably executed sometime in the winter of 1983, though Budanov says he doesn't know exactly when. "It wasn't our job. We just had to help the investigators with the materials they needed to make the case in accordance with the law."

It remained for Yurchenko to tell the West that its most productive mole had been silenced. He did this in his usual odd, peripatetic way. On August 1, 1985, he defected to the CIA in Rome. One of the first cases he was asked about was Vetrov's. Four months later he sauntered out of a Washington restaurant and sought asylum at the Soviet Embassy. Grinning through his mustache at reporters hastily assembled for a press conference, Yurchenko told them he wanted to go home.[16]

Yurchenko's message and the way he chose to deliver it has a stranger-than-fiction quality, but then so does the rest of the aftermath of Vetrov's case in the United States. Many of the nation's technological horses had been stolen, but getting America's government, academia, and industry to close their gaping barn proved to be a thankless task.

First, there was the orthodox view to contend with, one that the Carter administration and those before it had nurtured: No matter how much the

Soviets stole, their industrial base was so inferior and their bureaucracy so cumbersome that U.S. innovation would always leave them at least a generation behind in the arms race. This was patently not true. Vetrov's documents showed that some of Russia's copycat weapons, such as the Kirov-class cruiser, were being launched sooner than the U.S. systems they were copied from.

"Our argument from the White House was that somebody should put a stop to this because we're losing our shirt here," recalls Kenneth DeGraffenreid, a former Defense Intelligence Agency analyst who had pored over the Vetrov files as director of intelligence programs for the National Security Council.

The FBI, DeGraffenreid recalls, insisted the losses were overstated because it was their job, as the head counterintelligence agency, to protect the United States from such thefts. The FBI felt "they had their arms around everything," recalls Degraffenreid. Meanwhile, the CIA worried about its own turf. If the armies of Soviet students, scientists, and diplomats were expelled from the United States, American agents would get reduced access in Moscow, although at that point much of the Soviet Union was off limits to them anyway.

"It was a very hard case to make at the Pentagon," remembers Steve Bryen, then in charge of technology security policy for the Department of Defense. Defense technology experts argued that putting further curbs on openness would slow down the flow of new weapons systems. "Some people, especially the R&D people, liked the arms race."

Then there were the scientists. Bryen recalls many wrangles with the National Academy of Sciences. "Nobody on the Russian side ever traveled over here without being tasked [to collect something]. But their argument was that good ties with Russian scientists will lead to a more peaceful role."

Bryen recalls one prolonged fight with officials at Nellis Air Force Base near Las Vegas, Nevada, where he found that several Russian "students" were conducting research projects on a supercomputer—a machine useful for designing nuclear weapons and plotting missile trajectories. "We finally got them to stop it, but can you imagine such craziness?"

As for industry, Bryen remembers a "big push from the semiconductor industry not to place any rules on their ability to work with foreign employees. It was so necessary for them to have those people in order to keep ahead."

Vladimir Vetrov is dead. The arms race he knew is history. The secrets delivered by "Farewell" are locked in the CIA's vault. But that doesn't mean this story is over. The multiple routes to stealing U.S. technology that the Soviets pioneered and that Vetrov exposed are still in use. For other intelligence agencies, the case of "Farewell" is an appealing road map. Bryen, now a private consultant, is convinced that Iraq's successful forays for U.S. weapons-related technology in the late eighties were based on the same training and even the same shopping lists that Line X used in the early part of the decade.

DeGraffenreid, also in private business, believes that the next enemy who uses Farewell's techniques may not necessarily be a major power. In earlier wars, he notes, nations needed industrial bases and a sizable body of engineers and scientists to develop high-technology weapons. Now it may be that a country that merely has money can do it, "if they went to school on the United States. It's not like the information is locked in a safe. It isn't. It's a more difficult problem as time goes on. How do you know when to lock things up? There are a lot of people thinking about this."[17]

SEVEN

Spooky Business

October 1992: An airliner breached the seemingly permanent cover of gray clouds over Moscow's Sheremetyevo Airport and touched down gently. Gliding along the vast ribbon of concrete, it passed between the drab military transports that always seem to have business at Sheremetyevo. The plane's passengers, groggy and rumpled from the long international flight, stared out the window. Most of them were looking at a land they had never seen before. Yet they had spent their entire careers studying it.

They were an unusual group: sixty-one spooks, veterans of the Cold War from the CIA, FBI, the National Security Agency (NSA), Britain's MI-6, U.S. military intelligence, and others who had long careers in the shadows, watching, listening, measuring, and sometimes fighting an enemy that rarely showed its face.

Waiting to greet them in a VIP room just inside the terminal were the faces of that enemy: retired officials from various branches of Russia's KGB, men from a 500,000-member secret army, the largest and most powerful spy agency in the world. On the American side there were people like Keith Flannigan, a beefy, fortyish man who still won't say what he did or who he did it for. "Let's just say I did some things." He and the others bore years of accumulated suspicions about the KGB people gleaned from intelligence files where truth, half-truth, and paranoia were often inseparably mixed. It was a heavy layer of sediment that kept many fast friendships from blooming in the days that followed.

Still, curiosity did lead to a sort of stiff camaraderie. They each knew half of at least one good war story. There was this hunger to learn the other side from the faces that matched those in the files. They did a lot of that during the symposium on the booming private security business that followed.

"To sit and have conversations with them, their side and our side, it was like looking at old football game films and being able to talk with the other team," recalls Flannigan.

The Russians were mostly men like Flannigan, in their late forties and fifties; former atheletic types who had begun to thicken more than a bit at the waist. Their uniforms would have fit much better than their motley collection of poorly tailored civilian suits. Among them one man seemed to dominate: a husky, smiling, round-faced man wearing a black leather coat. Russians deferred to him. He seemed peculiarly at ease with some of the Americans.

He was Victor Budanov, the man who solved the riddle of "Farewell," the French mole who had exposed the KGB's economic espionage.

Two months before, Budanov had worn the two stars that signified he had risen to KGB lieutenant general. He was the head of external counterintelligence, the watcher of all the watchers. Then he had resigned, leaving his thirty-four-year KGB career behind him. Then he was the first president of something called The International Cooperative Business Security Association, a consortium of some fifty-six different and newly formed Russian security firms, most of them drawn from the ranks of fresh KGB retirees.

Budanov, now sixty, was more than just a face from the files to some of the Americans. At various points in the tense, high-stakes spy games of the 1980s, there had been a series of unofficial timeouts. Secret meetings were held in Vienna to hammer out the "rules of the road" between the East and the West. Budanov represented the KGB in these talks. Western spymasters respected him because there was no flimflam when it came to Budanov. He was the Other Side, the man who had caught some of the spies they had recruited.

Budanov had cut some interesting deals in Vienna. He had agreed that spy agencies would not torture or abuse each other's people. He had agreed to try to help the United States locate John Buckley, the CIA station chief in Beirut who was kidnapped and later tortured to death by terrorists in Lebanon. Budanov came to be regarded as a "straight shooter" by his counterparts in those talks; a tough customer for sure, but one whose word, once it was given, could be honored.

Now there was a new war brewing and it had no rules. The Russian veterans' hunger for contact with their former enemies grew from something more elemental than mere curiosity. Some of them were literally hungry. Under Boris Yeltsin, the former state security agencies were melting and newly forming Russian companies could not yet afford the specialized skills of the ex-KGB. Their hopes were pinned on business from the West. It is very important to know reliable private security companies in Russia, Budanov explained to a visitor. "Otherwise they [Western companies] would establish relations with companies controlled by criminals. It happens quite often here."[1]

The privatization of the former Eastern Bloc's spy apparatus has created a grand specter that will haunt business and political dealings with the West for years, perhaps decades to come. There was nothing quite like the KGB, whose sprawling apparatus conducted foreign espionage, provided internal security, performed military and police counterintelligence functions, operated the world's largest eavesdropping agency, protected Communist Party leaders and their horde of gold, ran scientific laboratories and psychiatric torture clinics, and safeguarded nuclear weapons.

"This was a real empire," explains Victor Yasminn, a former Soviet dissident who has spent the last twelve years studying the KGB. It had its own uniformed army: large parts of the KGB were border guards or uniformed troops who monitored nuclear installations. The key component that Yasminn worries about are the spies and the agents that they ran, both inside and outside Russia. The spies, he estimates, include some twenty thousand people. Their "helpers" may run into the hundreds of thousands, including a legion of Russian crooks who learned the ropes doing black market deals and other illegal favors for the party elite: the so-called criminals within the law. Unlike the former East Germany and other Eastern Bloc countries, where the files of informants of the secret police were turned over to the new authorities, the KGB's huge network of helpers remains hidden, and probably continues to be of use.

The KGB's ranks included the best and the brightest, men and women who had been allowed to travel abroad and who had the language skills and the manners that would appeal to a Western company. But it also had people promoted for ties to the Communist Party's reigning hierarchy, the so-called *nomenclatura*. There were sadists, killers, and goons, people with a boundless appetite for corruption, fraud, and disinformation.

Yasminn believes that spies of the old KGB have divided into three rough fragments: One-third remained in their old jobs in the new slimmed-down state spy agencies; one-third went into the private security business; and one-third went into business for themselves as "entrepreneurs, bankers, and wheeler dealers. Banks are their favorite area."[2]

Some of the new KGB-derived companies began rich and well connected. The KGB had used training sessions to help elect 2,756 of its officers to local, regional, and national legislatures in the 1990 elections.[3] The spy agency had thousands of "file companies" or well-capitalized fronts overseas that had been used to buy or steal foreign technology. In addition, the KGB is believed to have been given the task of exporting and hiding the Communist Party's gold, a war chest of some $15 to $50 billion that has never been found.[4]

Russia's largest bank, which is called MOST, has a security staff of 1,100 people overseen by 20 former KGB officials who, in turn, answer to a former KGB general. Vladimir Gusinsky, MOST's founder, recently shrugged off the connection in an interview saying, "My ties to the KGB are like the ties of any American corporation to the CIA. . . ."[5]

The distinctions between businessman, spy, and crook are not nearly as tidy as they may sound because in Moscow the new lines can be blurred, sometimes even nonexistent. Some of the new businessmen still function as spies—moonlighting as members of reserve units of Russia's new External Intelligence Service, the Sluzhba Vneshnei Razvedki, or SVR. "We see companies that are, on the one hand, legitimate, and on the other intelligence fronts. And on the third hand they are elements of organized crime-all simultaneously," says Admiral William O. Studeman, former deputy head of the CIA.

The emergence of this strange hybrid raises interesting questions for companies hoping to tap the new markets in Russia. J. Michael Waller, a Washington analyst who has written a book on the evolution of the KGB, warns that "American businesses have to understand that while it's necessary to hire ex-KGB for the short term, it's possible that the same people who are advising you are the ones who are stealing proprietary information to sell to the negotiators on the other side, or people who plant agents within your company for the long term."[6]

But there was no time for Western businessmen to sit and ponder such interesting questions. Moscow was rapidly turning into the 1990s version of Dodge City. Some 5,700 organized crime groups had sprung up around the country, of which 200 were large, sophisticated organizations. The addition of spy skills to criminal gangs had vastly expanded their reach and sophistication. The same month that the ex-spooks were getting to know each other at their business security symposium in Moscow, there was a second meeting in Prague where some of the larger Russian gangs were meeting with Italian Mafia leaders to form an alliance to carve up the drug business in Eastern Europe.

Meanwhile, Russian gangs had begun to appear in credit card frauds in the northeastern United States.[7] In California, officials were struggling to redesign the state's Medicare system after two Russian immigrants showed them just how creative Russians can be when it comes to defrauding big government. Using mobile laboratories that gave "free tests," they filed $1 billion worth of phony insurance claims to the U.S. state and private insurers. It was the biggest medical fraud case ever uncovered.[8]

While the press often refers to the "Russian Mafiya" as if it were one organization, it clearly isn't. In the months that followed, chaos reigned in Moscow and dozens of bankers were shot, poisoned, kidnapped, or beaten to death. Their bodies were a kind of macabre scoreboard for the crooks as they warred over turf among the two thousand newly privatized banks and various other lucrative fields where they had a piece of the action. Meanwhile, police forces were becoming rapidly corrupt. In 1993 alone, more than five hundred members of Russia's Interior Ministry were fired for selling police information to criminals. Ten billion dollars worth of raw materials, a colossal volume of traffic, was being illegally exported, trundled past border guards who had suddenly lost the ability to see.[9] And palace-like mansions were beginning to sprout in the suburbs around Sheremetyevo Airport and on Cyprus, which was rapidly becoming the Riviera for the new Russian elite.

To survive in the new Moscow, Western businesses desperately needed to trust somebody. They needed muscle to ward off extortion attempts, investigators who could spot frauds and criminals, reliable technicians who knew how to sweep offices for bugs. A huge new market beckoned, and the ex-KGB responded in droves. By the mid-nineties, there were some eight thousand private guard and security services registered in Russia, involving some thirty thousand people.[10]

Victor Budanov was a pioneer. He had formed his own small security company, picking a few younger operatives he had worked with in KGB counterintelligence. His company worked closely with five other small companies, and Budanov could also call on contacts among the fifty similar groups in the trade association he headed.

Together, the groups held themselves out as a sort of trusted network, a bridge over the chaos. It is possible, Budanov readily admits, that ex-KGB officers also joined Russian Mafiya groups. He regards them as "traitors." "They are youngsters, mostly, young people with big muscles. Among them are people from the specially trained forces [military commando units]. But not officers of my age . . . the most honest and reliable people are those who served before in the KGB. We know each other. There are files there."

While thousands of former Russian intelligence officers poured into top posts in Russian businesses or into the firms that guarded them, the job market was different on the American side. The United States wasn't the Wild East. Spy credentials did not readily translate into a cushy job in a bank. Even private investigative firms were picky about people coming in from the cold. "I had a lot of job applicants from intelligence people," recalls Leila Kight, president of Washington Researchers Ltd., one of Washington's larger competitive intelligence firms. "They not only had to be trained, but retrained. I interviewed one fellow who made a very strong case on the phone. I brought him in and asked him a hypothetical: Company X wants to know about a plant in North Carolina being built by a competitor. They want to know what size is the plant, what technology will it use. I said how would you go about doing that. Answer: He would hire a helicopter, fly over, and take photos. . . . The information I was asking him for is strictly public information. It would have taken one of my researchers three phonecalls. In five phonecalls they could have gotten the blueprints. The cost of his approach would have been monumentally expensive."[11]

Most ex-U.S. spooks who went into the business of security and joined the trip to Moscow, like Mr. Flannigan from Atlanta, found the competition in Russia discouraging. Flannigan was endlessly fascinated by little paradoxes he discovered. For example, room service usually didn't work very well in the Ukraine Hotel, a Stalin-era pile that looks like a gigantic bowling trophy. But there were some people in there who were very efficient. Every night Mr. Flannigan would carefully take apart the smoke detector on the ceiling of his room and remove the small, live radio transmitter someone had connected there. Every morning, someone would insert a fresh one. But there was no long-term meal ticket in Moscow for Flannigan. "American companies can hire a thousand Russians to do what they'd have to pay me to do," he says.[12]

The leader of the American delegation, Gerard P. Burke, a lawyer and the former chief of staff of the National Security Agency—the U.S. eavesdropping agency—thought differently. He had formed a cluster of security companies, the Parvus Group, headquartered in Silver Spring, Maryland, and he had corporate customers in Russia who were experiencing thefts and extortion threats. "We do a lot of background investigations on joint ventures. The Western company wants to know who he's getting in bed with," explained Burke, who had been thinking about getting a Moscow connection.[13]

Burke knew Budanov by reputation, and they hit it off during three days of meetings in Moscow. Budanov enjoyed hearing Burke, a former White House intelligence adviser to President Nixon, tell war stories, and Burke found that Budanov, who had been plucked by the KGB out of a class of newly minted civil engineers in Novosibirsk at age twenty-three, had managed to preserve a spirit of Siberian frankness and geniality that he found appealing. The Russian was eager to make a U.S. connection, but who was Burke getting into bed with?

Burke had some friends who might know. One of them is Robert B. Wade, a tall, lanky FBI officer who worked as Budanov's equivalent in Washington. He headed the unit that performed all FBI espionage investigations. "He [Burke] looked at Victor very hard. So did I," explains Wade, who had spent most of his career trying to decipher the KGB. During the 1970s, Wade ran a unit that followed the KGB's Line X spies in New York City. While the scientists and engineers in Line X were very good, they were also restless and produced a number of defectors. When Wade's team found a promising recruit, that eventually meant new business for Budanov.

Wade checked the bureau's files for Burke. Again, Budanov came off as a professional, a man whose word had been good and whose record appeared untainted. In 1993, Burke signed a joint venture with Budanov. The resulting company, Parvus-Jerico Russia, attracted a number of American companies that needed help in Moscow. It also attracted Wade, who retired from the FBI in December 1994 and joined the U.S. branch of Burke's company as a senior vice president.

Once again, Wade is generating new business for Victor Budanov. American companies in Moscow want a twenty-four-hour hotline to security people, they want armed Russian drivers who speak good English, they want detailed evacuation plans in case the political situation breaks down completely, they want to know why entire shipments—trucks, drivers, and cargo-can disappear repeatedly without a trace. Budanov, who now sits on the security committee of the American Chamber of Commerce in Moscow, can often deliver. "We depend a lot on Victor and his network," admits Wade.[14]

On his new beat in Dodge City for the Americans and other Western companies, Budanov has applied some of his old skills: research, patience, a network of trusted friends, and a fondness for small details. Every day there are new adventures. A rich twenty-seven-year-old metal trader appeared in his office with two hulking bodyguards. They wanted security training. Budanov sent them packing. The "metal trader," he discovered, was a convicted murderer who had just bribed his way out of jail.

There was the case of the Jittery Japanese. An army of crooks constantly harassed the Moscow branch of a Tokyo company: employees were followed; company property was vandalized and its executives received regular kidnapping threats. It was like a vendetta. Budanov discovered that a year and a half earlier, the Japanese had refused to pay one of their Russian drivers. He had turned to a gang for help. "We told them it was their fault. If you pay, as the law says you have to, they will go away. So they paid and that was it."

Vanishing acts are one of the more constant themes in Budanov's new life. One company complained that three straight shipments of imported goods trucked in from Germany had disappeared along with their trucks and drivers. The insurance company would have been satisfied with a perfunctory probe that verified the goods were stolen, but Budanov's people discovered that the company's freight forwarder had developed a creative new sideline. He would arrange for a two-day delay at the Russian border, giving him time to forge the documents necessary to ship it to someone else.

"Sweeps," or electronic bug hunts, are also Budanov's bread and butter. Bugs have been a fixture in Moscow since the Russian Revolution, but Budanov says the police don't eavesdrop much any more. His current worry is a rash of imported German bugs that businessmen are using to spy on each other. "It happens all the time because people are afraid of their competitors," says Budanov. He brings in technicians with strange devices who crawl around the offices on their knees, searching for tiny, telltale blips of radio energy. "Our people are very good."

Then there is the "roofing business." Moscow's new legions of extortionists have a common trademark: "They come in to your business and say, 'I wonder if anybody is making a roof for your company?'" "Roof" is Russian slang for protection, and at that point the customer is usually given a schedule of fees and a choice: Pay $25,000 down and $10,000 a month or bad things will happen to your people and your company.

Budanov has found that mobsters in the protection business don't seem to have the patience or the staying power of other crooks. Their phone numbers usually turn out to be pager numbers. When Budanov's agents show up on the scene, the crooks generally opt to find customers elsewhere. "They do not live here, these people. They are usually from other cities. They're afraid not only of the ex-KGB, but of local organized crime groups. That's why they work so fast."

The former KGB general freely admits that sometimes the business of chasing amateurs and colorful crooks makes him long for the old days, the more deadly games and the adrenaline rush that came with catching moles like Vetrov. Sitting in his shirtsleeves in his austere, two-room corporate office on the top floor of a seedy high rise in northwest Moscow, Budanov has the kind of inner confidence that comes from having proven himself in the big leagues. He does not yearn to become filthy rich, like some of his ex-KGB counterparts. He seems content to be Moscow's answer to Sam Spade, happy to take whatever comes in the door. "At this point I have nothing to lose," he says, grinning.

To be sure, there is plenty of adrenaline left in the ex-spy business. Deadly games continue. There are some good examples in what the KGB once referred to as its "sister services," the Eastern Bloc spy agencies that often did Moscow's dirtiest work. Yaroslav Basta, a former Czech dissident and an archeologist, was given the job of dismantling Czechoslovakia's secret services in 1991.

The largest one, the STB, had more than 10,000 members and 140,000 collaborators, roughly one spy for every 100 Czechs. Many of the top party leaders had installed their relatives in it. When Basta fired them, they went into business, calling on some of their many connections, including friends from the old KGB.

Basta remembers one of them, a former KGB general who came to Prague hawking his new wares—Russian oil, and packages of "clandestine technologies," including those related to the design and manufacture of nuclear weapons. Using such ties, he says, some of the ex-Czech spies are among Prague's new business elite. "In Eastern Europe it is nonsense that we have free market capitalism. We have nomenclatura capitalism. We pay for freedom by letting the nomenclatura people be the richest. It is a tax for freedom."

In late 1990, the job of digging down through the layers of Bulgaria's spy agencies fell to Dimitar Loudjev, a stocky, perpetually tired-looking history professor who had helped form the first democratic political party in Sofia. With some energetic assistance from the CIA, Loudjev identified the top officials and had their names published in a newspaper. "All of these people belonged to prominent Communist Party families," he pointed out.

As the newly installed Minister of State Security, Loudjev found and fired thousands of spies, but there were always more to be found when he overturned the next rock. In late 1991, when he was appointed Defense Minister, Loudjev discovered a large network of Bulgarian companies operating overseas. They were set up at the request of the KGB in the late 1980s to steal technology from the West.

Loudjev followed spaghettilike trails of government money that led to banks in Liechtenstein, Switzerland, and Austria. There were over two hundred of these companies. Packed with experts and offshore funds, many of them went directly into private business, later reappearing in Sofia as Bulgarian representatives for large Western companies. Loudjev, trying to recover state money, had only begun to untangle this mess before he lost his job in late 1992 as the result of an election. "Nobody knows what the situation is with these file [front] companies," he says.

In all, Bulgaria had 10,000 spy agency officers and 50,000 helpers to police a nation of only 9 million. As in Czechoslovakia and Russia, at the top of this pyramid was an elite that has taken care of itself. "All of them were quite well prepared with the language and education to go into business," Loudjev maintains. "They know each other because they are fellows from the security agencies. For example, in one of the biggest Bulgarian financial groups, 75 percent of their employees were recruited from the former security agencies. The reason was very simple and it's typical."[15]

Finally, not everyone has gone private. In February 1996, Boris Yeltsin assembled his security council in the Kremlin and ordered them to get the state's still-sizable spy agencies to focus on "technological rearmament," by collecting new ideas from the West and then seeing that they are applied more quickly in Russia. It was the old Cold War approach, but with a new spin. "It is better to have a leading technology than a leading ideology," Yeltsin said.[16]

EIGHT

La Guerre Economique

"Life is seldom monotonous for an intelligence officer."
—P.L. Thyraud de Vosjoli,
former Washington station chief,
French Secret Service

On a bright morning in May 1991, a guard standing behind the sprawling home of an executive of a large U.S. defense contractor happened to notice two well-tailored men tossing plastic bags of garbage into their van.

Guards in the exclusive River Oaks section of Houston see many things. It is a neighborhood of excess, of in-your-face wealth; a place where people hire consultants to make their lawns turn a preternatural green and where dogs have psychiatrists. But custom-collected garbage?

The guard jotted down the license number of the van as it sped away. It belonged to Bernard Guillet, then the French consul general in Houston. That brought the FBI into the case.

In the vast arena of economic espionage, Americans have been looted by the Russians, outplayed by the Japanese, and overwhelmed by the Chinese; but the French, they are different. They are a close match. Their adventures often wind up in headlines.

As it happened, M. Guillet had a ready excuse. He and an assistant were looking for grass clippings to fill a hole dug for a swimming pool at his nearby house. The pool couldn't be completed because of a zoning dispute. A swimming pool—how interesting. The French, for swimming pool is *la piscine*. And "La Piscine," as every good counterintelligence agent knows, is the nickname of the Direction Générale de la Securité (DGSE), the one intelligence agency in the world whose operatives made no bones about economic espionage. They just did it.[1]

Two years earlier, the Houston office of the FBI had its first brush with La Piscine. The Feds had helped Texas Instruments find and remove a French mole. He was a "sleeper," an engineer suspected of siphoning exotic secrets out of the company since 1976. The FBI's gumshoes were well aware that in the pedestrian, but fast-growing and lucrative area of economic espionage, one of the most effective tools was "TRASHINT," the smelly but sometimes rewarding craft of sorting through a company's trash.

But the case against M. Guillet turned out to be, well, mostly garbage. And the matter of holding a consul general of France on a minor charge would cause more diplomatic grief than it was worth. Still, the FBI knew how to hit the French where it hurt. They trashed Guillet. News articles using the incident as a symbol began to appear in the *Wall Street Journal*, the *Washington Post*, and the London *Sunday Times*. "FBI agents . . . believe the French were more interested in discarded company papers than in landscaping," said the *Post*.[2]

The pieces outraged the French, who had been able to cloak their campaign for over thirty years in what they call "*non-dit*." There had been incidents, yes, but the rules of the old and well-traveled diplomatic road between Washington and Paris called for them to be *non-dit*, or unspoken. There was Lafayette; thousands of French dead at Yorktown; and the tens of thousands of American bodies piled up in France during World Wars I and II to consider. French agents caught with their hands in a U.S. company's files were secretly "PNG'd" or sent home as persona non grata, and the alliance was perfumed, as it were.

But things had begun to stink as early as December 1962, when the French station chief in Washington, a short, trim, dark-complected man with the imposing name of P. L. Thyraud de Vosjoli, was suddenly summoned to Paris. In the bowels of La Piscine, then called the Service de Documentation Extérieur et de Contre-Espionage or SDECE, he was handed a detailed new order: three hastily typewritten pages. He was to organize a network to spy on "U.S. military installations and U.S. scientific research."

De Vosjoli was no parlor spook. He had run spy networks against the Nazis in World War II, and serving in Washington since 1951 he had built the connection between the newly formed SDECE and U.S. spy agencies. He knew how hard it was to put groups together and how easily they fell apart. Washingtonians admired him. De Vosjoli drank martinis in Georgetown with his friend James Jesus Angleton, the legendary counterintelligence expert who had infused the agency with his concern about Soviet moles. At the onset of the Cuban missile crisis, de Vosjoli even pitched in and volunteered to spy for the Kennedy administration. He sent Washington firsthand accounts from Havana about the movement of Russian missiles. In short, de Vosjoli was different. While the SDECE drew most of its men from the ranks of France's military, its man in Washington was a civilian. It was not his habit to respond to every order with a crisp salute.

De Vosjoli's orders in December 1962 struck him as incredible. "I could not believe my ears," he recalled. He protested that such spying would seriously harm the alliance between France and Washington. But his superiors were adamant. President de Gaulle was outraged because the United States had agreed to share nuclear weapons secrets with the British, but not the French—"we no longer consider America our ally, our friend," de Vosjoli was told. "France has no friends." De Vosjoli demanded a copy of the order. He was refused. The code of *non-dit* must apply; the original he held in his hand was to be destroyed because the mere existence of the paper "constituted a danger."[3]

De Vosjoli returned to Washington, and in the silence of his small office in the old French Embassy building on Belmont Road, he turned the problem over in his mind. Spying on Washington was stupid. It would be like a knife in the back for the friendly relationships he had spent eleven years building. But there were others who would do it if he didn't. He was still mulling this over the following September when Paris grew tired of waiting. De Vosjoli was told his replacement would arrive in a month. A desk job awaited him in Paris.

On his last official day in Washington, October 18, 1963, de Vosjoli gave in to his conscience. Rather than take a new job with an organization that now disgusted him, he would resign. This news was not well received at La Piscine. A month later, on November 22, de Vosjoli was preparing his papers to return to France when he received three electrifying pieces of news. First, President Kennedy had been assassinated. Following that by a half hour was a cable from the SDECE ordering him to fly to Paris immediately. Then a friend called from Paris to tell him: "Orders have been given to silence you by all means."[4]

De Vosjoli knew the SDECE had its goon squads, so-called Action teams that carried out death orders. Sometimes they used U.S.-designed tranquilizer dart guns whose darts had been reloaded with poisons that mimicked symptoms of a heart attack. (One member of the hit team was trained to rush up to the victim in a show of concern and then remove the dart.) De Vosjoli decided it would be wise to flee to Mexico. He alerted his friends in the CIA that he was defecting and wanted eventual asylum in the States.[5]

In the early 1970s, as the Soviet Union stepped up its clandestine campaign to raid the West for economic secrets, France learned some hard lessons about the new economic terrain. Great Britain and West Germany were beginning to muscle France out of its traditional markets, so the Eastern Bloc seemed to beckon as a new frontier for trade.

It was the first flush of détente, and Bernard Esambert, then President Georges Pompidou's thirty-three-year-old economic adviser, remembers helping his boss order some fifteen heads of large French companies onto a plane to Moscow. Their missions were to create new markets in a hurry. It was a frenzied juncture of diplomatic and economic missions: "I got the idea what we were doing was something very much like war." Esambert later wrote a book that was to be entitled *La Guerre Economique* (*Economic War*), but his publisher insisted on changing the title. "War" was felt to be too strong a word.

What was going on, though, was more warlike than he and Pompidou realized. The promise of new markets was often just bait. In Romania, Nicolae Ceausescu's intelligence service, the DIE, had developed what it called the "drool technique": Lure Western businessmen into negotiations for fat contracts to build huge industrial projects, and then artfully milk them of enough technical detail so Romanian engineers could build the project themselves.

It helped to have the businessmen stay at the KGB-remodeled Athénée Palace Hotel, which had so many bugs that the whole place was like a live microphone. DIE agents made up its entire staff. The payoffs in stolen secrets were "dramatic, by 1978 becoming the single most important component of the country's economy," according to Lieutenant General Ion Mihai Pacepa, the head of DIE.

While General Pacepa admits that some of Romania's claims for the program were exaggerated, it seems clear that among the standout suckers for Romania's spooks were French businessmen. There were negotiations for a polystyrene plant that dragged out for over a year. Six Western companies were eager to deal, but none so much as the French, who kept responding to Romanian demands for more documents. Finally, in a grand show of panache, the French trumped the opposition by bringing in blueprints for the entire plant. "Understandably cautious, the French asked that their key documents be locked up every night in the safes of the Athénée Palace Hotel," recounted General Pacepa. When removed and photocopied, he added, the blueprints were enough for a "Romanian solution" for the polystyrene plant.[6]

The Japanese were also a problem. Count Alexandre de Marenches, the tall, aristocrat horse fancier who ran La Piscine from 1970 to 1981, recalled how eagerly the French received free-spending hordes of visiting Japanese businessmen and government officials: "People are rushing along because there is talk of big contracts. Factories are thrown open to the visitors, who generally go in twos or threes with a couple of cameras swinging on their stomachs."

What the Japanese took from the French factory owners, however, were not contracts but pictures of machines and descriptions of processes that were later copied and improved upon in Tokyo. When the products of those stolen ideas emerged, they often underpriced French products out of their markets.[7]

It was not an entirely new game to the French, who had used hundreds of volunteer businessmen—so-called honorary correspondents—to spy on other countries for years. They worked sporadically, mostly for medals or patriotism, and de Marenches, for one, began to see that they were underutilized in the economic area. "In any intelligence service worthy of the name you could easily come across cases where the whole year's budget has been paid in full by a single operation," de Marenches points out. "Naturally, intelligence does not receive actual payment, but the country benefits."[8]

The count's successor, Pierre Marion, was an Air France executive and longtime honorary correspondent. He tried to promote more economic espionage. But the spy agency had developed a bureaucracy drawn from the lower ranks of the French military, who did not like outsiders making waves in La Piscine. There were cliques of former parachutists and artillerists who seemed more interested in fighting each other and creating sinecures for their friends than they were in providing intelligence. "His [de Marenche's] overseas agents were giving him reports out of the newspapers . . . ," Marion complained. "The whole comprised a mosaic of groups that were ignorant of one another."[9]

Marion brought in civilians from French industry to set up an economic information section focused on industrial technology. He began to hold meetings with French companies to get a sense of what foreign technology they needed. Wish lists were drawn up and spy tactics were devised to fill them: "interception of documents or telephone conversations, penetrations of hotel rooms, recruitment, manipulation and use of informants were the ways that were not neglected."[10]

As a sign that what was going on within La Piscine was major reconstruction, its name was changed to the DGSE in April 1982. But Marion found more obstacles. Mitterand's people regarded his agency as a "nest of spies."[11] For at least ten years, the KGB had high-level moles operating in the SDECE. Moscow learned of NATO secrets almost as quickly as Paris did.

When the case of "Farewell" provided the opportunity to use a mole in the heart of the KGB's economic espionage operation, Mitterand decided it was too sensitive to entrust to La Piscine. Instead, he had it run through DGSE's rival agency, France's internal security service, the Direction de la Surveillance du Territoire (DST) (See chapter 6). He made a point of not telling Marion about it. The news, when it finally came, shocked Marion. The "professionals" of the overseas spy agency regarded the DST's people as mere gumshoes. To have them handling one of the biggest spy cases in the decade was demoralizing. The final shock came in November 1982, when Mitterand fired Marion, giving him no explanation.

By now, "Farewell" had buried Mitterand's experts in documents exposing the KGB's various schemes to steal technology. Mitterand shared some of the secrets with President Reagan to ingratiate himself as a good ally, but it seems clear that at the same time he quietly gave the go-ahead for France's spooks to try out some of "Farewell's" tricks on U.S. companies.

During the 1970s and 1980s, moles were recruited and inserted in the French operations of at least three U.S. companies: IBM, Corning Inc., and Texas Instruments. Meanwhile, other moles, budding scientists and engineers, appeared in the United States. According to American officials, the FBI captured five of them in the eighties and found they had been given draft deferments by the French government to go to the United States and work for U.S. companies. In the words of one official, "they were encouraged to take what they could." Like most draftees, they received a small monthly stipend. Some of them didn't know that it came from the DGSE. The United States launched a diplomatic protest, supplying the French with affidavits from the captured "draftees" describing the scheme. The French apologized and the matter was kept *non-dit*. But the spying didn't stop. One reason, according to U.S. officials, was that the DGSE had for years enhanced its budget by selling what its moles collected to French companies for a fee. Economic espionage was good business for all.

Some of the best hotels in Paris took on aspects of the best hotel in Bucharest: some rooms were bugged; documents left in rooms were surreptitiously copied; information put in hotel safes for protection fell right into the waiting hands of the DST. Laptops—some packed with years' worth of vital company records—had a way of disappearing. There were even reports that business-class seats on Air France were bugged. In the 1990s, the U.S. State Department and the Canadian Security Intelligence Service took the reports seriously enough to begin warning traveling businessmen.

But during most of the 1980s, the West's largest economy was sleeping, ignorant of economic spies. The story of Farewell was closely held, and what was going on in France was subordinated to a more central interest of the two main U.S. security agencies: fighting with each another. La Piscine's skirmish with the DST was small beer compared with the trench warfare between the CIA and the FBI. Although the FBI's charter included counterintelligence, the CIA worked hard to keep FBI agents from coming overseas. In the eyes of the CIA, which recruited from Ivy League schools, the FBI stood for "Foreign Born Irish."[12]

By 1989, however, the two agencies had arrived at a kind of detente. CIA and FBI agents had begun training together to improve their counterintelligence skills. That year an IBM affiliate in France received a package. It had been sent by someone from IBM, but the address label had come off or was too blurred to read, so the French post office had dutifully returned it. IBM officials were stunned: It contained highly confidential company documents, apparently being sent to a competitor.[13]

IBM called in the FBI, and FBI investigators were sent to the CIA station in Paris where a joint team spent seven months tracking down at least three French moles. Such cooperation was, in the words of one CIA official, "unprecedented in Agency history."[14]

Of course, it was all handled by the rule of *non-dit*. Companies were sworn to silence. Moles were fired. Relations with the French were quietly patched over. Although U.S. companies appear to have suffered substantial losses at the hands of French competitors, stockholders and the general public were kept in the dark.

In the United States, a country that fairly bristles with lawyers, the matter of French moles running loose with company secrets is the kind of thing that one would presume would get dragged into court. That did not happen until four years later, in October 1993. And then it was only because a French company, the government-owned Cie. des Machines Bull, decided to sue.

Bull charged that Texas Instruments was illegally making a computer chip that Bull had invented and patented back in 1978. The French company demanded that Texas Instruments send technical drawings and marketing material for the American company's new series of microcomputer chips to France so Bull technicians could better assess how much the infringement payments should be.

Initially, Texas Instruments had agreed to consider payments, but somebody in the company noticed something odd: Bull's chip was "uncannily similar" to one that had been invented by Michael Cochran, a scientist in Texas Instrument's calculator division in 1974, four years before Bull patented it. Cochran's division happened to be where the alleged French mole, Jean-Pierre Dolait, had worked for a time.

Lights began to go on at Texas Instruments. When Bull brought suit, the American company charged that Bull was suing to collect damages for a chip that it had earlier stolen. "It is apparent that the French espionage agent discovered working as a TI employee in 1989 had been feeding information useful to Bull from TI's calculator division for thirteen years," the company asserted.[15]

M. Dolait could not be reached for comment. According to court records, he had had an interesting career. The holder of a Ph.D. in aeronautical engineering from the California Institute of Technology, he had been teaching at Laval University in France in 1976 when he decided to return to the United States and to work for Texas Instruments. Until the company fired him in 1989, he had held thirteen different jobs and had gained intimate knowledge of the company's research and development base in the United States as well as its marketing strategies in Europe.

A U.S. attorney for Bull, Hadrian Katz, called the spy story "a fantasy," but in January 1995 the two companies decided to settle out of court. It was a familiar ending: The matter of who paid what to whom for what was *non-dit*.

But the protocol of *non-dit* was about to come to an end. The mole episodes had been galling enough. Meanwhile the Clinton administration had begun focusing on another major irritation: French companies were aggressively using bribes to wrest contracts away from U.S. rivals.

The bribery problem had been simmering for years in the arms business.

U.S. companies are forbidden by the U.S. Foreign Corrupt Practices Act to line foreign officials' pockets, but France has no such law. In the words of one U.S. official, the French are "the best in the world" at bribing to win contracts, although Asian countries, particularly Japan, run a close second. The problem, which is estimated to cost some U.S. companies some $20 billion in lost sales each year, grew more worrisome as former defense contractors plunged into new markets to keep their order books full. In the parlance of the U.S. Commerce Department it was known as the "Battle of the BEMs"—for Big Emerging Markets.[16]

Bribery is extremely difficult to prove. One possible sign is a sudden reversal in a contract that was thought to have been won. A funny thing had happened to Hughes Aircraft Company, a subsidiary of GM Hughes Electronics. It had been competing against Aerospatiale of France to sell the Arab Satellite Communications Organization (Arabsat) two communications satellites, for $250 million. The Arabs awarded Hughes the contract on September 30, 1992.

On April 12, 1993, the Arabs reversed their decision. The contract was to go to the French. Nobody said a bribe was involved, although Hughes later put out a press release stating that "some manufacturers are willing to accept extreme risks to achieve market share."

From the U.S. intelligence community's point of view, the Hughes case was just the tip of an expensive iceberg. The CIA later revealed it had completed a study showing that "questionable business practices" had been detected in seventy-two cases within a seventeen-month period. This represented "about $30 billion" in lost contracts and jobs for U.S. companies.[17]

That same month, Frank Greve, a reporter for the Knight-Ridder newspaper syndicate in Washington, received a strange brown paper package in the mail. It bore no postage; somebody had hand-delivered it. It contained twenty-seven pages written entirely in French. Greve, who had previously done a story about reports of French espionage in the United States, didn't read French, but he overcame that obstacle with panache worthy of de Vosjoli. He went home and cooked sausage and creamed noodles while his wife translated the document. Greve had been given what appeared to be an entire espionage plan, drawn up by the French in 1989 or 1990, to target forty-nine U.S. companies, twenty-four financial institutions, and six U.S. government agencies for secrets of high technology.

Entitled a "collection plan," and prepared by the "Exploitation-Implementation Office of the Department of Economics, Science and Technology," the document established the "intelligence requirements and related targets based on guidance and studies for each section."

Such targets were graded one, two, or three, depending upon their priority. Near the top of the list was Hughes, with a number-one priority for the very telecommunications satellite it had failed to sell to the Arabs. Other prime targets were helicopters, space launch programs, U.S. bargaining positions in trade talks, and "all types of accords with Japanese financial firms or banks."[18]

Sensitive documents that come "over the transom" are often impossible for reporters to confirm, but Greve found that DIA and CIA experts were eager to confirm this one's authenticity. Aerospace companies such as Hughes had already received government briefings on the contents of the report by the time Greve called.

It was the eve of the Paris Air Show, a biennial gathering of the aerospace business, and Greve's story caused an enormous flap. C. Michael Armstrong, Hughes's chairman, called the report "the last straw," and ordered Hughes to pull out. "It is one thing to compete globally and lose because of business shortcomings. It is quite another to lose to an unethical advantage gained when our competitors collaborate with their national intelligence services," said Clint L. Howard, director of the company's security unit.[19]

The only people unprepared for Greve's call were the French. "There is nothing in this document to indicate that it was released by French government offices," stammered a French Embassy spokesman.[20] The French were shocked. Someone had broken the rule of *non-dit!*

There was more to come. In November 1993 R. James Woolsey, the Clinton administration's first CIA director, made a speech to businessmen in Chicago. He promised that the U.S. government would take steps to protect its companies against foreign espionage, cases that it had tended to ignore in the past. "Well, no more Mr. Nice Guy," he said, carefully refusing to mention any countries by name.[21]

The U.S. intelligence community, including the National Security Agency and the CIA, had been plugged into a big room on the third floor of the Commerce Department's headquarters in downtown Washington. It looked more like a Wall Street trading room than a government office. Desks and cubicles bore the names of a variety of government agencies that might weigh in on a pending deal. Clocks on the wall were set for the time zones of big emerging markets like Brazil, China, and New Delhi. The Clinton administration had a new Commerce Department study that showed

U.S. firms may have lost as much as $40 billion worth of business deals through bribes by foreign competitors in two years.[22] Cabinet officials, including the president, let it be known that they were ready to work the phones, even to hop on a plane to save a deal.

In January 1994 the new French prime minister, Edouard Balladur, flew to Riyadh in Saudi Arabia for what was thought to be a ceremonial signing of a $6 billion package that included arms, airliners, and maintenance contracts. But the deal had suddenly turned around. Balladur found that the contract was going to Boeing and McDonnell Douglas after complaints from Washington officials about bribery.

A similar scenario played out in Brazil six months later, when a $1.4 billion project to build a series of sensors for climatological research that had been leaning toward Thomson CSF, the French arms giant, suddenly veered to the U.S. competitor, Raytheon. A series of press reports in the United States and Brazil quoted unnamed officials as saying that French bribes might have been involved.

As Woolsey explained, "No more Mr. Nice Guy" did not mean that the United States had changed its policy against spying on behalf of specific U.S. companies. It meant that when "such foreign bribery occurs or is about to occur," U.S. officials would call leaders of the country involved and raise hell. "Most such companies never realize that they have received our assistance and even state publicly that they do not need it. This is fine with us. It is the nature of the intelligence business."[23]

René Descartes, France's Renaissance philosopher, might have understood Woolsey's logic. He once taught that two bodies could communicate without talking by a kind of synchronization; but that's not the message that arrived at La Piscine. The nature of the intelligence business meant it was time for plotting revenge.

Meanwhile at the Elysée Palace something odd was happening. Balladur and some of his officials brooding over France's 12 percent unemployment rate, the highest in Europe, had become seduced by a new school of thought. The belief was that it was stupid for France to think it could win economic wars with spy games. It was better to imitate Japan and play smarter and faster, using mostly open sources of information.

Although France remained periodically annoyed with Washington, it had a deepseated phobia about Japan that had begun in the 1930s when sharp Japanese traders took over major portions of the shoe business and made heavy inroads into certain canned foods. The Japanese would size up markets, target crucial technology, diffuse the necessary information to win, and then take over with better, cheaper products. "So Japan came to know European markets better than the Europeans," wrote Christian Harbulot, a young political scientist.

In his influential book *The Machine of Economic War*, Harbulot argued in 1992 that Japan was mounting a new "economic colonialism" developed from a mixture of British global empire-building policies of the Victorian era and Soviet-style disinformation. It allowed Japanese politicians to promote a "borderless" world while keeping Japan's borders tightly closed to imports. To Harbulot, Japan was the real enemy. And France and America were its victims; only Americans suffered more because they were kept unconscious. "As soon as an anti-Japanese campaign sees the light in the U.S., the Japanese mobilize immediately their network of influence to neutralize it."[24]

Japan, to Harbulot, is a "force without a flag which practices doubletalk" to seduce U.S. free market planners. Germany and Sweden, which also use Japanese-style tactics to mobilize government agencies, banks, and businesses to win market share at any cost, are high up on Harbulot's enemies' list, too. To defeat such enemies, he argues, France must stop imitating the losing tactics of the Americans and develop its own plans to deal with the Japanese.[25]

Balladur liked Harbulot's approach and appointed him to advise a high-level commission, headed by Aerospatiale's recently retired chairman, Henri Martre. Martre's commission raised eyebrows: it criticized France, the French people's penchant for secrecy, and the French government's preoccupation with professional spies. Japan, it noted, had no professional spies: "The problem for their [Japan's] Western competitors is that there are several tens of millions of amateurs: the community of Japan's intelligence is confused at each instant with the whole nation."[26]

Martre, a stocky, balding man who piloted the huge Aerospatiale for nine tough years as it emerged as a competitor to Boeing, says, "My group invented nothing." It was obvious that information was the key to France's future, but years of tradition stand in the way. "It is more of a cultural problem than a technological problem," Martre adds. For cultural reasons, the French people are individualists, not collectivists like the Japanese."[27]

Now Martre has been appointed to head a committee to help change the culture by promoting the sharing of information—no small order in a country with hierarchical layers of secrecy, no Freedom of Information Act, and no Internet. He wants companies to begin talking to each other, and seeks to bring bankers and academics in to help find ways to develop and promote French exports.

Wheels of policy appear to be moving. "I want you to be really convinced that, for us, this is a radical change of philosophy in our habits," Rémy Pautrat, deputy head of the General Secretariat for National Defense, which coordinates policy for defense and intelligence agencies, told this reporter.

"The image of France as a country of intelligence professionals is completely wrong," asserted Pautrat, a suave, intense man who once headed the DST. While the United States has developed such a profession, France has failed to attract more than 3 percent of graduates from its top schools into its spy agencies, he notes. "If you want to have a good career, you don't go into intelligence.

"If we had been efficient [at spying] we wouldn't have the need to carry out this," Pautrat continued, referring to the new policy to use open sources of information. He blamed the spy foul-ups of the past on a disdain the French policy elite has held for France's spooks. "Our politicians haven't given precise directions to the services, which left them free to do what they want." Pautrat believes the cultural change needed to correct things could take twenty years.[28]

Part of the new scheme involves the use of private intelligence companies to teach business people how to use open sources to their advantage and how to protect their companies against foreign espionage. The first one is called INTELCO, and it is run by J. Pichot-Duclos, a retired army general who, until 1992, ran France's military school for spies. Right under him is Harbulot, who seems to turn up at each stage of the new policy.

Switching to total reliance on open sources amounts to a sea-change for General Pichot-Duclos, who spent years as an attaché lurking around Prague and Warsaw, spying on the opposition. After that, he worried about the Americans. Sitting in INTELCO's new Paris office, he still fulminates about the U.S. government's intervention in the Brazil and Saudi Arabian deals. "I want to tell you in a friendly way that this is very angering to the French people. It is double talk," he says.

Gently, Harbulot keeps bringing the conversation back to the problem at hand, which is how to beat the Japanese and everyone else at the game of open sources. At almost every opportunity, the general emphasizes the sweeping nature of France's policy change. "Moles are a product of the Cold War. The Cold War is finished."

At the end of the interview, however, the general seems wistful. His company, which is 49 percent owned by the French government, has as yet no competition and few customers, because French companies haven't become adjusted to the new ways. "We are pioneers, it is like the Old West. It is sad."[29]

On February 22, 1995, the DST settled an old score. It revealed that four U.S. diplomats and a fifth person had been caught spying on the French government, trying to get a preview of trade negotiation positions.

As spy stories go, it wasn't much. It evolved around the alleged machinations of a fiftyish Dallas public relations woman, Mary Ann Baumgartner, who had paid a young French official $400 to do a study. But the French press frolicked in a veritable cascade of leaks. It was a "purely intellectual" relationship, explained the magazine Le Point, "for the American 'spy' is clearly not structured along the lines of a Mata Hari."[30] Meanwhile, the CIA was strangely silent. There were some things it couldn't deny. The CIA's inspector general was called in to investigate and later acknowledged that the affair of the aging "Mata Hari" had been a major foul-up. His report was kept tightly classified, however. The policy of non-dit had suddenly returned.[31]

The mastermind who caught the United States spying, reportedly, was none other than Bernard Guillet, the man who made headlines in Houston in 1991 for collecting other people's garbage. Mr. Guillet's new post was diplomatic adviser to the overseer of the DST, Charles Pasqua, then France's Interior Minister.

By 1996, a kind of detente had emerged. According to U.S. counterintelligence officials, after over thirty years of spooking around in the United States, the French seem to have stopped. "They appear to have turned off their collection programs. They are not focusing on our technology right now," said one official who did not wish to be named. After a sometimes hamhanded, shadowy struggle that has lasted almost as long as the Cold War, this news will take a while to sink in for the U.S. intelligence community. The French were one enemy we could understand. "The question could be when do they turn this back on again," the official added.

NINE

War by Information

In the winter and spring of 1995, many of Washington's best defense minds assembled to take part in a series of six war games. As they took their places around large rectangular tables, there was usually a breezy familiarity within the groups, and a comfortable optimism about the game.

For these people—a mixture of older Cold War veterans and younger whiz kids—war games are old-hat. Over the years they had played many different scenarios. Some of them had planned, played, and won the high-tech battles of the Gulf War. There were generals and admirals, seers from government think tanks and laboratories, a smattering of high Defense Department officials, and experts from many of the companies that produce the computers, the guidance and communications systems, and other electronic gear that makes the United States the most formidable military power on earth.

A familiar scenario began to unfold before them:

It is mid-spring in the year 2000. Iran, after unsuccessfully demanding that the Arab oil states cut production by 20 percent, begins mobilizing for war. Meanwhile, there are serious signs of unrest in the kingdom of Saudi Arabia. Tension gathers like gasoline fumes over the Persian Gulf until two Saudi missile boats ignite the crisis, firing on two Iranian warships found lurking near a Saudi naval base. Saudi F-15s and Iranian MiG-29s tangle at 30,000 feet. An Iranian missile frigate locks its radars onto a patrol plane from the hulking new U.S. carrier, SS Ronald Reagan, and fires. F/A-18 bombers from the

carrier sink the frigate and send three of the MiG-29s spinning into the chop-
py green-gray water of the Gulf.

Juices in the room began flowing and old, warrior reflexes were aroused
as the RAND Corporation visionaries who planned this game explained that
an imaginary president was just down the hall waiting for the group—his
top national security advisers—to recommend how the United States should
respond. The people at RAND, an Air Force think tank, then trotted out
some proposals. On the conventional side there was GREEN HORNET, an elaborate plan to send at least five divisions of U.S. troops and three carrier battle groups in time-phased segments to the Gulf region.

On the unconventional side was NET MASTER, a scheme to use computer
attacks and sophisticated jamming to destroy Iranian telecommunications,
energy, transportion, banking, and information systems. It contained a
package of electronic moves designed to bring Iran's economy to its knees
without bombing buildings or killing many civilians.

The scenario continued:

U.S. peace groups express vehement opposition to any U.S. involvement. The
telephone system for Northern California and Oregon suddenly fails. A U.S.
Army base at Fort Lewis, Washington, reports that thousands of incoming
phonecalls from computers have paralyzed its switchboards. A high-speed
Metroliner heading for New York plows into a freight train that has been mys-
teriously misrouted onto its track. CNN, in the midst of reporting the train
crash, suddenly drops off the air for twelve minutes. The New York Stock Ex-
change tanks, losing 200 points in one day as institutional investors panic to
get out of electronically controlled markets. A French Airbus airliner making
its final approach to O'Hare International in Chicago crashes into a suburb
after its electronic controls go dead. Pentagon technicians find that an elec-
tronic "worm" is injecting spurious information into the database of the com-
puters controlling the time-phased deployment of U.S. military units.

Overseas, the Bank of England reports that it fears a massive loss of funds
because technicians have just found devices called "sniffers" in the computer
system that controls money transfers. An errant process-control computer trig-
gers an enormous explosion near Saudi Arabia's main oil-pumping system at
Dhaharan. As Saudis watch the blaze on government television, the nation's
two most prominent newsanchors are surprisingly transformed. Their faces
become the faces of the leaders of a prominent underground group. On the air
they call for the peaceful overthrow of the kingdom. Saudis race for their

phones, but the kingdom's newly installed cellular system has gone complete-
ly dead. . . .

In each of the six games, the tension and the confusion simulated in the Gulf erupted in the game room after this scenario. Players began to argue with each other. Some of them argued against the scenario: "The U.S. is the sole surviving superpower". . . . "They wouldn't dare" . . . "They're too dumb."[1]

Cooler heads in the room quickly got to the nub of the problem: Who were "They?" The facts of the scenario didn't offer much help. The U.S. intelligence community and law enforcement agencies were like a compass that pointed in all directions. The wizards at the National Security Agency with its huge, computerized eavesdropping apparatus doubted that Iran had the sophistication to foul up U.S. computer systems. The FBI's counterter-rorism experts suspected domestic groups that "may or may not be con-nected with the unfolding events in the Persian Gulf."[2] Security and Exchange Commission investigators said unknown players using banks in Europe and the Middle East had caused the stock market crisis. France's Interior Minister told the U.S. Justice Department that two top suspects in the plane crash were U.S. extremists who had received large cash payments through a Swiss bank "from a foreign but unidentified source."

The RAND game often led to a "paralytic effect" because the players within the groups could not agree on what action to advise.[3] Tangled in a myriad of computer foul-ups, GREEN HORNET disintegrated into what one planner described as a "goddamned mess."[4] Groups usually voted to keep NET MASTER on the shelf. How could the United States deter an enemy from mounting computer attacks if it was itself more vulnerable than the enemy was one strong argument that kept NET MASTER out of the game.

For many of the players it was a rude introduction to what the Pentagon has come to call "Information Warfare." Leon Sloss, a former State Department nuclear weapons strategist who served as a discussion leader for one of the groups, described the general tone as "bafflement," saying, "In the real world we would have been forced to make decisions, but I think everybody would have been very frustrated with the thin basis we had upon which to make them. The decisions would have been, well, retaliate against so-and-so, when we didn't know for sure who so-and-so was."[5]

One of the many ironies of the game was that the main tools used by the enemy—whoever it was—had been perfected by the Pentagon, beginning with the Internet, which was devised by the RAND Corporation in the mid-1960s, as a national communications system that could survive a nuclear attack. As the Pentagon began to develop the system during the seventies, it became a convenient way to help scientists in U.S. weapons laboratories share computer databases. In the late eighties, as commercial use of Internet began to explode, hordes of new users appeared.

Not all of them were benign. Most of the attacks simulated in the game have already occurred, often in computer "hacker" incidents masterminded by teenagers or college dropouts. And, just about as often, the identities of the victims and the extent of their damage has been covered up. In the nineties, U.S. experts began to worry that the nation's unique and ever-growing reliance on computerized information has become a kind of Frank-ensteinian vulnerability, one that, as the RAND game suggests, can be turned upon its master.

The very idea that information can be used as a weapon is foreign to most people. Certainly it was a foreign idea to a group of students at the Massachusetts Institute of Technology who were caught carrying a giant female nipple in December 1978. MIT claims to be the originator of hacks, or clever tricks carried out by using science and engineering skills. But MIT's overriding rule, according to Warren Seamans, director of the MIT Museum, is that hacking is never supposed to hurt anybody.

The giant nipple—a pink, paper-and-chicken wire monstrosity about the size of a car—was designed to fit on top of the huge breast-shaped concrete dome that covers MIT's main administration building. After they were caught twice more by campus police, the perpetrators built a collapsible nipple that could be carried in segments, in backpacks. Then they snuck the segments into the building after hours, picked locks on office doors, and rewired an elevator so it could lift them to a place where they could climb out on the dome. The hack was completed the following August when fresh-men being assembled for orientation week looked up one morning and saw a proud pink nipple on the dome.

When the idea of using computers for hacking began to spread beyond the neighborhood of the Great Dome, the perpetrators didn't always follow the MIT ethic to do no harm. The potential for great harm didn't sink into the various layers of the Pentagon until the buildup to the Gulf War in 1990. A group of Dutch hackers calling themselves "High Tech for Peace" approached diplomats in the Iraqi Embassy in Paris. For a payment of $1 million, the Dutch hackers offered to foul up the network handling logistics messages between bases in the United States and U.S. military units in Saudi Arabia. The Iraqis rejected the idea.

It was one offer Saddam Hussein should have accepted. Twenty-five percent of the message flow coming into Saudi Arabia during the war was running in the open, uncoded, on the Internet. After the war, Pentagon planners began to see the possibilities that had lured the Dutch hackers. Messages for vital spare parts could have been destroyed, rerouted, or simply changed so that the whole supply apparatus could be thrown into chaos. At the time, the Pentagon's notion of Information Warfare was a growing body of electronic tricks that could be played on the enemy. Defense officials ordered a seldom-seen maneuver, a U-turn at full throttle. In the mid-nineties the emphasis suddenly shifted to the defense.

"We're more vulnerable than any other nation on earth," was the way Vice Admiral John M. McConnell, director of the National Security Agency, put it during a symposium on military intelligence in June 1995. The nation's banks, its Federal Reserve, and the growing global financial market, he noted, all have come to depend heavily on computer systems that can be attacked.[6]

Aside from the great difficulty of figuring out who the enemy is, there are other odd aspects of Information War. Unlike most other forms of attack against a major power, entry into the game is extremely cheap. According to a secret report by the White House's National Economic Council, "In recent years foreign intelligence services—including small, poorly funded services—have increasingly used computers against U.S. economic targets." They have acquired hacker techniques from computer bulletin boards, recruited agents who had access to computers, or recruited hackers to invade computer systems via the Internet.[7]

There were times when the enemy wasn't even an enemy, merely a bright teenager looking for thrills. "I know there are hackers out there that trash systems and cause havoc," explains Rop Gonggrijp, who edits *Hack-Tic*, a magazine for Dutch hackers. A man in his middle twenties with a wispy blond mustache and a mischevous grin, Gonggrijp says he hasn't broken into any computers for at least five years, but he can understand the motivations of those who do.

"Most of these breakins are actually fourteen- and fifteen-year-old kids. It's their way of graffiti." Cruising into the United States at the speed of light over the Internet and hitting the stern message that marks the gateway to many U.S. government computer systems—a message to the effect that unauthorized intruders will be prosecuted by the FBI or the Secret Service—is something like cow-tipping or drag racing was to earlier generations of Americans. It presents a challenge.

"U.S. computers are so much fun," Gonggrijp continues. "If you get further in than this it's a federal offense and you can have your house taken away and God knows what; that's fun. If you're in Holland and so far away from all that. . . . The feeling is, you can't catch me, I'm invincible. It's a phase in people's lives. Imagine, you can do graffiti on the Secret Service and no one comes after you! It's like the ultimate graffiti."[8]

To hundreds of American corporations that have been victimized, this isn't funny at all. But another odd thing about Information Warfare is that, as far as U.S. corporations are concerned, it is a crime that is only rarely reported. According to James C. Settle, who formerly headed the FBI's computer crimes squad in Washington, hacker cases he investigated involving intrusions into U.S. government systems often encompassed whole daisy chains of U.S. corporations, which begged to remain anonymous. "If we had an airplane crash, they would send everybody and his brother out to get a fix on it," points out Settle. "With computer problems, we don't even know they happen. When you think about it, it's stupid."[9]

In September 1993, John Ward, the computer systems manager for the U.S. National Weather Service, found himself being sucked into this electronic netherworld. From his control panel he could see that hackers were rummaging around in the big computers that function as the electronic brains for U.S. weather forecasters.

He called in Settle's FBI squad and arranged to keep the computers running, programming a series of subtle changes that isolated the hackers' access to a relatively unimportant sector of the agency's huge database. Because he was the sole keeper of the system's secret passwords, Ward realized he had to do much of the detective work himself. He couldn't confide in fellow employees at the agency.

For some reason, the attacks always came down the Internet from a laboratory at MIT. Ward found an ally in Jeff Schiller, manager of the university's computer network. The two rigged up an alarm system. When the intruders entered the MIT system through an account that they had, somehow, compromised, a door chime would ring at the Weather Service's center at Camp Springs, Maryland. If the hackers reached the machines at Camp Springs, a bell that sounded like an alarm clock would go off.

When they reached Camp Springs, a suburb of Washington, the hackers always went straight for the Weather Service's secret password file, words that allowed access into major files in the database. They were all written in code, but that did not prove to be a major obstacle. Ward's computers had excess capacity and the hackers soon set it to work, using a special software program called a "hacker's dictionary." It used millions of calculations to crack the more obvious passwords.

Then Ward made another discovery: Those weren't just his passwords being cracked. The hackers were bringing in passwords from U.S. companies. Their reach was amazing. One night they brought in passwords from a computer network in South America. Another night they were trundling back data hacked out of companies somewhere in Europe. "We'd just sit here and watch them do it," explained Ward. He and the FBI promptly notified the owners of the other networks that their systems were compromised.

It was a nightmarish experience. He was in charge of computers that do 95 percent of the nation's forecasting. If the hackers, whoever they were, could jump over the makeshift electronic fence he had created, forecasting would stop. Without weather forecasts, the airlines would soon have to shut down. Then the damages would quickly begin to mount—"We could be talking in terms of tens of millions of dollars per hour."[10]

Ward's is one case, though, where the hackers came to learn they were vincible. Very early on a Saturday morning in November 1994, the door chime at Camp Springs went off and meteorologists called Ward's pager with a prearranged message: "They're back."

Ward jumped in his car. When he arrived at the computer room, he discovered that this was his lucky day. Often the hackers just popped into his machines for a moment, as if to see that it could still be done. Even when they lingered, their tracks were lost in Boston because the phonelines coming into MIT were extremely busy, making calls hard to trace.

But this time Settle's FBI techno-slueths had gotten the call traced to a Boston SPRINT office. And SPRINT supervisors quickly traced the hackers to Denmark. This was a shock to Danish police, who were investigating thirty-six recent hacker attacks on university, government, and business systems there. "The first time we saw this, we thought it was hackers from the Unites States coming into Denmark," explained Jorgen Bo Madsen, the Danish government's security consultant on the case.

Now the question was, where were they in Denmark? This was tougher. Unlike the electronic phone system in the United States, Denmark's phones still relied on mechanical switching stations. To trace a call, a technician must be present at the switching center near where it originates. The Danes put thirty-five investigators on the case.

Through sheer luck, on December 8, one of them was standing in a switching station at Roskilde, in the suburbs of Copenhagen, when the alarm clock rang in Ward's computer room. Seven young men with such colorful cyber nicknames as "Wedlock," "Zephyr," "Dixie," and "Le Cerveau" were arrested. Their ages ranged from seventeen to twenty-four.

According to Madsen, their operations were global. They jumped from computer networks to telephone lines and back to reach computers in Japan, Brazil, Israel, and Europe, as well as thirty-two different systems in the United States. While they did little damage to computers, according to Madsen, they financed their electronic joy rides with over $1 million worth of credit card calls charged to AT&T customers in the United States. Through a process hackers call "social engineering," the Danish hackers had developed a ruse to get the U.S. holders of the cards to reveal their PIN numbers. They would call, identifying themselves as operators in the ATT "security division," and say the numbers needed to be changed.

Hackers are often portrayed in the U.S. media as being near geniuses, but Madsen says the Danish hackers simply copied most of of their tactics from bulletin boards on the Internet: "These are in fact not particularly inventive people, nor do they possess an advanced computer education."[11]

In another hacker case at about the same time, one that involved one hundred different victims—again, many of them undisclosed U.S. corporations—the U.S. Air Force had to shut down two hundred computers at an intelligence and communications laboratory in Rome, New York, a move costing over $500,000.

This was a "sniffer" attack—like the one portrayed in the war game on the Bank of England—so the case was far more serious than the mere cost of downtime and repairs. Sniffers originated as software programs used by operators to monitor the traffic on a network of computers. They simply store the first portions of incoming electronic messages called "packets," enough to disclose the passwords and names of people using the system. Later, when the sniffers are queried, the operators get a list of people using their system. When the programs for sniffers were published on bulletin boards, however, they fell into the hands of outsiders who could use them to collect passwords.

Prowling through the electronic innards of thirty systems at the Rome

Laboratory, Air Force technicians found six sniffers. Like so many electronic leeches, they had been sitting silently for weeks, sucking up passwords of various users. Then whoever had planted them would enter, download the memories of the sniffers, and leave. It was simple, like emptying a crab pot or a parking meter. The attacks on Rome usually came from computers owned by two private companies—one in New York City, the other in Seattle, Washington. The calls went all over the world. One penetration involved military secrets stolen from South Korea's Atomic Research Institute.

Again, it was a lucky hit that nailed one of the perpetrators. Somebody remembered a hacker named "Data Stream" bragging about his exploits on the Internet and told the Air Force. When detectives from Scotland Yard finally found the home of his parents in London and pulled him away from his computer, the hacker curled up in a fetal position on the floor and cried. "Data Stream" was sixteen.[12]

The Air Force has found that Data Stream had an older mentor, someone known only by the cybername "Kuji." A more sophisticated and cautious hacker, Kuji told Data Stream which military-related computers to attack and then took all the resulting information from him. Investigators believe Data Stream and Kuji never met, conversing entirely via the Internet. While Data Stream may have been a curious, thrill-seeking teenager, Air Force officials suspect that Kuji was a spy, working for a foreign government collecting U.S. military research information.[13]

By December 1993, sniffers had been installed on primary computer networks that carry much of the world's Internet traffic. The Pentagon's Defense Information Systems agency estimated that the devices had stolen access codes from over 100,000 Internet users, codes that were then used to install more sniffers.[14] The plaguelike nature of the devices was the reason why the Bank of England was immobilized by sniffers during the RAND Corporation's war game. Access to passwords that can enter bank computers can cost millions.

In August 1995, two months after the last RAND game had been played, officials of Citicorp charged that a twenty-eight-year-old Russian chemistry graduate, Vladimir Levin, had somehow used a computer in St. Petersburg, Russia, to break into the New York bank's computerized cash management system and illegally transfer $12 million. Of that, according to the bank, $400,000 was stolen.

"It's purely by grace of God that this hasn't happened before," says the

FBI's James Settle, who has since resigned and gone into the computer security business. One way to defeat sniffers, he notes, is to install one-time password generators that give legitimate users a new password for each entry. Another defense is to use code. "Ninety-nine percent of the time," he says, companies "are not doing either one of them."

While companies don't talk about their vulnerability to hackers, the Pentagon has tested its own systems, so we have a rough idea of whether the vulnerabilities exploited in the RAND game are widespread in a big organization. Using techniques derived from hackers, military technicians attacked twelve thousand Department of Defense computer systems. Eighty-eight percent of the time, they gained unauthorized entry; and in 96 percent of those cases, the attacks weren't detected.[15]

Could a foreign power shut down the telephone system for an entire region? Young hackers prosecuted in Atlanta, Georgia, in the so-called Legion of Doom case later told investigators that because they had gained control over Bell South's computers, they "had the ability to shut down phone systems throughout the entire southeastern United States."[16]

Several of the tricks that shocked the players at RAND's game are ancient history to hacker-watchers. The use of computer-generated calls to jam switchboards started back in 1990 when Kevin Lee Poulsen, styling himself "Dark Dante," used over 102 calls to take over the 24 phones on a radio station's switchboard and win himself a new Porsche in a promotional contest.[17]

The "worm" that fouled up GREEN HORNET in the game has been around since 1988, when Robert Morris, Jr.'s, worm slowed traffic on the Internet to a crawl.

As for the matter of taking over another country's broadcasting networks, the United States has been secretly doing that to its enemies for decades. According to Colonel Thomas Kuhn, vice commander of the Air Force's 193rd Special Operations Group, the capability emerged in the late 1960s as a response to the Cuban missile crisis.

The unit, run by the Pennsylvania Air National Guard from Harrisburg, Pennsylvania, has only recently been permitted to talk about itself. It uses six strange, gray C-130s that carry bulky electronic pods and that trail long arrays of antennas from their tails. In effect, they are flying television and radio studios that can simply take over the frequency of local stations by substituting a more powerful signal. The planes, long known to insiders by a code name—"Command Solo"—can be a powerful propaganda weapon.

According to Colonel Kuhn, twenty thousand Iraqi soldiers surrendered to Command Solo planes in the Gulf War after voices, coming out of their own military radios, told the Iraqis that if they gave up, the B-52 bombers plowing swaths of bloody destruction through their formations would stop.

"We can broadcast color television on all worldwide standards. It's quite an engineering marvel," says Kuhn. He is well aware that a recent innovation in videotape editing, called "morphing," can actually change the faces of people on television. That would make Command Solo an even more powerful propaganda tool; but, historically, Kuhn notes, the U.S. military has stayed away from fiction. "We've found that the truth is a very powerful weapon."[18]

The truth of the RAND game and the games that hackers continue to play is that fixing the nation's leaky information systems will cost everyone a lot of money and take a very long time. For openers there is MISSI, the "Multi-level Information Systems Security Initiative," being led by the hyper-secretive NSA. Designed to bring much tighter security to the systems used by U.S. military and intelligence agencies, this will cost "several hundreds of millions of dollars" through 1999, according to James J. Hearn, a former deputy director of the NSA.[19] MISSI will offer "superencryption" to the government's most sensitive information; that is, coded words will coded again, and again.

But MISSI would just be a start because Pentagon planners estimate that in future military crises, given the huge demands for communication, as much as 60 percent of the military's messages will have to go over the Internet and the U.S. telephone system. The cost of developing systems for encryption and verification of that traffic would be somewhere between $15 to $18 billion, and it would take eight to ten years, according to Emmett Paige, Jr., assistant secretary of defense for communications and intelligence. "That is even if we had the money to fix it, which we don't."[20]

Even with the fix, DOD security officials had better not relax. Unauthorized people who gain access to a terminal on a secure system can have what amounts to the keys to the safe. Captain Joe Garmon, an Air Force computer expert, gave the Navy proof of that during a military field exercise near Boston in September 1995. Using a simple desktop computer from his tent, Captain Garmon went over a military equivalent of Internet, called Siprnet, and found his way into the computer system that controlled a U.S. Navy warship patrolling in the Mediterranean.

According to an Air Force spokesman, Captain Garmon couldn't actually steer the ship, but he could begin giving it spurious information. "If their computer was tracking a sub, he could make the sub disappear or appear somewhere else." The Navy has since closed the loophole in Siprnet.[21]

As for the commercial sector, the protectors of most of the U.S. economy, RAND game planners assumed that through the year 2000 they will continue to try to ignore the problem while becoming much more reliant on vulnerable systems like the Internet and cellular telephones. It seems like a good bet.

If so, the job of fixing things may go by default to lawyers, who tend to be the nation's answer to expensive, intractable problems. They are likely to drive up business costs still further, suing computer systems operators found to have left loopholes or mismanaged passwords, and perhaps suing companies that fail to tell other companies when they know their passwords have been compromised. "Civil liability is likely to create incentives for improving security of information systems," is the way a task force studying the problem for the White House's Office of Management and Budget recently put it.[22]

As for the hackers, a generation of juveniles who have cut their teeth on notions of easy fraud, vandalism, larceny, and trespass—crimes with no apparent victims—they will grow older and hungrier, but perhaps not necessarily wiser. Don B. Parker, consultant to a large research firm, SRI International, thinks the age of harmless tricks is over. He has interviewed over two hundred hackers and has found a "big cultural battle" going on between the older ones, who claim they don't harm anyone and only explore computers out of curiosity, and the younger ones. The younger ones say, "That's all fine, but we want to make lots of money."

The problem, according to Parker, is not far from a notion of war. "It's like giving very large armaments to juveniles when they're very idealistic and unpredictable. We have . . . an increasingly dangerous situation."[23]

TEN

Mining the Air

"I'm shocked, shocked to find that gambling is going on here."
—Captain Renault, in *Casablanca*

On Monday, October 15, 1995, Ichiro Fujisaki was shocked. He was the political minister for the Japanese Embassy in Washington, D.C., and, over the weekend the *New York Times* had quoted an anonymous "senior" U.S. official as admitting that a U.S. intelligence agency had eavesdropped on Japan's trade negotiators.[1]

Fujisaki grabbed the telephone and called the U.S. State Department. If this was true, Fujisaki warned, it would "hurt friendship and mutual trust between Japan and America."[2]

U.S. trade negotiators, who believe their deliberations have been bugged by Japan for at least fifteen years, thought it was an amusing response. "A bit hysterical; maybe they didn't have anything better to do that day," offers retired Ambassador Michael B. Smith, who handled trade talks with Tokyo from 1981 to 1988.

Clyde V. Prestowitz, Jr., another former negotiator, figures it had to be a face-saving gesture, part of the theater of diplomacy. Fujisaki wasn't shocked; he was lying. "It was one of those cases where they're lying, we know they're lying, and they know we know they're lying." Both countries have enormous eavesdropping capabilities and regularly use them, he notes. "It's there. It fashions your life."

In the rarefied world of trade negotiations, coping with bugging is part of everyday life, especially in Tokyo, which is emerging as the capital of the world for high-technology eavesdropping gear. It starts where U.S. officials normally stay, at the Hotel Okura, an aging, sixties-era establishment just down the street from the U.S. Embassy. Room rates begin at $260 a night— by Tokyo standards, a bargain. There is a quiet garden where guests can escape the nerve-jangling pace of the city, and a very alert, attentive staff. In fact, American guests have long suspected that the Okura gives them more attention than they want.

"I'm told we would regularly send people over there to sweep the place and, routinely, they found bugs," recalls Ambassador Smith. "Nobody in their right mind would make a serious telephone call from the Okura," says Prestowitz.

Both men found ways to cope. Prestowitz took colleagues to noisy bars to work out negotiating strategies. Ambassador Smith preferred the outdoors: "You just go out and take a walk in the park. They can't bug the parks."[3]

Perhaps not yet. But Japanese firms are working hard to create and dominate a global commercial eavesdropping industry, applying simplified engineering, quality assurance, and mass production to exotic technologies developed by the United States and Russia during the Cold War. Then they are driving the price down to the point where high-quality devices—tiny, concealable radio transmitters or tape recorders, hard-to-detect telephone taps, and television sensors shrunk to the size of a fifty-cent piece—sell for a few hundred dollars, quite affordable to the business or even the home next door.

In the summer of 1994, Tokyo police raided a private detective agency and recovered 166 tapes of recorded telephone conversations. The agency's clients included: an enemy of a candidate running for mayor in a small town; the competitor of a Yokohama auto parts dealer; and the president of a newspaper who had his sister's telephone tapped as part of an inheritance fight. "All detective agencies tap telephone wires," the head of the detective company reportedly told police. Meanwhile, the victims who heard their taped conversations were once again described as being "shocked."[4]

They shouldn't have been. Manufacturing and selling bugs is legal and flourishing in Japan. Tokyo's Akihabara district is a rabbit warren of electronic goods outlets that sell bugs for all occasions, as well as manuals such as *Tocho-no Subete* (*Wiretapping from A to Z*). "How customers use listening devices is up to them. We sell the goods on the assumption they won't be used for illegal purposes," one storeowner told a reporter.[5]

In the not-too-distant future this phenomenon will fashion the lives of U.S. business people, just as it has done for trade negotiators and government officials for years. It has already begun to turn American cities into electronic Casablancas where a few callused experts hear and see the play on the ethereal battleground of electronic thievery. As for the rest of us— which includes most U.S. business executives—there will come a day when we are shocked.

William E. De Arman, a U.S. undercover Customs agent, got a glimpse of this future in June 1994 when he lured a slim, graying, bespectacled Japanese man to a meeting in New York. As the president of a Tokyo company called Micro Electronics Ind. Co., Ltd., Tatsuo Hinata is the Henry Ford of bugs.

By downsizing and improving the circuitry on a bug first developed by the CIA in the sixties, Hinata's company has come to dominate the U.S. and world markets. Micro's bugs have turned up in such diverse circumstances as new businesses in Moscow, a kidnapping and extortion plot in New York City, and inside a half ton of cocaine, disguised as hard candy, sent by the Cali cartel to Miami. During the seventeen months ending in February 1995, Customs investigators estimate 4,367 Micro bugs were smuggled into the United States, where they fetched some $2.9 million from people who put them to various uses.[6]

Like Ford and his cars, Micro sets the standards for bugs. They broadcast on three precise UHF frequencies, frequencies that have since been adopted by Micro's many imitators. For his meeting with De Arman, who was posing as a U.S. wholesaler, Hinata smuggled in a sample of his handiwork. It looked like a standard plug for a telephone jack, only it was capable of broadcasting both sides of a phone conversation. Because it feeds off of telephone current, it can operate virtually forever.

But De Arman, the undercover Customs agent, was fussy. He wanted a more powerful bug that could be concealed in a electrical power strip, the kind that are used to hook up most personal computers. Hinata said he would think about it when he returned to Tokyo. A week later, De Arman received a fax: a sample bugged power strip was on its way.[7]

Japan's bugs are becoming part of the American way of life. Although they have been outlawed since 1988, they are sold by a network of "spy shops" under the ruse that they are for sale only to law enforcement agencies and overseas customers. According to the U.S. Customs Service, Micro imported them as "electronic equipment" and used two sets of invoices to understate their price. Among the "overseas" customers who buy them are lawyers and investigators in divorce and child custody cases.[8]

Some evenings, as he cruises the streets of Charlotte and Raleigh, North Carolina, Dave McCall, a former U.S. Special Forces electronics expert, punches buttons on a radio scanner he has in his car. They are set for Micro's frequencies. It is a rare evening, he says, when he doesn't pick up a conversation.

The sound of bugs talking means business for McCall, who operates a security company in nearby Fayetteville, and frequently instructs law enforcement officials in how to use and defend against bugs. But some of Micro's newest bugs, he admits, make it hard to figure out a defense. For example, there is Micro model no. PK-300: a ballpoint pen that actually writes. It is also a radio transmitter that transmits conversations up to a block away.

"Say a guy goes into a conference room for a negotiation. He makes a proposal to the other side and then goes out to the men's room. He leaves his pen on the table. In the men's room he pulls out his earphones or maybe his car out on the street has an automatic recorder going. He gets instant feedback. Very rarely do businessmen check someone's inkpen to see if there's a transmitter in it. It's not polite."[9]

Hitachi, Sony, and other Japanese companies also lead the world in so-called pinhole surveillance television cameras that are being installed in wall clocks, eyeglass frames, smoke detectors, no-smoking signs, and loose-leaf notebooks. New technology has made them virtually invisible, shrinking the electronics down from a lunchbox to a fifty-cent piece in about ten years, explains Herman Kruegle, an electrical engineer who sells the cameras for a New Jersey firm.

"You can buy all of these devices and become a high-tech spy overnight," says Kruegle. While companies have a legitimate need to use them for security purposes, Kruegle worries about other uses because few people are aware of them. "I don't like to have my privacy invaded." So far, though, he's not aware of any law on the subject.[10]

The owner of an electronic equipment store in suburban Washington used to make a tidy business selling exotic items to U.S. intelligence agencies. Now his market is much broader, thanks to new Japanese-built scanners and computer software built to tune in on cellular phone conversations.

In the 1960s, the hyper-secretive National Security Agency spent billions of dollars to build football field–sized computers and giant antennas to monitor international telephone traffic. The antennas would suck the traffic in and the computers would scan for phone numbers that would allow the agency to sift out important calls.[11] The equipment storeowner displays a scanner the size of a breadbox attached to a laptop computer. Together, they perform the same function as NSA's gargantuan machines did for a mere $5,000.

The scanner taps cellular phones, a market that has literally exploded. There were 4.4 million cellular phones in 1990; today there are over 30 million. The storeowner has customers who spend a lot of their time tapping their neighbors' calls. He demonstrates, punching a button on the scanner. *Bip.* Two businessmen are discussing each other's reputations. *Bip.* A woman is negotiating the sticky part of a real estate deal. All the voices have that soft, confiding sound of people who assume they are talking in strict privacy.

In fact the law protecting them is a soufflé of loopholes. It is illegal to own such a scanner, except for scanners like the storeowner's, which was made before the law was passed in 1992. New scanners still come in from Japan, supposedly equipped with wiring that blocks the cellular telephone frequencies. "Clip one wire and you get complete coverage," says the owner. It is also illegal to listen to cellphone conversations, but it is an act that is undetectable and usually unprovable. "I doubt if people are going to be coming to our door right now," he tells a visitor.[12]

Wiretapping used to be a young man's game. FBI agents known as "wires 'n pliers" specialists climbed down dusty air shafts and traced tangles of wires across moldy basement ceilings. No more. New computer-run switchboards are designed so that the systems operator can monitor any call with the flip of a button. So can outsiders who know how to enter the system's computer and manipulate the software. Most office phones now have built-in microphones that can be turned on without ringing, which means no more crawling around. The phones themselves can become the bugs. Just who gets to eavesdrop depends on the software.[13]

This presents a serious problem for the FBI and other U.S. intelligence agencies because Japanese-made switchboards often underprice their U.S. competitors. As federal purchasing rules require them to take the lowest bidder, this means spy agencies must now use their "wires 'n pliers" people to tear apart their own switchboards and probe the software for bugs. "Phone technology has evolved to the point where they [bugs] are much more easily used to collect information," notes one U.S. official.

Because Japanese companies make the devices and regularly use them on each other, Japanese businessmen have a much higher awareness of bugging than their U.S. counterparts. In fact, companies like Micro have succeeded in standing George Orwell on his head. In his terrifying novel *1984*, Orwell warned millions that "Big Brother" was listening. Ten years after his totalitarian future was supposed to arrive, it is increasingly Little Brother who is doing the listening.

So far, the law has made only a few small dents in this problem. In February 1995, U.S. Customs agents arrested Ken Taguchi, the head of Micro's U.S. operations, who pleaded guilty to a conspiracy to smuggle in bugs. Customs is also prosecuting a network of forty U.S. spy shops involved in the case. As for Little Brother's great friend, Tatsuo Hinata, he's still getting the bugs out from Micro's plant in Japan. A U.S. arrest warrant has been issued, but, according to U.S. Customs, the Japanese government has not been cooperative in processing it.

It is not the case, though, that Big Brother has gone out of the business. Far from it. According to U.S. officials, the Japanese government is building a nationwide phonetapping capability. Regional systems, such as Tokyo's, are already operating. One U.S. official tells the story of an American telecommunications company executive who recently put his company's newly designed scrambler telephone to the supreme test. He plugged it into the telephone jack in his Tokyo hotel room. The phone, designed to transmit conversations in code, worked perfectly. Two hours later, a very polite but insistent serviceman from the Nippon Telegraph and Telephone Corporation appeared, unsolicited, at his door.

SERVICEMAN: There is something wrong with your telephone.
AMERICAN: No, it works fine.
SERVICEMAN: But we can't understand what you're saying.
AMERICAN: That's the point.
SERVICEMAN: It is not compatible with Japanese standards.

Japan's Big Brother is called Chobetsu. It is the island nation's equivalent of the U.S. National Security Agency and has the power to eavesdrop on all of Japan's neighbors, including China, the Koreas, and Russia. Chobetsu's staff is expanding along with those of many other national SIGINT, or signals intelligence agencies, because the amount of useful information being sent via satellite links is like the cellphone market. It, too, has simply exploded.

Although Japan has taken the lead in Little Brother activities, Chobetsu has nowhere near the global reach of the NSA. And the NSA's activities are dwarfed, in turn, by the original Big Brother, the eavesdropping apparatus of the former Soviet Union. According to Desmond Ball, a professor at Australia's National University and one of the world's foremost experts on SIGINT, the Soviet Union invested at least $25 billion in eavesdropping facilities, making it the largest and most comprehensive SIGINT agency in the world.[14]

Few Americans think about the profitability of a machine that can "mine" the airwaves for commercial information, but the Russians have thought about it for many years. Harry Rositzke, a former CIA official, asserted that by tapping microwave relay transmissions in Washington in 1972, the Russians were able to orchestrate the massive Soviet wheat deal. They monitored calls from U.S. traders to the U.S. Department of Agriculture, so they were ahead of their trading partners at every step of the delicate trade. It caused a sudden jump in U.S. wheat prices that punished some of the traders, but Moscow had secured its share of the crop before the price shift, at bargain rates.[15]

Raymond Tate, a former deputy director of NSA, told an audience at a seminar at Harvard in 1980 that the Soviets were investing in a capability that had "nothing to do with national security in the military sense." They were interested in making money.[16]

The first focus of the Soviet efforts were microwave relay transmissions, phone conversations that are beamed from tower to tower in many cities. While the beams are cheaper and more efficient than using telephone cables, they have a "spillover" effect. At the receiving end, the beams are much wider than the antenna "dish" that catches them. The beams are so wide, in fact, that anyone in a tall building in a major city who can stick up an antenna within the general vicinity of a transmission can get them. If he or she hooks up the right equipment, the eavesdropper can scan numbers and collect particular calls.

In the mid-1980s, Swiss intelligence experts became so concerned about this that they brought in Ball, the Australian expert, as a consultant. Ball spent months in Zurich and Bern reading transcripts of the Swiss government's wiretaps of KGB transmissions to Moscow and talking to Swiss bankers. His assignment was to assess the value of information the KGB had collected in its eavesdropping of various banks and traders offices. Ball left Switzerland unimpressed. "They [the KGB] had inside advantage because they had inside intelligence, but their knowledge of how to move money around to play the good capitalist game was so bad that it didn't seem to help them that much," he maintained.[17]

But the Soviets kept trying. By the eighties, the rooftops of the Soviet embassies in Washington and New York and at least a half dozen other Soviet-owned U.S. properties bristled with antennas. The United States responded by trying to raise the awareness of American companies. "We'd go to a company and say, 'Oh, by the way, did you know someone is reading your mail?'" recalls Jan P. Herring, who was then working for the CIA's counterintelligence branch. Because the Russians were active in negotiating deals in oil, metals, diamonds, and other commodities, they were, naturally, eager to know the negotiating position on the other side. As time went on, they learned about commodity markets and also studied the financial operations of U.S. companies—knowledge that could be used in the stock market. "The Soviet KGB has been in markets for years and has made money on it. We tumbled onto this in the early eighties," adds Herring. He believes the KGB's trading profits went into the Soviet military.[18]

The job of cleaning up the microwave "spillover" in the United States fell to Noel D. Matchett, a mathematician and an NSA information security expert. He designed the "Protected Communications Zone" (PCZ) program. It amounted to putting microwave relay signals back on telephone cables or installing machines that turned the signals into code in Washington, San Francisco, and New York City. It was a massive effort, but the Reagan administration thought it had to be done. The bill, some $400 million, was paid by the Pentagon, according to Matchett, who now heads a Silver Spring, Maryland, company, Information Security Inc. The encryption ended several years ago, he believes.[19]

But the Russian effort hasn't ended. In the late 1970s, U.S. satellite photos and other intelligence showed that Russian army technicians were building a 28-square-mile "antenna farm" at Lourdes, a suburb just east of Havana, Cuba. It has since grown into the largest electronic listening post in the world. While the Cold War wound down in the late eighties, the size and number of arrays at Lourdes has increased by 40 percent. The NSA developed a code name for Lourdes: it is "LOW EARS."[20]

What LOW EARS hears are phonecalls transmitted by satellite communications. Over 80 percent of international telephone calls are now made by satellite. Radio beams carry the signal up to an orbiting satellite, the so-called uplink. Next, the conversation is beamed down to a large, dish-shaped antenna somewhere else on the earth. This is the "downlink." While the electronic "spillover" associated with microwave relays might be a few thousand feet, the spillover from beaming signals down from space is enormous.

In the case of tightly focused military satellites, the beam sprawls over an area of tens of thousands of square miles. And in the case of commercial telecommunications satellites, the downlink can cover an entire continent.[21] Lourdes, only ninety miles from the Florida coast, is positioned to get calls downlinked almost anywhere in the United States. Desmond Ball, the Australian signals expert, believes that information sifted from the airwaves by the facility may be worth as much as $1 billion a year to the Russians. It includes not only voice conversations but faxed blueprints and designs for new technology. "Much of the telex, facsimile and data traffic is either unencrypted or only encrypted to standards which are within Soviet/Russian decryption capabilities," says Ball.[22]

It doesn't take a SIGINT expert, however, to figure out that whatever LOW EARS is hearing, it is extremely valuable, and it probably doesn't often involve military matters. Russia has pulled back its military forces all over the world, including units from Cuba, with the single exception of Lourdes, where fifteen hundred army technicians remain glued to their earphones. In November 1994, General Mikhail Kolesnikov, the chief of the Russian military's general staff, told reporters that the need for the facility was "permanent." He attempted to minimize the annual payments that his cash-starved government makes to Cuba for Lourdes.

"It is not too big, less than $200 million a year, and not in money. This amount will be covered by Russian supplies of fuel, timber and spare parts for various equipment, including military," he stated.[23] An unnamed senior Russian diplomat later imparted some additional spin, explaining that Lourdes is necessary as a "confidence-building" measure to monitor U.S. compliance with arms control treaties.[24]

Meanwhile, the KGB's former Eighth Directorate, which oversaw most Soviet eavesdropping operations, has put on a pin-striped suit. Its new name is the Federal Agency for Governmental Communications (FAPSI), and Big Brother's reach, which was already breathtaking, now extends into many new Russian businesses. In 1991, the KGB unit was estimated as having 350,000 people and 500 ground stations in the USSR and 82 other countries.[25]

FAPSI's computers today keep track of Russia's trade in diamonds, gold, and other precious metals. It is selling special telephones to businessmen designed to secure their information.[26] FAPSI controls the electronic information network that interconnects Russia's new private banks and has bought a large block of stock in Relkom, a company that operates Russia's largest E-mail network.[27] And FAPSI maintains an organization of reservists—retired officers who now work in private business, both in Russia and overseas.[28]

Lately, apparently as part of President Boris Yeltsin's effort to gain control over the upper levels of his government, there has been an influx of imported Japanese- and German-made bugs and miniaturized television surveillance equipment. To workers in the Kremlin, it is a case of Big Brother meets Little Brother. According to an account in *Izvestiya*, their meetings are now held according to a protocol that would make Orwell smile:

"As a rule, the oral dialogue in such cases consists of bland sentences about the weather and each other's health, with the interlocutors scribbling away furiously during the pauses. In this process, index fingers are used either to touch the lips or to point at air ducts, chandeliers and other places where 'bugs' might possibly be concealed."[29]

The Kremlin workers are ahead of the game. At least they know they are being bugged. Most victims don't. Former U.S. officials talk about an American company in Japan that regularly lost bids to Japanese competitors by a fraction of a percent. When the company replaced a microwave phone link with a cable, it began winning. Sometimes the listeners give little hints that something strange is going on.

Mark W. Goode, manager of a Texas consulting firm, LaunchTech Inc., travels the world investigating foreign companies for U.S. firms contemplating a joint venture. He collects war stories.

There is the case of the Swiss broker receiving a telexed bid from a Moscow shipping company responding to a proposal to haul some oil to the United States from the Middle East. The response had all the details right, except one: the Russian company hadn't been sent the initial proposal. Then there is the large U.S. trading house that found one of its secret moves published in a French newspaper shortly after it telephoned its Paris office.

America's eavesdropping agency, NSA, gets more than mere hints of funny business. Members of the Senate Select Committee on Intelligence were recently shocked to learn that the agency has overheard Japanese companies preparing to "dump" commodities in the United States at below-market levels. U.S. corporate victims of such moves, however, are not warned, because such revelations would violate the rule which says U.S. intelligence can't spy on behalf of a specific U.S. company.

Some corporations have developed policies to deal with eavesdropping. All of them are time-consuming. Henri Martre, the former head of Aerospatiale, says that his company's negotiators, faced with a new turn in an overseas deal, are required to return home rather than trust the phones for new instructions.[30]

Northern Telecom, the Canadian telecommunications giant, requires the final stages of sensitive negotiations to take place in its home offices. "In Europe we assume that certain locations are subject to interceptions, and that in hotel rooms and public areas, eavesdropping is going on," says David Tostenson, the company's security chief.[31]

But most Americans seem to be different. "We're babes-in-the-woods when it comes to economic espionage," complains Noel Matchett, the former NSA expert who directed the $400 million effort to protect U.S. phone systems from the Soviets. Now in private business, Matchett has developed Noisebath 4000, a $9,000 loudspeaker system contained in a briefcase. It surrounds negotiators with a carefully concocted spectrum of noise, including lots of mindless cocktail chatter and frequencies designed to overload small microphones. Because modern eavesdroppers can use computers to filter out old spy movie tricks, like turning on a faucet or a radio to mask conversation, U.S. negotiators in Bosnia used Noisebath. The Canadian Royal Mounted Police have tried it to thwart sophisticated bugging by drug gangs, but so far there has been little interest from U.S. businesses.

Mark Goode, the Texas consultant, puts it this way: "In the U.S. community, it's a cultural problem. Our country's economy is managed by individuals, most of whom have never been in a war or in close geographical proximity to one. Their competitors have. They view economic espionage as a natural outgrowth of competition. To them it requires no major conceptual leap. . . .

"U.S. companies have never been consumers of this class of information. It's like: 'Wouldn't you like to have the trading position of company X?' Americans say, 'Gee, I didn't know it was possible to have information like that.' We're like the British foreign secretary who said, 'Gentlemen don't read other gentlemen's mail.'"[32]

Meanwhile, people continue to be shocked. A Washington electronics expert, one of the city's hundreds of graying veterans of the eavesdropping battles of the Cold War, admits he occasionally turns on the scanner in his car to break the monotony of long drives. "I've heard things on cellular, women talking in detail about things that make me blush, even at my age. I heard a guy talking to his mistress in D.C. while he was driving home to Pennsylvania to his family. She was suicidal. She didn't know if she could make it through the night. And he made light of it. I could have killed that guy if I'd gotten my hands on him!"

ELEVEN

Data Rape

O ne day in 1988, three executives from a South Korean shoe factory drove out to McLean, Virginia, an upscale suburb of Washington. A consultant had told them about Ardak Corporation, a tiny company they found tucked away in a medicinal-smelling office building crammed with doctors' and dentists' offices.

Located far from the downtown corridors of lawyers and influence peddlers, Ardak isn't flashy or stylish, but the South Korean shoemakers soon realized they had found a good fit. They were eager to enter the U.S. market and knew almost nothing about it. With a few keystrokes on his computer, Mac McCutchan, Ardak's president, laid out the entire U.S. industry for them: the top one hundred leading shoe sellers, both in men's and women's shoes. "We told them, this is it. Here's your competition. Here's their market share. To the Koreans, this was amazing. They'd never seen anything like it."

After they left, McCutchan, a portly former Navy submarine commander then in his mid-fifties, began to have misgivings, as he says he often does with foreign clients. During the later stages of his Navy career, McCutchan gave up submarines to explore even murkier waters. U.S. intelligence agencies were the world's first users of big computers, and Naval Intelligence wanted someone to find a way to use them to search through tons of available data about worldwide shipping movements. McCutchan became the designer-pilot of a new weapon, a software program that could collect and analyze billions of bits of information—bits that yielded a picture of all of the ships at sea on a moment-to-moment basis.

After resigning from the Navy in 1982, McCutchan tinkered with the program. Once it looked overseas; now McCutchan focused it inward, getting it to explore another ocean of data: the U.S. government's sprawling bank of information on 74,000 different companies that sell it some $170 billion worth of goods or services every year.[1] In intelligence, McCutchan had learned how to uncover a vital military secret—the location of an enemy ship—by electronically reshaping, then sifting through huge banks of disheveled information. Applying the same techniques to the publicly held procurement records, McCutchan found ways to tease out a close estimate of a company's most competitively sensitive secrets, such as its rate structure and its overhead. Using the data, McCutchan says he has been able to give hyper-secretive French and Israeli defense contractors an accurate picture of what it would take to outbid an American competitor.

As with the Koreans, he had misgivings, commenting: "They all know us better than we will ever know them. Other countries don't allow that kind of stuff to get into the public domain."

The United States is database heaven. To McCutchan and thousands of others working in the exploding field of information brokerage, U.S. citizens live in a glass house that makes them peculiarly visible. Although tools and skills initially developed for the spy trade are spilling into the commercial sector all over the world, no other economy provides the amount of data on its citizens and its businesses that the United States does. A lot of what Americans have long assumed to be private is now on display to others, or soon will be, for a price.

"Some of this [information] has no business being in the public domain, from my point of view," grumbles McCutchan. "I have watched the government spend billions of dollars trying to get information from closed societies, data that is just given away over here because we're an open society." But the information *is* in the public domain, and while it is, McCutcheon makes a tidy business out of it.[2]

He is certainly not alone. Traffic in the ocean of public data that McCutchan prowls in grows heavier by the day. In 1982, there were 600 commercial databases; today, there are over 8,000.[3] In 1984, there were 334 information brokers, people who make their living ferreting out information, mostly from databases. Today, there are at least 1,700.[4]

Most of the databases and brokers are found in the United States, where many state governments have begun putting records on motor vehicle registration, property, business and corporate records, and workers' compensation claims into publicly available databases. Florida has set up a one-stop system in which, with a name or a Social Security number, all of the above comes tumbling out of its memory banks. "When you've got somebody in Florida, you can write a book on them," exults Norma Tillman, a former Nashville, Tennessee, vice squad detective, who now runs a bustling business finding lost family members, using five commercial databases.[5]

"The openness of the United States is simply amazing," exclaims Rop Gonggrijp, the leader of a group of Dutch hackers. "You can get more information on people there than anywhere else in the world. For a few thousand dollars' worth of equipment, you can put together an unbelievable amount of information on somebody without breaking into anyone's computer."[6]

It was certainly amazing to M. L. Carr, coach of the Boston Celtics. In 1993, he allowed the *Boston Globe* to hire research firms that, starting with just his name, dug out the appreciated value of his house, a description of his two cars, a speeding ticket, records of three failed businesses, and a minor criminal violation stemming from a fight when he was a teenager. For a $69 fee, a Florida firm dug out his unlisted phone number in less than an hour.

Carr felt violated. "I'm a very public person and, when I go home, that's my refuge, the place where I can kick back and just be daddy and hubby. . . . If you can't have refuge in your house, where can you have it?" he exclaimed at the time.[7]

Since the clients of databases are kept confidential, there is no way of knowing who uses the electronic information; but from the very beginning, foreigners have found them to be invaluable windows into the United States. The matter of who information brokers are is equally unclear. The business started out with a heavy influx of librarians, but Helen Burwell, a Houston-based former librarian, thinks that aging hackers, like Gonggrijp, who is twenty-six, and victims of corporate downsizing (disgruntled former executives with extensive knowledge about a particular industry) are now getting into the field in some volume.

Burwell publishes the *Burwell Directory of Information Brokers*, which attempts to keep track of the growing field. She is currently trying to figure out how to develop a code of ethical standards for information brokers. One of her concerns is the new entrants into the game—"Those folks are not going to have an interest in standards that librarians would be setting."[8]

While the big computers and their early uses have their roots in secret government programs, some industries very quickly caught on to the potential of electronic browsing. In the late 1950's Eugene Garfield, a chemist, sensed the hunger in the drug business for a quicker, more effective way to keep track of scientific literature. After going to library school, he began setting up databases for big drug companies, feeding thousands of punch cards into the early IBM computers.

It didn't take long for Garfield to realize he hadn't reinvented the wheel. After publishing several papers on his methods, Garfield received an invitation to visit the Soviet Academy of Sciences in Moscow in 1961. There he found a huge operation, thousands of people working in a cavernous building, sorting out U.S. scientific and technical literature by category. Since the Russians didn't have computers at the time, it was all done by hand, but Garfield was impressed, commenting that "Russian scientists are incredibly well informed in the literature, in many ways better informed than American scientists." Managers of the Soviet operation, which went under the acronym VINITI, told Garfield it had twenty thousand people gathering information for it. "I had no doubt they would be under the mercy of the KGB," he recalls.[9]

In 1964, Garfield set up the Institute of Scientific Information (ISI) in Philadelphia to market his own database of scientific literature. It caught on very quickly with some customers. "I got two orders in the same day," he says. "One was from China, the other was from the CIA." Later, he visited China's version of VINITI. "The Chinese pirate a lot of information. . . . They had a massive place where they do all this reprinting. They do it in such a way that it looks like the original."

At about the same time Garfield began exploring the field, Japan was developing a formidable database called the Japanese Information Center of Science and Technology. As the Congressional Research Service later put it: "Systematic accesss to foreign literature has been a fundamental reason for Japan's rapid progress in both basic and high-tech industries since World War II."[10]

Garfield proved there is a great deal of money to be had in the information business. ISI currently brings in some $70 million a year from its clients, 55 percent of whom are foreign-based. He also helped pioneer more exotic search techniques that, like McCutchan's, could penetrate secrets. One, called "co-citation analysis," uses the computer to find and track clusters of scientists who publish scholarly articles together, or who have established mentor-protégé relationships.

The CIA and other intelligence agencies later adapted the cluster-following technique to hunt for so-called black, or clandestine weapons projects. When one of the clusters suddenly disappears, that's important. Richard Clavens, another database expert, explains: "Let's say you're looking at Iraq and you've got a history of top scientists working there. You notice that so-and-so hasn't published for three years and is currently working in a baby milk factory. It's the old story of 'listening to silence.' You infer that either the man's suddenly become stupid, or there's a black project working there."

Clavens's company, Center for Research Planning, also in Philadelphia, uses the technique to help inform drug company clients about potential research moves by their competitors. "It's a matter of where are you going to place your bets: Which [scientific] communities are you going to place your bets on? Which communities are your competitors placing their money on?" Clavens goes on.[11]

In the hands of a skilled researcher, big databases, powerful as they are, are only one tool. They produce pieces of a puzzle for a client. Some researchers then go on to complete the picture. "We have an optimism about finding information," explains Leila Kight, president of Washington Researchers Ltd., the large Washington, D.C.,–based research firm. "We simply go out there and ask."

The typical client, according to Kight, is a large corporation, say, Wolf Co. Wolf Co. wants information about a competitor—Sheep Co.—but Wolf Co. does not want to be seen mounting an investigation. Kight begins with a database search. To fill in the blanks after that, she sometimes calls Sheep Co. directly and asks lower-level employees specific questions about prices and products, blending sensitive questions into what might sound like a harmless market survey.

When that doesn't work, she grills lower-level employees of Wolf Co. Often, she has discovered, they know what Sheep Co. is doing, but nobody ever asks them. "You talk to sales representatives, the purchasing people. Ask them what the competition is buying at what prices. What résumés do you get from the competition? People in companies in the United States don't think competitively," says Kight. "They're concentrating on their jobs."

While Kight's company works for foreign clients, she has discovered that some of them, particularly the Japanese, bridle at her prices because what she does they do for themselves. With their instinctive knack for competitive intelligence, Japanese companies get a huge boost from the U.S. government's openness, particularly through databases and the Freedom of Information Act (FOIA).

FOIA was created by Congress in 1966, largely pushed by newspaper, magazine, and television editors intent on widening the public's view of government records. Since then, however, it has become a much bigger business, driven primarily by corporations seeing what government files can tell them about their competition.

Harold Relyea, an information specialist for the Congressional Research Service—Congress's in-house information gatherer—estimates that 60 percent of FOIA's users are now business firms or business firms working through law firms. Foreign companies usually operate through the cover of law firms. "What they're finding out is a mosaic, a few bits and pieces here and there, and they put the pieces together." Relyea estimates there are 600,000 FOIA requests per year, requests that cost taxpayers between $60 and $100 million a year to answer.[12]

The resulting government-subsidized openess, Leila Kight argues, is a "huge disadvantage" to U.S. companies being investigated by foreign competitors, particularly competition from Japan, the United Kingdom, and Germany, which have no equivalent of FOIA. She advises clients to tighten their security by assessing how much "overdisclosing" goes on in filling out government forms, "particularly when you're applying for something."[13]

To help offset the relative blindness of U.S. companies, Kight founded a professional association called the Society of Competitive Intelligence Professionals (SCIP) in 1986. SCIP has grown from 150 members to near 1,000, and has evolved a code of ethics to give the field a professional gloss. Selling the idea is still uphill, missionary work, Kight admits. Only about 5 percent of U.S. corporations, she estimates, have created formal business intelligence operations.

In some industries, competitive information gathering doesn't have any gloss at all. In the oil business, where secrets can mean millions of dollars, there is a long history of theft, bribery, and corruption. Robert Wanstall, an engineer for Exxon, got a good whiff of it one summer day in 1990, when he was invited to lunch by one of Exxon's equipment suppliers.

The setting was a posh restaurant overlooking Hyde Park in central

London. During the meal, Wanstall's host quietly pushed a fat envelope over the table. It contained $10,000 in cash, a bribe to get Wanstall to settle a contract dispute on favorable terms. The envelope, Wanstall was told, was a mere hors d'oeuvre compared to the money he could make selling Exxon's internal information to another guest at the lunch, a Swiss broker named Michael Szrajber.

"What do you want me, er, to deliver to you?" Wanstall asked.

Szrajber confided that his business starts with a vendors' list; equipment companies likely to bid on millions of dollars' worth of equipment needed by the oil company for various drilling jobs. "Next thing, you know, [find out] who's most likely to get the job. . . . Once the bids come in, we need . . . prices, deliveries, commercial terms, et cetera. Then keep our vendors informed, put them in the number-one position."

A company that knows its bid is lowest, Szrajber explained, can raise its bid almost up to the next-highest bidder. That meant higher profits and more cash for the source of the information.

Wanstall was interested. So was Exxon. So interested, in fact, that they had agreed to let Scotland Yard put a tape recorder on Wanstall for the lunch, creating a base of evidence that led to Szrajber's conviction for paying the bribe to Wanstall. Szrajber's diaries and other documents seized by British police exposed a network of well-paid spies operating in such companies as Shell, BP, Marathon Oil, Mobil, and Statoil, Norway's government-owned oil company.

Among the buyers of the information were two major *sogo shoshas*, (big Japanese trading companies): Itochu Corporation, and Marubeni Corporation. An Itochu employee was tried before a British jury, but acquitted. A Marubeni official was arrested and later left Britain after posting bail. Itochu told the *Wall Street Journal* its man paid a broker for internal BP documents, but had no idea they were obtained illegally. Two big German equipment suppliers, Thyssen AG and Mannesmann AG, were also identified as information buyers. (Thyssen said it was investigating its use of information brokers. Mannesmann conceded that in one case it made an improper payment.)[14]

The case offered a rare glimpse into a private intelligence world that is almost unknown to U.S. intelligence agencies. During the seventies and eighties, at a time when the U.S. steel, machine-tool, television, and semi-conductor companies began losing market share to hardball-playing competitors in Japan, the CIA and its sister agencies maintained an almost tunnel vision on Communist countries. Much of the rest of the world, and most of its trade, was blurry, outside their focus.

"We didn't know much about our own economy," recalls Alan William Wolff, who frequently asked for intelligence information when he was deputy chief of the U.S. Trade Representative's Office in the late 1970s. There were some exceptions. The U.S. government, he found, knew a great deal about the international wheat and aerospace markets. But when Wolff needed help on something else, the nation's $28 billion-a-year intelligence apparatus was often clueless.

"If you called up somebody and said, 'Tell us about the steel market. What's world capacity? What's excess capacity?' nothing much the agency provided was ever any good," Wolf complains. "The United States, for the most part, isn't close to commercial endeavors. Foreign governments are. . . . We have a citizenry that doesn't want government involvement, therefore the government doesn't know much about what's going on in the U.S. economy. So it's not terribly surprising that we don't know much about other countries' economies either."[15]

Ignorance of trade matters later became embarrassing after a federal judge in Atlanta, Marvin H. Shoob, demanded to know how much U.S. intelligence agencies knew about Iraq's clandestine procurement of U.S. equipment prior to the Gulf War. Some of the equipment used by Saddam Hussein to make weapons fired at U.S. troops was also financed in U.S. markets through the Atlanta, Georgia, branch of an Italian government–owned bank, the Banca Nazionale del Lavoro (BNL). It presented an infuriating picture: U.S. reservists, slaughtered by a SCUD missile that hit their barracks, may have unwittingly helped to finance the missile through their pension funds.

What did the U.S. government know and when did it know it? the judge demanded. The answer, provided later by the U.S. Senate's Select Committee on Intelligence, was: Very little before the fact and not much more afterwards.[16] Out of ten reports of Iraq weapons-buying activities before the 1989 federal raid on BNL-Atlanta, only one mentioned financial connections to the effort, and it didn't point to the Atlanta bank.[17]

After the fact, U.S. spooks suddenly appeared to be much more knowledgeable, but under closer scrutiny they didn't really know much. The Defense Intelligence Agency provided "mainly café conversation and speculation about material appearing in the newspaper." The CIA dug up sensational information, including the assertion that the Italian government was in on the deal. But the sensation was short-lived: the spy agency's source of the information, which was never proved, turned out to be an article in London's *Financial Times*.[18]

Vice Admiral John M. McConnell, director of the National Security Agency, later offered a reason for U.S. intelligence's peculiar view of the world, a view that tended to exclude such factors as Italy, Iraq, and banking. In a nutshell, he explained, the strategy was that countries with nuclear weapons required big intelligence coverage; countries without nuclear weapons didn't. What that meant, in terms of the Gulf War, he added, was that the day after Saddam Hussein's surprise August 1990 attack, "We had 2,000 people working Iraq, up from two a month before."[19]

To be sure, some U.S. intelligence operatives did innovative things to broaden economic intelligence coverage during the 1980s. After years of frustration over trying to convince U.S. policy makers that the theft of U.S. technology was militarily and economically harmful, Jan Herring left the CIA in 1983 to set up an intelligence operation for Motorola.

Herring found that his biggest challenge was bringing the cost of intelligence gathering down. In the CIA, he had enjoyed whatever resources it took to monitor the Soviet Union; in Motorola, Herring had an overall budget of $1 million. Making major use of commercial databases and employing a staff of ten, he set up an intelligence unit in the electronics company that some consider the industry's benchmark.

Commercial espionage is like most government spy work, he explains, full of grinding, unglamorous research and journeys that often end in blind alleys. Nothing much developed from some of his efforts, Herring admits. But in one case Herring's unit found that an acquisition candidate—one that Motorola thought it had lost—was still in the market. The deal was worth $40 million. After four years at Motorola, Herring joined The Futures Group, a Glastonbury, Connecticut, consulting firm that develops intelligence strategies for companies.

"Most of these guys [industry executives] have never had any experience with intelligence, other than spy novels or movies. So when they think about it, they don't know how to think about it," says Herring.[20]

In 1988, Robert D. Steele, another CIA veteran, was hired to develop a computerized intelligence system for the Marine Corps. The intelligence community's view of the world was troubling to the Corps, whose missions often put it in Third World countries—almost guaranteed to be intelligence voids under the U.S. policy that said intelligence assets should be focused on countries that have nuclear weapons. Steele was budgeted $10 million to fix this problem.

Steele, a former Marine himself, knows what it's like to work in intelligence voids. He faced death threats running a spy ring for the CIA in El Salvador. He set up an elaborate computer hookup between the Marines' intelligence center at Quantico, Virginia, and the NSA, DIA, and CIA. It could also bring in satellite images from the National Reconnaissance Office. Almost as an afterthought, Steele spent $20,000 on a personal computer and hooked it up to the Internet and a commercial database. After a few weeks, he discovered that 80 percent of the information he needed was coming from the PC. "What we had failed to realize was that the paradigm had shifted. The world of secrecy was no longer the best place to go for the majority of our information."[21]

Aside from the cost difference, which was substantial, Steele found another advantage. Since the information from his PC was not secret, he could get it right out to the troops. Information that is classified "Secret," on the other hand, is difficult to move quickly. During the Gulf War, pilots were sometimes denied access to satellite photos of their targets because they lacked the proper security clearance. Weather reports used during the war are still secret.[22]

Steele left the Marines in 1993 to start an organization called Open Source Solutions (OSS), Inc., which he uses to lobby for changes in what he sees as a bloated intelligence bureacracy, lagging far behind the accelerating flow and depth of electronic information. A squarish, bearded man in his mid-forties, Steele enjoys provoking his old colleagues, saying: "The intelligence community of today is trapped in an underground bunker of its own making."[23]

As Steele began hammering on the outside, inside the "bunker," U.S. intelligence officials were absorbed in a secret fight against a policy change that will soon open yet another window into the lives and activities of U.S. citizens. The Pentagon and intelligence agencies were opposing the commercialization of U.S. spy satellite technology. They were overridden by the Commerce Department, U.S. defense contractors, and, finally, President Clinton, who signed a presidential directive, PD-23, authorizing the change. According to officials involved, the most telling argument was stark and simple: Unless the United States changed its policy, competitors including France, Russia, Canada, and Japan would take commercial markets and, some day, the technological lead, from the U.S. satellite industry.

As was the case with other intelligence tools, commercial versions of spy satellites will further swell the ocean of public data, providing a new level of detail that will change people's lives, whether they know it or not. U.S. intelligence and defense officials opposed the move because detailed, commercially available photos from space will give an enemy advance warning of surprise attacks, such as the U.S. Army's famous "Hail Mary" flanking maneuver that struck Iraqi forces from an unexpected direction and brought an abrupt end to the Gulf War.

Satellite terrain mapping, initially perfected at the cost of billions to give target information and navigation guidance to U.S. cruise missiles, may someday be used by enemy missiles to find targets in the United States. "One of the major features of the world of tomorrow is that this technology will no longer be proprietary to the U.S. and our allies," warns William O. Studeman, former deputy director of the CIA under President Clinton.[24]

Several consortia of U.S. defense contractors are preparing to sell what has been, up to now, a spy's view of the world: electronic images of any spot on earth with a level of detail ten times more revealing than currently available pictures from space. The imagery will reveal objects as small as a garbage can—or, perhaps, a crisp closeup of Boston Celtics coach, M. L. Carr relaxing in his backyard hot tub. It could sell for prices as low as $100, making satellite photos far cheaper and thus more widely used than aerial photography.[25] Despite a good deal of commercial puffery about potential consumer uses—such as viewing vacation sites via the Internet—so far, according to the industry, most of the clients are foreign governments seeking a look at their neighbors.

Behind the imagery providers will come the experts, men like Daniel B. Sibbet, who can further parse the data, making it see the unseen. Sibbet spent nine years studying space reconnaissance photos for the Defense Intelligence Agency. Now he is general manager of Autometric Inc., an Alexandria, Virginia, company set up to consult with corporations on the many potential uses of satellites.

At a 1994 symposium in Washington, Sibbet projected a detailed overhead view of a shipyard on screen, showing how easy it is to see the methods and the pace of ship construction. "If this is your shipyard, you have a signature here," he said, referring to the likelihood that company secrets will be naked to satellite surveillance. "If it's not your shipyard, it's your competitor's. You can find out what he's doing."

There are lots of tricks to learn in the trade, noted Sibbet. He showed an overhead view of a railyard: "You can tell the difference between individual freight cars." He showed how an estimate was made of the output of an Iraqi uranium ore-processing plant by studying an ash pile next to it: "You can tell the difference between what has settled and what's recently settled."

Sibbet explained he has no idea what the eventual price for satellite imagery will be, but he believes that by 1999, major corporations will use it. Some will do so because they're curious; others will be driven to it because their competitors are peering at them and they will need to know what to camouflage.

As in the case of databases, the United States, with its huge infrastructure of high-tech facilities, will be a prime showcase. Few people will know who is peering down at them from above because tools of the spy trade are designed not to leave marks. Sibbet put up an infrared picture of a power plant, showing how the measure of the heat plume in the plant's cooling water revealed its capacity and output. "You can have some information about that plant and its operator will have no knowledge that you were ever interested," he remarked.[26]

TWELVE

Follow the Money

The American phase of Sun Ming's adventure began when he stepped off an airliner in San Francisco in September 1992. A tall man, and well muscled, he carried a visa identifying him as a poor laborer from the Chang Yi Tung Wood Product Company in China's Shandong Province. It said he was temporarily entering the United States for training.

Ming did not work with wood. He was a clever trader and master forger, who could make his visa or any other official documents say whatever he wanted them to say. He had used bribes, fictitious trading documents, and a forged rubber stamp bearing the official government "chop" of the Bank of China to surreptitiously borrow $157 million from the bank. Then, after a time, he had put the money back and Beijing was none the wiser. It was the largest, most carefully planned bank fraud in China's history. What Ming worked with was other people's money.

If there was one last white-knuckle moment left in Ming's plan for the perfect crime, this was it. As a sleepy U.S. Customs officer perused Ming's visa and punched Ming's name into his desktop computer, the poker-faced "woodworker" carefully swept the busy Customs Hall with his eyes. If anyone was looking for him, they would have to be watching now, preparing to grab him. But no eyes met his. The Customs officer pushed his visa back through the slot in the window and motioned for the next person in line.

Ming took his visa and his cheap hand luggage and disappeared into the crowd milling outside the exit door—another illegal immigrant planning a new, permanent life in the United States. But this one was prepared to enjoy the American dream a bit sooner than most.

Careful preparation was the key to everything Ming did. His preferred method of hiding was to be a drop in the ocean, a pebble on the beach. The United States, with its porous borders, was the perfect place. He knew he could blend into the estimated 4 million illegal immigrants living in the United States: laws were lax, enforcement sporadic. As for money, America is the world's ocean. At least half of its $300 billion worth of currency sloshes around somewhere overseas, the Treasury Department doesn't know exactly where.[1] A good part of the former Soviet Union and countries like Panama and Colombia all have economies that are fueled with dollars. The currency's sprawl is such that U.S. intelligence officials dismiss reports of enemy nations or crooks manipulating the dollar: there are so many players in the currency's global market that they cancel each other out; or so they argue. Rumors of a conspiracy to produce billions worth of nearly perfect counterfeit hundred-dollar bills or "Supernotes" somewhere in the Middle East are minimized by U.S. Treasury officials who point out that the ocean of money is much bigger than that.[2]

Indeed it is. Nearly $2 trillion worth of bank wire transactions zip electronically in and out of U.S. banks each day. That was the part of the ocean where Ming hoped to hide his profits—some $42 million he had gained from the fraud. His millions were being artfully "laundered," or blended into normal commercial flows to obscure their origin. He knew the risks were much lower than passing counterfeits. The laws for detecting "dirty money" are mostly paper, and enforcement is a rare, lucky event. "Your chances of getting caught are close to zero," explains Jack Blum, a Washington lawyer who worked on major money-laundering cases as a Senate investigator.[3]

But Ming was not a man who trusted to luck. He tried to foresee all the obstacles. One was that private individuals in China were not allowed to keep dollars. If anyone in the United States *was* watching, the kind of money Ming wanted to bring in from Beijing or Hong Kong might spark some interest. So Ming had shopped the world and selected what appeared to be the most compliant third country where he could bank his millions. Then, when he fed the money from there slowly into the U.S. banking system, there would be no sign that it came from China.

There remained an infinitesimal risk that someone might be able to backtrack his steps, untangle the hundreds of seemingly different transactions, and, somehow, connect them. But as Ming headed south for the protective cover of large Asian communities in the Los Angeles suburbs of Arcadia and Monterey Park, he was quite pleased with himself. The tiniest risks he could live with.

U.S. officials now estimate that in any given year some $300 billion worth of dirty money circulates the globe electronically, looking for a home. Taken together, it dwarfs the gross national products of most of the world's 170 countries. Of this, $80 billion could be drug money; the rest comes from tax evasion, smuggling, and various kinds of fraud and black market activities, such as Sun Ming's "business."[4]

"Follow the money" is a hoary adage that generations of fledgling detectives have written on their shirtcuffs. It is Investigation 101. But actually doing it is hard, and this huge pool of dirty money presents a mysterious, uncharted new world. Before the 1980s, national laws tended to prohibit such large amounts from forming. New financial instruments, the globalization of money markets, and the widespread removal of trade barriers to cross-border transactions have changed the geography of money. Now, with the flick of a computer key, money can leap from country to country at the speed of light. The police usually don't move quite that fast.

Nor do bank regulators or governments. By 1992, there were plenty of warning lights that something major was wrong. The International Monetary Fund (IMF) found "serious and progressive deterioration" in money flow reports from countries. Where inflows and outflows should balance, there were unexplained discrepancies of as much as $60 billion. Substantial activities of global corporations, offshore hedge funds, and booming new offshore money centers such as Hong Kong and the Cayman Islands were being underreported. The world's ocean of money had become so roiled and murky that an IMF working group reported it had been "unable to identify" which countries were involved in illegal currency flows.[5] Two University of Florida professors, Simon J. Pak and John S. Zdanowicz, asserted that money launderers were moving billions in and out of the United States by grossly underpricing or overpricing imports and exports. Using computers to delve into U.S. trade statistics, they produced thousands of examples of bizarre trades.[6]

Ming was headed toward an area that troubles governments the most: the accelerating seepage of dirty money into legitimate businesses. Crooks are buying banks in Russia, insurance companies in Germany, and construction and trucking companies throughout Europe and South America.[7] The net effect is more than criminality; it is "a danger of a much higher order," as one U.S. intelligence official put it. The power of the new money is seen, he explained, in visitors from unnamed foreign countries who are, at one and the same time, ministers, owners of vast multinational businesses, and crooks. "These people have the abilities to move billions around, but you can't arrest the minister of country X," the official explained.

"You wake up some days wondering who owns the nation's trucking industry," adds the chief of intelligence for one of Europe's richer Common Market countries. "We never had to worry about things like this before."

Although U.S. attempts to curb illegal drug money began in 1970, for the first twenty years the law produced little more than a mountain of paper reports from banks on cash transations, some 52 million of them. There were so many that the Feds couldn't begin to read them all.[8] Meanwhile, the nation's banks regularly argued before Congress that further attempts to tighten the law would be similarly cumbersome, enormously expensive, and would hinder trade.

Others countered that the nation's inability to see or stop the flood of dirty money results in horrendous damage, a level of harm that is quite comparable to war. For example, between 1988 and 1991, as the Bush administration wrestled with money laundering, 27,112 Americans died from drug overdoses—more than all the U.S. soldiers killed in the Korean War. In those same years, 1.6 million Americans with drug problems filled hospital emergency rooms, almost three times the number of Americans wounded in World War II.[9]

Moreover, when it becomes heavily invested in legitimate businesses, dirty money can light the fuses for future wars. Stanley E. Morris, director of the Treasury Department's Financial Crimes Enforcement Network (FinCEN), agues: "What is central to the foreign policy of this country is to establish democratic institutions and the creation of free enterprise. That is what we are selling, that is what our national goal is, and organized crime can subvert both of those."

As for the people who don't count their cash in billions, the little crooks like Sun Ming, they can be like Ninja Warriors when they suddenly drop into legitimate fields of business. Competitors can find themselves beaten without any warning or explanation. "When you are competing against low cost or no cost money, there is no way legitimate players can compete," explains Morris.[10] Further, at a time when government services are being sharply cut, business fed by dirty money means billions of lost tax revenues.

FinCEN was the Bush administration's attempt to stop yet another variation on the theme of economic war. Set up in 1988, this is the nation's newest, smallest, and oddest intelligence agency. Although its purpose seemed obvious to some twenty nations who rapidly copied it, the new kid on the block has had trouble getting heard among the big shoulders of the CIA, the Pentagon, the FBI, the State Department, the Internal Revenue Service, and other agencies it was designed to huddle with.

FinCEN's job is to function as a bridge between law enforcement, banking, intelligence, and diplomacy, using computers to wire together databases that have, for years, been unable or unwilling to talk to each other. It is an ambitious task, and FinCEN—located in a suburban Virginia shopping center in an office building whose facade is marked with a flamboyant, four-story inverted U—has taken a while to develop the clout to handle it. In Washington's alphabet soup of agencies, some powers are given the name of their buildings. There is the Pentagon; the White House. With a staff of only two hundred and a relatively minuscule budget, critics began referring to FinCEN as the "Toilet Seat Building."

Some of those critics were banks, which had doggedly fought the initial reports required by Congress on cash transactions. When that failed, they turned to computers, automating their processes so reports were automatically filed on anything even vaguely connected to the law. The literal mountain of reports that resulted paralyzed investigators and made some Treasury officials grumble about "malicious compliance." FinCEN's first task was to find a way to dig itself out. In March 1993, the agency fired up "FAIT," the FinCEN Artificial Intelligence Targeting system. For the first time, its large Sun work stations gave the government the power to follow the movement of millions of chunks of cash (amounts over $10,000) as they flowed from casinos and businesses to banks. The cash's owners could be checked against FBI and state criminal records and IRS files. So far, FinCEN has distributed over ten thousand case reports, some providing multicolored flow charts of complex criminal cases-a godsend to local prosecutors.

But the case of Sun Ming never emerged on the big screens of the "targeting room" in the Toilet Seat Building. Ming was in a bigger league, where the players move money with bank-to-bank wire transfers. In China's sprawling, cumbersome bureaucracy, only certain businessmen could get government permission to change Chinese currency—the renminbi yuan— into U.S. dollars, the currency needed to import most foreign goods. As China's economy exploded in the late 1980s, the demand for dollars became enormous; yet China's precious hoard of dollars remained small, rationed by the State Administration for Exchange Control (SAEC), a regulatory arm of the Bank of China. The SAEC would examine each import application to see whether the company had the cash and the government authorization for the deal. Then it would apply its "chop," or stamp, to the document. The chop meant the lucky importer could get funds from account no. 921, which was where China's dollars were kept.[11]

Sun Ming worked as a trader for a small company that facilitated import-export deals. In seven years his annual salary never rose above $1,000, but he made one very lucrative discovery: clerks at the 921 window usually accepted phony papers bearing a forged chop. That meant that Ming and an accomplice could borrow dollars at the bank's low rates, loan them at high prices to importers, and then later repay the Bank of China, pocketing the difference. At times when the bank's clerks balked, Ming would simply bribe them "to look the other way" as the import contracts, bills of lading, and various government agency approvals (all fictitious) got the bank's official seal.[12]

Wire transfers are cryptic electronic messages sent via computer between major banks. Ming sometimes wrote the wiring instructions into the deals he submitted to the bank. Bank wire transfers have always been a kind of netherworld to U.S. investigators. They know that's how the big money transactions move, but they don't have access under current law. The power to monitor them "absolutely would be helpful," explains Robert Van Etten, who runs the Customs Service's largest money-laundering probe as the agent-in-charge of its New York office. Access would allow federal agents to track money to accounts in offshore tax havens, where it tends to lose any criminal identity. Then they could follow the laundered money back into the United States and see where crooks invest it. "Law enforcement agencies have been pushing for this for several years," he says.[13]

The American Bankers Association has always been pushing against them. Kawika Daguio, Washington spokesman for the powerful trade association, says trying to follow the 400,000 wire transfers that go in and out of the United States each day would be impractical. Even with computers, he explains, "you'll be spending huge amounts of money which I can't even begin to estimate. It's likely that the banking industry would be bearing significant costs which they would never be compensated for. It's difficult for people whose background is law enforcement to understand the complexities of banks."[14]

The Bush and the Clinton administrations tended to keep faith with the banks; but Washington abounds in heretics. On this issue they were in the Pentagon, which financed some studies by the MITRE Corporation, an Air Force think thank. MITRE's people approached the problem of dirty money coming into the United States as if it were an enemy attack.

True, there were 400,000 daily bank wire transfers to deal with, but MITRE's computer jocks played with numbers like that in real time. They had developed the powerful software necessary to do that for President Reagan's "Star Wars," the anti-missile defense that supposedly could follow thousands of incoming Soviet warheads at once. The full "Star Wars" plan, as described in the early 1980s, was mostly propaganda. But the program's awesome software, that allows targeters to plot and prioritize the tracks of incoming missiles instant by instant, was real—a weapon looking for a war.

The software was adapted for following money transfers, and versions of the MITRE scheme made their way to the Toilet Seat Building. Richard Harms, then one of FinCEN's top financial intelligence experts, was enthusiastic. Once it is laundered and begins moving in the stream of wire transfers, dirty money poses an extremely hard problem. Needle-in-a-haystack doesn't begin to describe the difficulty; investigators sometimes refer to it as finding a needle in a stack of needles. MITRE's was a radical, new approach. "We needed something like that," recalls Harms. "You could see a couple of countries, Colombia and Panama, are almost held hostage by narco dollars. When the laundry process is completed and the money gets back here in the form of shopping centers and hospitals and so on, you really have a situation that takes the economy out of our hands." But Harms's bosses didn't share his enthusiasm. The project was scuttled during a 1991 budget-tightening exercise, and Harms quit in frustration. He decided to become a college professor.

On March 30, 1992, an unemployed thirty-five-year-old cab driver, Ren Peng, incorporated a new company: Perrich International Business Co., in a suburb of Sydney, Australia. A day later, he opened an account in the name of Perrich at a nearby bank. He deposited $200. The following October, Guo Jianling, twenty-eight, a newly arrived graduate student from China, registered the S.J. International Trading Company in a suburb of Melbourne. She put $1,000 in an account for the company in a Melbourne bank.

The cab driver went on to open at least eight other accounts around

Sydney in his, the company's, or his wife's name. The student—a trim, supremely confident woman—set up at least two more in Melbourne. By early 1993, money began flowing into the accounts from China. First it came in trickles, but by midsummer the stream had swollen to about $25 million.

It was the beginning of Sun Ming's laundering scheme and it was designed to raise no suspicions: two seemingly unconnected people in two different cities, who scattered the money through a dozen unrelated accounts. Of course, as the flows grew, there were questions. The woman told bankers that she was in the textile business and the cab driver said he dabbled in computer components. "The banks loved them and thought they were good customers," recalls Mark Standen, an investigator for the Australian National Crime Authority.

Meanwhile, in Los Angeles, Sun Ming scrupulously kept to his cover as a poor Asian immigrant. He sponged off of friends for lodging. He dressed casually and limited his purchases to one small Honda, which he drove daily to a local health spa for strenuous workouts. For Ming, a splurge was an occasional game of pool.

Of course Ming's bankers knew he was more than just a factory laborer. One of the first things Ming did was to fly to Flushing, New York, where he opened an account at a Citibank branch for $1.3 million. And Jian Tang, who let Ming stay in his house in Arcadia, soon had cause to know that his guest was an expert in something besides woodwork. According to court papers, Ming loaned Tang and Tang's brother $711,570 for an aircraft business they ran.[15]

Ming went on to open ten more bulging accounts at various banks in New York and California. When bankers asked, he told some he'd made the money selling cigarette filters; others learned he'd made it playing the Hong Kong stock market. The bankers were discreet. And so is Jian Tang. "I can't talk about it," he said, when asked about his dealings with his former house guest. For a year, as Ming's money began to flow in from Sydney and Melbourne, U.S. officials remained unaware.

But there was one development that Sun Ming hadn't taken into his calculus of risk. Australia was reeling from a series of scandals involving a corrupt labor union and prominent businessmen who had used wire transfers to suddenly shift hundreds of millions of dollars overseas, beyond the reach of tax assessors and unpaid creditors. Voters were outraged and the government in the early 1990s passed tough new laws prohibiting money laundering.

Teams of experts were sent to Washington to examine the evolving U.S.

system. The Australians visited the Toilet Seat Building and decided there was no way they would adopt a system that wallowed in 52 million paper bank reports. They wanted something computerized that could track wire and cash transfers almost instantaneously. They liked the MITRE approach and hired Harms to help implement it in Australia.

By the spring of 1993, the Australian Transaction Reports and Analysis Center (AUSTRAC) had been established. Inside AUSTRAC, Harms and Tony Rossiter, an Australian computer engineer, were tinkering with a simplified version of the MITRE plan. Called ScreenIT, it allowed them to see the cash transfers among eighty banks and all the bank wire transfers going in and out of Australia.

Using computers to crunch five years' worth of previous bank transactions and two years of wire transfer traffic, they established what the normal trading patterns looked like. Then they set up a series of rules that instructed the computers to pick out and rank the most suspicious transactions. For law enforcement, which had previously had to know what it was looking for in order to subpoena wire transfer records from a bank, ScreenIT was revolutionary: They could see the universe of transactions and had a way to gauge the patterns in it. "It was like turning on the lights on a public square," said Rossiter.

In May 1993, a report arrived from a bank that had finally grown suspicious of the huge activity in one of the cab driver's accounts. It was only a crumb of information, but it gave ScreenIT something to chew on. By August, Tim Sage, head of the Sydney office for the National Crime Authority, received a Chinese puzzle from AUSTRAC. The computers had followed some of the money to a California account and then backtracked all the wire transfers going into that account. Sage could see money flowing from the Bank of China into the maze of accounts held by the cab driver and the student, and then flowing out again to one account in California. It belonged to a man named Sun Ming.

On August 23, Sage paid a call on the manager of the local branch of the Bank of China. By that time, AUSTRAC had watched $30 million from the bank come into the Australian accounts. Was there anything wrong? he asked. After two days, the answer came back from Beijing: There could be no such problem. The Bank of China's records were in perfect order.

A week later, Sage recalls, "they [the Chinese] rushed into my office." The allegedly fictitious trades by Sun Ming had been uncovered. "We then started a very close dialogue with the Bank of China."[16]

Money-laundering cases are different from homicides in that "the body won't just lie there until you can dust it," explains one veteran investigator. The Australians learned this in September when they seized over a dozen accounts. A clerk at one of the banks had casually mentioned to one of Sun Ming's operatives that police had been by to ask questions. All but $4 million of the money was suddenly wired to California.

China threw over one hundred detectives into the case, according to Richard Kendall, one of a team of lawyers from the high-powered New York–based firm of Shearman & Sterling retained by the Bank of China to follow and collect its money. "What was remarkable to me was how quickly China got up the curve on what was a very sophisticated operation," Kendall says.

Armed with information from Australia, the lawyers got a court order freezing all eleven of Sun Ming's U.S. accounts. For a moment they thought they had finished their job, but Sun Ming was still one step ahead of them. He had just wired $1.4 million from the Citicorp account into another New York bank. When they arrived there, the money had gone to several other banks.

While the hunt for his money went on, Ming appeared in Federal District Court in Los Angeles where the Bank of China was suing him in a civil case to collect its money. Other than citing his Fifth Amendment rights to remain silent, he said almost nothing. Kendall remembers him as a "very charming person with an ingratiating smile."

There was enough evidence to arrest Ming, but the authorities still held off. "He wasn't hunted because everyone knew where he was; it was his money we couldn't find," adds the lawyer.[17] The FBI, alerted by Australian authorities, began to follow Ming, hoping that he would lead them to his remaining stash.

And so through the fall of 1993 and into the spring of 1994, Ming resumed his old patterns, seemingly oblivious of the FBI tail that went with him to the gym and the pool hall. One thing changed: Ming enrolled in an English course at the Edgewood Language Institute in Monterey Park. Again, he didn't raise any suspicions.

"For all the money he was supposed to have, he was very frugal. The way he dressed, the car he drove—it was just very plain," recalls Florence Chan, the school's director. School officials, she says, were not aware of the multimillionaire in their midst.[18]

Just why Ming went to the language school baffled the FBI. He already spoke fluent English. Later they learned from the bank's lawyers that Ming had recruited several Chinese students at the school into opening accounts for him in their names. In all, the U.S. lawyers chased the $1.4 million through forty different accounts and never caught up with most of it. A large chunk is believed to have been wired to a bank in Taiwan. When presented in court, the flow chart for Ming's tangled accounts looked like the plumbing for a large oil refinery.

The FBI could find no evidence that Ming had committed a financial crime in the United States, so in March 1994 the U.S. Immigration and Naturalization Service (INS) arrested him on the one charge the Feds had that would stick: his forged entry visa. Between numerous INS hearings, at which Ming asserted that the $42 million was legitimately his and requested political asylum, Ming charmed his guards by volunteering to act as translator for other Chinese prisoners.

And then one day in July, while nobody was watching him at the jail-like San Pedro Service Processing Center, Ming carried out his next move: a soaring, ten-foot vault from the top of a basketball backboard to the top of a new, supposedly escape-proof fence. From there he disappeared, but guards later found him strolling nearby.

"We still have questions about how he could do that, physically. It was an amazing feat," exclaims Richard Rogers, the head of INS's Los Angeles office.[19]

Sun Ming had one more move left. Placed in solitary confinement after his escape, he changed his plea from asylum to a request for voluntary deportation. He had learned that under U.S. procedures he could opt for any country that would have him. So Ming produced an official-looking letter from Africa's Ivory Coast, granting him asylum.

"He was always worried that he would be executed," says Bob S. Platt, Ming's attorney, who insists the letter was genuine.[20] According to Rogers, however, the Ivory Coast told the INS it was not, and that it would refuse asylum. As a result, in September 1994 Ming was given a one-way plane trip to Beijing, where he resides in a prison for major criminal offenders. According to Kendall, Ming confessed the fraud and has spent a lot of time showing the Bank of China where its weak points are.

Although it closed without fanfare, law enforcement officials still talk about the case of Sun Ming. Standen, Sage, Rossiter, and the other Australians who broke the case were stunned to hear FBI director Louis J. Freeh claim credit for it at an international conference on organized crime in Boston the following March.[21]

"It's not a big issue for us other than as a kind of responsibility we have as an international citizen. It's an example of what we can do," explains Graham Pinner, director of AUSTRAC. He says ScreenIT—one of the odder examples of recent technology transfer from the U.S. military—has turned into a kind of money machine for the Australian government.

"We are throwing out about fifty major potential cases a month. Right now the law enforcement agencies can't handle all that, so a lot of that material goes to the tax office. As far as they are concerned, they're just about all good cases."[22]

As for Harms, one of the first Americans to see the promise of using "Star Wars" technology to follow the money, he has been re-recruited by FinCEN and is back in the Toilet Seat Building trying to find a way to help U.S. authorities catch up with Australia.

The U.S. government says it is determined to follow crooks and their dirty money. President Clinton has told the United Nations: "We must not allow them to wash the blood off profits from the sale of drugs, from terror or organized crimes."[23] According to FinCEN's current director, Stanley Morris, doing what Australia has done won't be easy or quick. The U.S. banking system, with eleven thousand banks, dwarfs Australia's, and it doesn't have uniform rules for wire transfers as is the case down under. Plus, there is the strong opposition from U.S. banks to consider. "We're going to try and find a friendly bank. We want to look for patterns, set up an artificial intelligence set of rules for wire transfers that would basically pitch out some things, not to us, but to the bank. Then the bank would say, 'Here is X sending $40,000 every two weeks to the Cayman Islands.' That's what we want to do," says Morris wistfully.

THIRTEEN

Higher Learning

It took the Japanese just over a year to find Harvey Pollicove's little laboratory, tucked away in a corner of a science building on the campus of the University of Rochester, New York.

Pollicove, an optical engineer, was sitting on a breakthrough, a device potentially worth billions to U.S. industry and thousands of American jobs, once it was fully developed. This invention is an almost perfect glass lens, made without grinding or polishing flaws. It can be fashioned into almost any shape and still retain its optical qualities; and it can be made relatively cheaply because it comes from a computer-controlled machine, not from expensive, skilled hand labor.

But the idea was still in its infancy. A group of seven U.S. companies headed by Kodak had come up with the concept, and in 1990, the university had agreed to become its incubator. Life support was a shaky stream of funding from the U.S. Army. A year later, Pollicove had just produced his first lens. What he desperately needed was two more years of obscurity to perfect the process and to generate more funding. Suddenly his door opened and there were ten Japanese, the competitors he fears most in the world. Experts from Nikon, Canon, Olympus, and a half-dozen other Japanese companies trooped into his laboratory, led by a man from Japan's Ministry of International Trade and Industry.

This is normal—a scene that repeats itself almost daily on American campuses. Although American industry is losing markets in steel, automobiles, television, computers, and electronics, the U.S. university system keeps pumping out new ideas. It still regards itself as being "unarguably" the world's leader in basic research, and it has been the source of most of the technology that built America's economic lead after World War II.[1]

And the Japanese are the best in the world at finding new technology on U.S. campuses—better than most U.S. companies. It is the source of many of their "breakthroughs." This is why Pollicove, an optical engineer in his early fifties, was not surprised by his visitors. "You can't be afraid of this stuff. You need to welcome it because it makes you move faster," he says firmly. "If you want to sit around and enjoy what you've done, you're going to be outclassed. The Japanese don't sit around, why should we? Everyone is trying to win the war and we need to win a number of strategic battles to win. . . . You get too busy slapping yourself on the back and you get punched in the mouth."

The "war" in Pollicove's lab is economic. "You're not trying to kill anybody. You're trying to take their business. It's a battle for survival of your economy." His objective is to bring back factory jobs to America. High hourly wages for skilled lens grinders have sent their industry overseas. "The systems we're inventing will make it much more plausible that U.S. factories will use U.S. suppliers," Pollicove adds. In the meantime, however, he must deal with a steady stream of curious foreign visitors, most of them from Asia.

It is a very strange sort of war. There is a certain etiquette. First, Pollicove can't throw his visitors out. The law requires university laboratories that enjoy public funding to grant access to companies paying U.S. taxes, and all the Japanese companies qualify.

The ten Japanese return every year. "It's like a puzzle, they get more pieces every time they come." In return, Pollicove gets to visit Japanese laboratories. Unlike most of his U.S. visitors, who speak English, Pollicove doesn't speak Japanese, so his opportunities for finding pieces of puzzles in Japan are limited. What he finds is hospitality: "They treat us better than we treat them. When we go over there, they are extremely hospitable."[2]

In order to prosecute World War II, the United States created thousands of Japanese-language speakers. They generated the intelligence that helped General Douglas MacArthur, a lifelong student of Japan, to craft the strategies to defeat the island nation. By the last decades of the century, however, MacArthur and the knowledge base he used had both faded away. Japan had gone global. It was America that was becoming insular. In 1981,

Richard Samuels, then a graduate student at Massachusetts Institute of Technology, noticed that "waves of Japanese researchers were coming through." Having freshly returned from studying in Japan, Samuels's job was to translate for them and to show them research in progress as part of MIT's Industrial Liaison Program. Samuels soon discovered he wasn't needed.

"They knew English well and they knew exactly what they were looking for," he says. "I realized that the numbers of Americans who had similar capabilities you could count on two hands in all of Japan. It was something that was just crying for redressing."

Fifteen years later, it is still crying. Samuels later established MIT's "U.S.-Japan Program," the nation's largest applied Japanese studies program. Designed to create what Samuels calls the "Japan-aware professional," the program sends sixty science and engineering students a year to Japan. But it, and a few other programs like it, he acknowledges, are like lighting a match in a cavern of darkness. "We're still two orders of magnitude short. If we're sending hundreds to Japan, they're sending tens of thousands."[3]

In 1990, there were 29,840 Japanese students attending U.S. universities; meanwhile 1,485 American students were studying in Japan.[4] The ratio, which remained about the same during the seventies and eighties, means that in a war of the best and the brightest, the United States has elected to fight with a bag over its head. Japanese visitors, on the other hand, who were often educated here, see things with a practiced eye, and have the use of what amounts to a military-style campus intelligence system.

The U.S. Commmerce Department recently discovered that there is a network of at least 224 Japanese research and development companies in the United States, more than twice the number of any other country.[5] Most have been established in the last ten years and many are quite small, often located near universities where they keep an eye on cutting-edge technologies, especially those getting some of the $70 billion worth of annual research funding doled out by the U.S. government.[6] Sometimes they endow chairs and hire moonlighting professors and promising graduate students.

Exactly how they function is unknown. "We're still in the really basic stages of this," explains Donald Dalton, a U.S. Department of Commerce researcher, who said the size of the network was pieced together from newspaper clippings, company statements, and some interviews. "We see bits and pieces of it, but it's hard to put together."[7]

They spend what seems like a lot of money. According to one study,

Japanese government and business organizations gave more than $175 million to U.S. universities between 1986 and 1991, two-thirds of which went to scientific research and teaching.[8] While the money looks good to cash-starved universities, for the United States as a nation it is probably a net loss, according to Dr. Allan Bromley, a former assistant to President Bush for science and technology.

Bromley points out that "the Japanese have gotten some tremendous bargains. When Sony gave the University of Illinois $4 million to endow a chair in electrical engineering, everyone said, 'Oh my God, isn't that marvelous.' We read the fine print of that and found it gave Sony access to both electrical engineering and physics at the University of Illinois. That was a fantastic deal.

"The same sort of thing happens at major universities all across the country. Japanese officials or representatives of Japanese corporations say, 'Would you like to have several Japanese postdoctoral researchers working in your lab at our expense?' And of course most people leap at that like trout. When the researchers sent faxes back home written in Japanese, nobody around the unviersity was the wiser. An awful lot of technology went back to Japan that way."[9]

Dr. Bromley, currently dean of engineering at Yale University, like other officials at U.S. universities also worries about the rapidly rising percentage of doctorates in science and engineering going to foreign students. In 1991, for the first time in history, 51 percent of U.S. doctorates in science and engineering were awarded to students from Pacific Rim countries, up from 21 percent just ten years earlier. While Japanese students flooded the campuses in the eighties, the new wave is coming mainly from the two Chinas. In 1981, the People's Republic of China had no doctoral candidates in the United States; ten years later, it had 1,596.[10]

The Chinese students tend to be super-bright, an elite skimmed from a nation of over 1.2 billion people.[11] They have come to dominate the lower levels of faculties in many universities and they regularly win highly prized research and teaching assistantships, which means their education is subsidized by the schools and U.S. taxpayers. The situation has reached a point where American undergraduates frequently complain that they can't understand their teacher's English.

The change is stark and shocking to old-timers who helped build the United States lead in science. In the 1930s, when William C. Norris, founder of the computer pioneer Control Data Inc., was learning electrical engineering, it was rare to see even one foreign student. Now he has a grand-son taking computer courses at the University of Minnesota who has a problem: "Half of the teaching assistants he had, he couldn't understand them. It was very frustrating for him."[12]

"In my university there are five hundred students from the People's Republic of China studying enginering, probably more than there are U.S. students," says Ronald A. Morse, director of international projects at the University of Maryland. "The Chinese are going to do the same thing to us that the Japanese did, because they're putting in the same structures." Morse, an expert in Japan studies, blames a "techno-arrogance" that has left most U.S. companies and universities unconcerned that the nation's technological lead is being eroded.[13]

The problem is the same for the nation's multi-billion-dollar complex of federally run laboratories. "Almost any non-classified laboratory you go to would say that, by far, they get more foreign people going through than U.S. visitors. We couldn't run our labs without our foreign students," says Joe Allen, director of the National Technology Transfer Center, an agency established by Congress to help U.S. companies find publicly funded research.

"When U.S. industry funds research at a laboratory, they will only rarely put their people in there," Allen goes on. "Foreign people have a different idea. They are very willing to put their top people in our facility. You don't lose your place in a Japanese company by putting in two years at Stanford. . . . That's just a cultural difference." While the U.S. government produces warehouses full of statistics, the matter of how many foreign visitors and researchers enjoy the riches of U.S. labs—funded by seventeen different federal agencies—remains unknown. "Nobody is really tracking it," says Allen.[14]

Dr. Charles M. Vest is a slim, softspoken mechanical engineer and an expert on holography, which uses laser light to make pictures in three dimensions. During his career he has seen all three dimensions of the evolution of U.S. science and engineering. In the sixties, when he was an undergraduate at West Virginia University, he learned from the veterans who founded the U.S. technological base. Many of them had gone to universities in Germany and England. "We totally imported science to this country until World War II," Vest points out.

In the late sixties as a doctoral candidate at the University of Michigan, Vest saw the huge, post-Sputnik wave of federal spending on research and high technology hit the campus. President Kennedy had exploited the "missile gap" and sent Americans students flocking to engineering schools. "That's when American science started getting really strong."

In the late eighties, Dr. Vest, as vice president for academic affairs at the University of Michigan, began seeing some signs of decline. U.S. college applicants for science and engineering programs had started to drop, while foreign interest in U.S. schools accelerated. There were the first stirrings of awareness in Washington that something was wrong. A House Government Operations Committee subcommittee, then headed by Representative Ted Weiss (D–NY), began investigating MIT's Industrial Liaison Program.

Annually, MIT, the nation's most prestigious science school, received over $500 million of federal funding and produced a cornucopia of new ideas. Corporations that joined its liaison program received an exclusive preview of MIT's newest work. The Hill probers found that the program, which generated an extra $8 million a year for the university, was being used primarily by the Japanese.

True, slightly more than 50 percent of the companies in the program were American, but most of the contacts of the 337 faculty members were with foreign companies. Of those, the Japanese were by far the heaviest users. Under a salary bonus system, professors received greater incentives for consulting with foreign companies, even though they paid smaller fees than American corporations.

The Japanese were not unappreciative. Koji Kobayashi, then the chairman of the NEC Corporation, credited his company's success in cracking the computer market to his access to MIT research. And Paul Gray, then the president of MIT, received one of Japan's highest awards, the Grand Cordon of the Order of the Sacred Treasure, for promoting the program in Tokyo.[15]

At the time, Gray explained that Japanese companies were simply "more assiduous" in going after new ideas. MIT appointed a faculty committee which absolved the institution of any blame, saying, "Weakness in the translation of research to the commercial market [in the United States], the causes of which in significant part lie outside the university, should not be used as a reason to limit openness of university research."[16]

The MIT dons did note that because of the decline of academic quality in U.S. public schools, the nation's universities and its companies had become addicted to a continuing stream of foreign students and foreign-trained scientists. However,, they reasoned that since 60 percent of the immigrant scientists remained in the United States, they "enhance the intellectual climate and research base."[17]

In 1990, Dr. Vest, who had watched the probe of MIT from afar in Michigan, was appointed head of MIT. Now he sits in the president's big wood-paneled office and ponders problems like the one in Pollicove's lab. One of his major goals is to get MIT professors more involved with U.S. companies; but the companies, increasingly, don't have research funds to support the professors, and are reluctant to send their technicians for extended visits to MIT.

"Companies won't send their best people," Vest complains. I've talked to CEOs and they absolutely agree with me, but when it gets down to the lower level, they won't do it . . . I really wish we could crack that on the American side."

Japan's technicians, on the other hand, are eager to come for long-term visits. Dr. Vest insists that MIT continues to benefit from such exchanges, but says he's trying to promote "a philosophy across the laboratories that when you have a visitor, you should have a reason for him or her to come here. And that person is expected to share his knowledge in seminars."

Meanwhile, another phenomenon has increased MIT's dependence on bright foreign doctoral students and faculty: Many of MIT's best American undergraduates are shunning careers in science to go to better-paying jobs on Wall Street. The students, Vest has discovered, prefer the quicker pace and decisions of commodity and currency markets to spending long hours, weeks, and months inventing something in a laboratory.

The money is good, but some angst comes with it. Dr. Vest recalls a recent meeting with an MIT alumni group in Hong Kong. Most of them, men in their late twenties and early thirties, worked for banks or trading firms. One of them, a prodigy who had entered MIT at the age of fifteen and blew away long-standing academic records, opened a long, soul-searching debate with the question: "Is this a socially useful way to be spending our lives?" The debate that evening over a sumptuous meal in Hong Kong still replays in Dr. Vest's head. Why do MIT graduates prefer to engineer deals on Wall Street? "It's a kind of cultural thing," says Vest. "It's of deep concern to me."

As to the overall health of the nation's research base, however, Dr. Vest remains optimistic. One of his favorite themes is the "leaky bucket theory," first propounded long ago by someone in the Pentagon: "Here is our knowledge bucket. It is going to have some leaks in it. Instead of plugging leaks, the really important thing is to keep the bucket full. We are in a globalizing economy."[18]

The idea that the United States can continue to depend on a "bucket" filling with bright foreign scientists and engineers, most of whom elect to remain in the country, is a popular idea one on campuses. It fits with the long-held notion of the American melting pot. It also fits with the careers of a great many senior U.S. scientists, who can select brighter researchers from overseas to do their research papers and their teaching, often at a fraction of the cost of a U.S. student.

Unfortunately, it is an idea that appears to be wrong. For years, the myth was that most foreign science graduates remained in the United States, but the U.S. Immigration and Naturalization Service kept no records on this. "It's not something we're interested in because it doesn't help with our work," explained a spokesman for the agency.[19] Recently, Michael Finn, an economist at the Department of Energy's laboratory at Oak Ridge, Tennessee, found a way to solve the puzzle. Checking students' Social Security numbers ten years after graduation, he found that between 50 and 60 percent of the graduates no longer worked in the United States.

"We definitely hear more anecdotal evidence that foreign countries are putting more efforts into recruiting students to come back," says Finn. One exception is the People's Republic of China, which, according to Finn, appears to have made a decision to keep a pool of talented scientists working in U.S. companies and university laboratories, a pool that China can draw on later.

One reason may be that the United States pays their salaries as they continue to learn. Plus, according to Finn, the "vast majority" of Chinese students in American science and engineering schools are supported by assistantships or other means provided by the universities, usually through U.S. government funding.[20]

Some people believe that the "leaky bucket theory" may also be wrong in another respect: they question whether trying to keep the "bucket" filled with foreign students is a good long-term policy. David North, an expert on immigration issues, argues that the policy uses U.S. funds to train foreign competitors who later take market share away from U.S. companies.

Meanwhile, he asserts, U.S. universities and companies use the influx of super-bright Asian scientists and students as a kind of cushion. In his recent book, *Soothing the Establishment*, North asserts that the cushion means more cushy jobs for faculty because it allows graduate schools that would have otherwise had to shrink to grow. It allows downsizing companies to fire senior scientists and hire younger, much cheaper foreign substitutes. It depresses the salaries that might have attracted more American students into science. Finally, the "cushion" tends to postpone the messy and expensive problem of fixing the nation's faltering public schools—the system that once kept America's knowledge bucket brimming.[21]

This last issue resonates strongly with at least one MIT graduate, Frank L. Morris, Sr., now dean of graduate studies at Morgan State University in Maryland, a predominantly black school. Morris notes that while foreign doctoral candidates often enjoy subsidized assistantships and the close mentorship of U.S. experts that usually comes with them, the relative handful of American black students who make it into doctoral programs often must pay their way, learn at a distance, and graduate with big debts.

"We have subsidized our competitors while we have not supported our own," Morris maintains. "Many of these are in the sciences that have military applications. We train some of their best people in sciences here so they can do it themselves. With China, it's crazy. In this new economy, what's critical is human power, and the availability of heavily subsidized foreign students has not encouraged the universities to develop our own. That's where I get off. We are weaker because we haven't developed our own person power. Only in America can this sort of thing happen."[22]

It certainly couldn't happen in Japan, which runs one of the most closed academic systems in the world. While U.S. campuses abound with thousands of foreign teachers, in 1994 there were forty-one foreign teachers with permanent positions among fifty thousand Japanese teachers in Japan's public university system. Five of them were Americans.[23] Some 380 foreigners in higher-ranking temporary positions were being sharply reduced as a way to carry out a government-sponsored budget-cutting exercise.[24]

"Access is very grudging," says Ivan Hall, a Princeton-educated historian who has taught in three different Japanese universities for a total of ten years. "It is very hard, even for people here on a short-term basis. There is an almost total lack of long-term [teaching] opportunities here and almost no foreigners at all in universities in the sciences."[25]

Although Japan passed a law in 1982 allowing foreigners to be hired as teachers, sharp-elbowed faculty politics within Japan's universities keep most foreigners out. Dr. Hall, who lost his job over a tenure dispute at Tokyo's private Gakushuin University two years ago, has mounted a campaign to get it back, receiving support from the U.S. Embassy on the issue of reciprocal openness.

When he was President Bush's science adviser, Dr. Bromley thought he had hit on a way to give U.S. companies a peek inside Japan's research establishments. He started a program that translated a large number of Japanese research papers into English. There was a wealth of material. "Our translations were sought by European companies and other companies from all over the world," Bromley says. "They were even examined by the Japanese, who wanted to see how good our translation abilities were. But there was not much interest from American companies."

This know-nothing attitude compounds the problem posed by the visiting delegations of Japanese. "In negotiations with the Japanese, they knew exactly what they wanted from us, but we were not sure what we wanted from them. We lost a lot of technology without getting much in return."[26]

In 1991, Dr. Bromley decided to draw a line. Japanese visitors were hunting through U.S. laboratories, piecing together research on a new generation of supercomputers. These are computers that use light beams to store vast amounts of information, and research on them is very heavily subsidized by the U.S. Defense Department. It was too much to simply give away. Dr. Bromley sent Dr. Eugene Wong, then associate director of the White House Office of Science and Technology Policy, to wangle something in return out of MITI.

This was a difficult chore. Legally, Dr. Wong had no way to close U.S. labs to Japanese companies, and the MITI representatives quickly pounced on that point. "They said if we really want to do this, will you try and stop us? I said the answer was no," Wong admits.

In Dr. Wong, however, MITI was dealing with a close student of Japan, its science and its culture. The inventor of one of the first computer databases, and the former head of the computer science department at the University of California at Berkeley, Dr. Wong knew that in Japan's camera industry there were experts in exotic mirrors and lenses of a type that were needed for the "opto-electronic" computer. He proposed a joint facility to make them in Japan.

"Initially, they were quite skeptical. They didn't want to do it," Dr. Wong recalls. Wong put the matter of reciprocity to MITI's experts as a matter of pride. "I tried to be genuinely non-threatening. I think people always respond to a sincere effort. One has to have vision and one has to pursue it with a good deal of persistence." And Dr. Wong was persistent. In the end, after a great deal of bargaining, the United States got the joint facility, and—Wong's objective—a window into Japan's program.[27]

It is not a solution that will work for most companies or most universities because they will not have an expert like Dr. Wong. For that matter, the

United States no longer has Dr. Wong. What happened to him afterwards presents the next problem with the "leaky bucket" school of thought. He was hired to be the vice chancellor of the new Hong Kong University of Science and Technology, a school with a $3 billion endowment that intends to become a Far East copy of MIT.

A similarly well endowed school is under way in Pohang, South Korea. The government of Taiwan has built the Hsinchu Science Park, described as an Asian version of Silicon Valley; it is spinning off companies run by returnees from California. The companies are said to have made $5 billion in the first six months of 1995 selling integrated circuits and computers.[28]

These new institutions are "attracting the best and the brightest, senior people who have been in the United States for twenty years or so," explains Robert Sullivan, an expert in manufacturing technology and former dean of business at Carnegie Mellon University. "They are paying them salaries that match the best in the world. Right now higher education in the United States is very much like the automotive industry was in the 1970s. We didn't take competitors very seriously until they really kicked us."

Thus the U.S. knowledge bucket is no longer merely leaking; chunks of it are being exported. And when the MIT clones rising in Asia approach the level of excellence of Dr. Vest's school, larger parts of it may rapidly vanish. Bright Asian students will no longer have a reason to leave home. But the "kick" that Dr. Sullivan sees coming to the U.S. economy may still be some years away. The White House's Office of Science and Technology Policy lists twenty-seven technologies as being "critical" to the economic health or the security of the nation. The office's most recent report to President Clinton notes that the United States retains the lead or is equal to competitors in all of them, but adds, ominously, that "the size of the U.S. lead has either declined or remained constant between 1990 and 1994. . . ."[29]

"It's like a gradual disease. It's not happening fast enough to feel the pain," says Sullivan, now the head of a small institute that explores technological innovation at the University of Texas at Austin. He believes the full-blown problem, when it emerges, will force U.S. politicians and parents to fix their own public school system. "It's not a simple problem because all of the ways we do business are changing. You can't erect barriers to protect poor American students."[30]

Then there is the changing American culture to consider. It means that, for American science and engineering, the future will not be like the recent past. Consider the experience of Dr. Fang Chen Luo, who immigrated from

Taiwan in the 1960s. He learned electrical engineering at Northwestern University, and like many Asians, paid more than his dues to America's "knowledge bucket." He was a key player on the Westinghouse Electric research team that first developed flat panel displays. It was a stunning breakthrough in the 1970s that, Westinghouse predicted, would soon lead to computer screens with the thickness of a sheet of glass and television sets that could be hung on the wall, like pictures.

The technology is still coming, but it is coming from Japan, where companies invested more money and developed marketable products as American companies failed to capitalize on a new idea. Dr. Luo continues to work in his laboratory, but his twin sons, both top-scoring American students, won't follow him there.

They were interested in science until a high school counselor told them, "Don't waste your brilliant talents on engineering activities," recalls Dr. Luo. Now both are at Harvard, one studying economics, the other interested in political science. Dr. Luo has had long discussions with each of them, but he can't lure them back to the profession he loves. His nightmare is that they'll become consultants.

"Lots of students go into consulting. They look at issues from a very superficial, global point of view. They can make presentations, but none of them know more than a superficial aspect. But they make more money. It's more glamorous." Dr. Luo pauses, giving a kind of verbal shrug. Then he adds: "The culture of the U.S. today is like that. Fortunately, we have these foreign students, otherwise the whole system would collapse."[31]

FOURTEEN

Virtual Justice

A t 9:00 A.M. on a crisply cold winter morning, a red sports car pulled into a parking lot in downtown Denver, Colorado. Before the driver could get out, FBI agents spilled out of several waiting cars to surround it. They told the driver he was under arrest.

Andrew Wang, a short, round-faced man with wire-rimmed glasses, emerged from his car, blinking in surprise. As he did so, an agent handed him a card printed in Chinese. It said he had the right to remain silent. In case Wang wanted to talk, though, a Chinese interpreter, hired for the day from the U.S. Air Force Academy, was positioned at Wang's elbow. The FBI, it seems, had thought of everything.

It was February 24, 1994, the start of what might have been one of the biggest economic espionage cases in U.S. history. Wang, a thirty-five-year-old computer engineer from Beijing, found himself accused of stealing a cutting-edge software program worth "much more" than $1 million from a former employer, a small Boulder, Colorado software company called Ellery Systems Inc.[1]

In a nation of voluminous laws, stiff criminal penalties, and packed jails, economic espionage cases are an extremely rare event. It often amounts to stealing knowledge, yet there is often no specific criminal law against stealing someone's idea, despite the fact that America's ideas are a rich lode. The FBI estimates that the United States—both government and industry—spends $249 billion on basic research every year. "More than anything else,

[what] the American economy has to sell to the world [is] its genius," explains Louis J. Freeh, director of the FBI.[2] But corporate victims rarely complain. The thefts often involve something valuable but intangible, like a trade secret, a marketing plan, or, in Wang's case, a pattern of electronic blips that might someday serve as part of the basis of the nation's computer-driven "Information Superhighway." Legally it is, as one FBI official put it, "similar to a murder investigation without the body."[3]

In this case, the FBI had been extremely lucky. It had Geoffrey Shaw, Wang's former boss, a Vietnam War veteran and a very presentable witness. Shaw was eager to explain how his company and the nation had been damaged by Wang's alleged software theft. "A lot of people sweated blood and bullets for something others now have access to," he told a reporter. "The idea of having other nations steal that work; you're talking about stealing jobs."[4]

And the FBI got luckier as the day wore on. Ignoring both the offer of the interpreter and the reminder of his constitutional right to remain silent, Wang tried to explain the case in his stuttery English to the agents right there in the parking lot. He told them he had moved the software out of Ellery by using the Internet, and where and why he had sent it.

Later that day, FBI agents watching Wang's suburban house saw Wang's wife, Min Zhu, leaving with two plastic shopping bags. After getting a search warrant for the bags, the agents found documents showing how Wang had been promised $500,000 by a Chinese government-owned company, Beijing Machinery Import Export Co., to finance a software company to be started by Wang and two Chinese partners. There was a printout of a portion of Ellery's software code. Best of all, the FBI found a letter, signed by Wang, that told the Beijing company: "the common practices of the Americans" should be used "to defeat them in their own competition."[5]

It became a very high visibility case. The Justice Department in Washington was interested. Henry L. Solano, the U.S. attorney for Colorado, put two of his best prosecutors on the case. They had Wang indicted with the strongest possible charge, interstate wire fraud, which carries up to ten years in prison and a $250,000 fine.

For the FBI, it was a gratifying moment: a case showing how it was fulfilling its new mission—protecting U.S. companies from economic espionage. For the U.S. software industry, it was a highly symbolic event. The United States produces more than half the world's software, and piracy of software programs is spreading worldwide like a plague. It cost the industry an estimated $8 billion in 1994—and the nation with the highest piracy rate is China.[6]

Twenty months later, the case against Andrew Wang suddenly collapsed. Like some crumbly old apartment building wired by the wreckers, it came down one day in a cloud of dust and hot air. This was yet another highly symbolic event, a lesson painful to almost everyone involved: The United States has staked its economic future, in part, on the Information Age, on sophisticated computer programs that can collect information and send it around the world at the speed of light. But the laws and the legal system that protect the heart of this new technology, its so-called intellectual property rights, could hardly be termed sophisticated. They still ride on horseback. And, more often than not, the road ends at the U.S. border.

Legal experts have talked about this problem for years. "We have these voids in our law, these pockets. You're driving along, and all of a sudden there is no law," says James P. Chandler, a professor at George Washington University Law Center. As Chandler explains to his students, in the U.S. system, legal wisdom develops and is refined through the consideration of many cases. Because victims of economic espionage rarely complain, however, that makes a significant difference. "Nobody writes about the voids because there are no cases to discuss."[7]

The voids in the case of *United States* v. *Andrew Wang* weren't apparent to anyone at first. Wang, sitting in a Denver jail, wondered how he would explain his situation to his father, once a respected professor of mechanical engineering at a university in Beijing. During the early 1970s, at the height of the so-called Cultural Revolution, the elder Wang was summarily thrown into jail for four years and his family was sent to do farmwork in the country.

While Andrew Wang was ruminating, the prisoner in the next cell, an accused counterfeiter, reminded him of the essential difference between the two legal systems: in America, Wang could fight back. While most criminal lawyers wouldn't know where to begin with Wang's case, one might, the prisoner suggested. His name was David Lane. Wang looked up his phone number.[8]

In the overloaded U.S. criminal justice system, career defense lawyers don't try most cases. They bargain with prosecutors. It's more efficient because many of their clients are guilty. "Nine out of ten times in a criminal case, the issue is to get the best deal you can for somebody," explains Lane. His first look at the complex mess Wang had gotten himself into convinced Lane this case would be no different. "Frankly, he looked guilty."[9]

But Wang insisted that it was all a huge misunderstanding. In his halting English, in which he appears to stutter while he searches for precisely the right words, Wang explained that he had come to Denver in 1989 to take a temporary job with a Denver software company called Unidata Inc. Software companies had begun to proliferate in Denver and nearby Boulder, but Unidata was peculiar in that its founder was Ming Yue, an engineer from Shekou Shenzhen, China's economic zone outside Hong Kong and one of the world's centers of software pirating.

Yue proceeded to import other Chinese engineers, including Wang, by then a professor in computer science at a Beijing university. Wang says he agreed to come to the United States for only three months to work on a particular problem at Unidata; but when hundreds of demonstrators were shot by the People's Liberation Army in Tiananmen Square, Wang decided to linger. Unidata offered him a full-time job.

Computer experts in China tend to be a close-knit community. Wang found one of his Beijing friends, Jing Cui, working at Unidata. They became roommates, living in a tiny apartment. One topic of frequent discussion was their salaries. Among Denver's software firms, Unidata was regarded as an intellectual sweatshop; it paid its largely Asian engineers little more than subsistence wages. Shortly after Wang decided to stay in the United States, his wife arrived, having won a scholarship at Denver University. Soon she was pregnant. Wang decided to get a better-paying job.[10]

He answered a newspaper ad placed by Ellery, a Boulder company that was developing a software program for the National Aeronautics and Space Administration. NASA wanted to enter the age of distributed computing, a rapidly evolving field that uses elaborate software programs to connect multiple databases and thousands of computer users. Wang had written two books on the subject in China, and Lowell Schneider, Ellery's top computer expert, liked him.

They made an odd combination. Wang, polite and genial, did his level best to look like an American business professional. Schneider, a tall, gaunt, graying man in his forties, wore his long hair in a ponytail and favored jeans and high-topped basketball shoes. According to Wang and others who have dealt with him, Schneider is a man of very few words, a workaholic who preferred to spend twelve-hour days in silence, hunched over his computer terminal at Ellery.

Schneider was one of the founders of Ellery, which had grown out of an earlier company that had designed software for U.S. intelligence agencies. Schneider's secretive ways may have come from working on exotic, top-secret programs designed to find patterns in large quantities of information that would show whether Warsaw Pact nations might be mobilizing for war. At night, everything had to go back into the safe.

But by 1992 it was a whole different world. There were no government-controlled security safes at Ellery, which was trying to position itself on the cutting edge of distributed computing. It had a new chief executive, Geoffrey Shaw, a businessman who had helped form a consortium of high-tech companies called the National Information Infrastructure Testbed. The testbed was building a prototype for the Information Superhighway. Shaw felt certain it would lead to a billion-dollar market.

The idea was all the rage in Washington, where Al Gore was one of its chief enthusiasts. It had also attracted interest in China, which had sent an official from its education ministry to Denver in December 1992 to shop around. Wang and Cui brought him to Ellery, but after listening to the company's sales pitch, the official didn't buy anything.

At the time, Ellery was working on something called the Ellery Open Systems distributed computing program. It was designed to give a large company or a government agency its own information highway. NASA had helped finance the research on the theory that it could later license the software from Ellery; but Ellery's program had gotten too fancy to suit NASA, which had a dwindling budget.

"There was just too much stuff we didn't need. We could do just as well by writing our own very simple package," explains John Good, an astronomer who was managing NASA's data system program. What Good wanted was a software program that would allow NASA's astronomers and astrophysicists to communicate and to dip into all of the agency's databases. Good found that Wang was interested, so Ellery agreed to let Wang work on the idea in his spare time.[11]

The potential for big money was certainly there, but distributed computing never quite seemed to get off the ground at Ellery. "They had fifty irons in the fire, but nobody came through with the money," recalls Good, who says that NASA's funding of the company was scheduled to be cut in 1994. "They knew it was coming."

So did Wang, who had begun thinking about getting another job. He and his former roommate, Cui, and another Chinese friend in Denver—Xin Shulin—had talked about setting up their own company to sell distributed computing software. It would be called D.C. Nology; but they needed some-body to finance it.

In December 1993, Shulin's wife found a potential investor, a Chinese businessman connected with Beijing Machinery. According to Wang, the businessman originally wanted to make a personal investment, but soon the company itself became interested. The following month, on a trip to Beijing to visit his sick mother, Wang struck a deal with officials of Beijing Machinery, a conglomerate of 158 newly "privatized" companies owned by the city of Beijing.

Beijing Machinery signed an agreement—a letter of intent—to put up $550,000 for a 52 percent share of D.C. Nology. The first portion of the money was due in March 1994; meanwhile, Wang returned to Denver and told Shaw and Schneider he would be leaving Ellery. A Denver software firm had offered him a higher-paying job and Wang's plan was to work there until D.C. Nology got off the ground.

D.C. Nology was still a secret, but Shaw and other Ellery officials sus-pected something odd was going on. They believed Wang may have engi-neered a separate deal with the visiting Chinese official. Wang had made at least fifty calls and faxes to Beijing, all billed to the company. In early February, as he cleaned up his remaining work, Wang became a watched man at Ellery. Shaw had begun collecting copies of Wang's faxes, written in Chinese. He had them translated.

One of the jobs Wang wanted to finish was the software code, called "Andrew's version," that Wang was working on for NASA. It had a number of serious bugs. One of them was that Wang couldn't transmit it. A comput-er manufacturer suggested it might have something to do with Ellery's com-puters and said that Wang should test it on somebody else's system.

According to Wang, he proposed the idea to Schneider, who was sitting in his office as usual, tapping away on his computer keyboard. Schneider didn't bother to look up, Wang says. "He just says yes. You can give them whatever you want."

So Wang gave Cui, who was still working at Unidata, the passwords he needed to enter Ellery's system and download the code. The data transfer, which went out over the Internet, took three hours. It amounted to 1,714 printed pages, including Andrew's version of the code, which, in turn, included a fragment of Ellery's software. There was also, according to Wang, a lot of "garbage," including a computer magazine written in Chinese.

When the transmission was completed, Cui saw he had a problem. Some of Ellery's software had copyright notices on it, which might raise problems at Unidata. So he allegedly deleted them.

Three days later, when the transfer showed up on Ellery's daily log of computer operations, Shaw and other company officials pounced on Wang. They terminated his computer password, had him sign a "termination agreement," and told him his work for the company was finished. He could go home.

Wang was not that worried. He had a $50,000-a-year job waiting for him in Denver. The demand for software experts in the area was substantial and there were not enough skilled Americans to fill it. The former Beijing university professor knew he had the right credentials, so he was not surprised to get a call, early on the morning of February 24, 1994, from someone who identified himself as an executive of a head-hunting firm. "He said he heard I was looking for a job. I said I got a job. They said are you interested in a better one? I said why not? I'm interested." The head-hunter would call Wang back when he arrived at his office. When would that be? At 9:00 A.M., responded Wang.

Wang's "head-hunter" turned out to be the FBI. Schneider and Shaw had complained that Wang had stolen almost the entire source code for Ellery's new product. It was the "most strategically important" link between "major telecommunications and computing," Shaw told the press. "Stealing the source code is like stealing the plans to an airplane."[12]

John Gedney, the FBI's chief agent on the case, told U.S. District Judge Daniel Sparr that Wang's dealings fit an FBI profile of "Chinese intelligence operations." The judge was impressed and ordered Wang kept under house arrest, citing "potential matters of national security."[13]

It was the espionage threat that kept Wang confined to his tiny house for seven months, attached to an electronic leg bracelet that would set off an alarm if he left. His father, the victim of China's Cultural Revolution, took the news of his son's disgrace stoically. "He said it was history repeating itself." But the younger Wang often found himself deeply depressed, sitting in the house with his wife, an elderly mother-in-law who was too afraid of America to go outside, and his infant son. Wang seriously considered suicide. "How can I explain to my son that his father is a criminal?"

David Lane, Wang's attorney, had spent sixteen years defending criminal cases, first as a public defender in the tough, crowded courts of New York City, later in private practice in Denver. His first instinct was to get rid of Wang's case by pleading guilty to a lesser offense. A copyright violation would be perfect. The law carried a mere slap on the wrist, up to a year in jail, a maximum $2,500 fine.

But for Wang, a guilty plea also probably meant deportation, and Lane decided he didn't want that on his hands. He had come to like Wang, and at Wang's suggestion, called John Good, the NASA astronomer who had sponsored the Ellery research. Good, Lane found, believed Wang had to be innocent.

To Good, the charges simply didn't compute. When it came to computers, he knew Wang was not stupid. The Chinese engineer had total access to all of Ellery's systems. If he had wanted to steal the company's software, Wang could have simply put it on a tape and walked out with it in his pocket. Or he could have sent it out on the Internet and then erased the log. "He did absolutely nothing to cover his tracks. This was absolutely the most visible way possible for someone to do this," Good said.[14]

It was a start. Now Lane had a potential witness. Next, he did a little research on the law. Prosecutors had charged Wang with two counts of wire fraud, a law written to punish misleading radio and television advertisers in the 1950s. Both counts required an out-of-state transmission. But Wang's transmission only went thirty-five miles, from Boulder to Denver. It was all in Colorado.

Lane explored how the Internet worked. Basically, it was a series of transmissions between various U.S. government computer stations. Information was broken into manageable chunks called "packets," and the electronic packets were usually switched via the most direct route. But Lane discovered that, once again, the FBI had gotten incredibly lucky. On the day of Cui's transmission, February 1, the switching mechanism on a U.S. Department of Commerce computer handling the feed into Denver had been faulty, and some of the incoming packets from Boulder had been rerouted through a NASA computer in California.

Lane was pretty sure that when he raised the issue, the government couldn't prove that Wang's specific packets went through California; but that wouldn't spring his client. With prosecutors putting the scent of espionage in the air, he explained, "we were not going to win with that. Juries just hate to see people get off on technicalities."[15]

The lawyer decided to try some psychological warfare on Ellery. Lane sent the prosecutors a letter, in which he threatened: "As I'm sure you are aware, any and all aspects of the Ellery code will almost certainly be disclosed during the trial of the matter."[16]

Ironically, the letter came at the same time that Ellery was trying the same ploy on Beijing Machinery. Shaw sent Li Wu Quan, the company's chairman, a letter noting that the trial of Wang could damage Beijing's "esteemed reputation as an honorable trading partner." All of Wang's dealings with the company would be made public, Shaw noted, adding, "Unfortunately, we expect the level of press coverage to increase significantly as Mr. Wang's trial draws near." One way to avoid such an airing of secrets, Shaw suggested, would be for Beijing Machinery to "immediately" agree to license Ellery's software. Shaw would grant an exclusive license for $1 million. Shaw noted that he had sent copies of the letter to Vice President Al Gore and Senate majority leader Robert Dole.[17]

By the summer of 1994, Wang's prosecutors were struggling with a damaging little secret of their own. One of the chief pillars of their case, Xin Shulin, was beginning to crumble. Shulin was the business student who had agreed to form D.C. Nology with Wang and Cui. In return for leniency, Shulin had agreed to testify against them, but now he had informed the prosecutors that he would be leaving for a new job in Hong Kong in July.

That sent the prosecutors rustling through their law books. While the United States finds it easy to trade with China, legal dealings with the world's last remaining large Communist state range from merely difficult to impossible. If Shulin went back to China, the prosecutors discovered, a U.S. subpoena to get him back as a witness might well be ignored.

As a precaution, the prosecutors videotaped Shulin's testimony in July. It was a disaster. Earlier, Shulin had told the FBI that he agreed with their version of the case. In the videotape, however, Shulin said that Wang hadn't stolen anything and that D.C. Nology had nothing to do with Ellery's software.[18]

At about the same time, Lane was learning how tough it is to make legal dealings with China. He wanted to go to Beijing to take depositions of witnesses who had volunteered to testify to Wang's character and his reputation as a software expert. Lawyers at the Departments of State and Justice advised that the effort would be futile because China regularly rejected such requests. If Lane tried to do it anyway, he risked being arrested and deported for "a violation of China's judicial sovereignty."[19]

To ease Ellery's fears that Beijing Machinery would market its software, Judge Sparr issued an injunction against the company. He later dropped it after lawyers for the Chinese company argued that Wang had no legally binding agreement with Beijing, that the company had not received any

Ellery software, and that, in any case, the U.S. court had no business telling Beijing Machinery what to do.

By December 1994, the case against Wang weakened further. Good, the NASA astronomer and computer expert, had been hired by Judge Sparr to go to FBI headquarters and make a detailed examination of the software that Wang allegedly stole. Good concluded that there was only a small portion of Ellery's proprietal software in the transmission received by Cui. "What he [Wang] was saying made sense and what Ellery was saying didn't," Good says he reported to the judge.

Under the laws being used to prosecute Wang, however, a stolen fragment was all that was required. But on December 28, 1994, a federal judge in Boston reinterpreted the laws, throwing out a case against David La Macchia, a twenty-one-year-old MIT student. He had been accused of stealing more than $1 million worth of copyrighted software programs and putting them on the Internet.

The problem with legal voids, as Professor Chandler and other experts point out, is that they often result from a dearth of cases where a few odd decisions tend to control opinion. The characters in the cases leading up to Wang were certainly odd. First there was Paul Edmond Dowling, a California man charged with mail fraud for advertising his large collection of bootleg Elvis Presley records. In 1994 the Supreme Court threw the case out, concluding that it was merely a violation of U.S. copyright laws.

Now the Boston judge had done the same thing with La Macchia, who had asserted that he put the software on the Internet out of altruism and took no profit for himself. Although La Macchia had been "nihilistic, self indulgent and lacking in any fundamental sense of values," the judge concluded, there was no way he was going to send the student to the slammer for wire fraud.[20] Under the precedent set in *United States* v. *Dowling*, it was, at most, a copyright violation.

Having struggled with Wang for almost a year, federal prosecutors were determined they were not going to be defeated by a case involving bootleg Elvis Presley records. They went back to the grand jury in Denver with a whole new legal theory: By allowing Ellery's software to go out over the Internet, Wang had set off a chain of events that resulted in wrongly depriving Ellery of Wang's "honest services." That also constituted a charge of wire fraud, which carried up to five years in jail and a $250,000 fine.

"It is incumbent on us to try and be aggressive," explained Henry Solano, who supervised the two federal attorneys working the case. Settling the Wang case for a mere copyright violation, he noted, "wouldn't do much to deter people who would otherwise be engaged in theft or fraud."[21]

Lane and Cui's attorney moved to dismiss the case against Wang, based on the La Macchia decision, but Judge Sparr ruled against them. He appeared to be determined to see the Wang case go to trial. That was troubling to Lane. When it comes to cases where espionage is charged and a foreigner, like Wang, is sitting in the defendant's chair, juries tend to be patriots. To fully protect his client, Lane had to find a way to kill the case before it got that far.

He began by examining the last remaining prop holding the case up: Lowell Schneider, Wang's reclusive supervisor. Schneider was a key witness, but nobody had talked to him yet. The prosecutors were dealing with Ellery matters through Shaw, but Wang believed that Schneider, when pressed, would tell a different story.

By September 1995, Solano's prosecutors were in the final preparations for trial. It promised to be a mind-glazing case. They had rounded up twenty-three witnesses. The gamut ran from an expert on Chinese culture, who would testify that Asians have little respect for intellectual property rights, to a government Internet engineer, who would explain that the shortest E-mail route from Boulder to Denver is, fortuitously, sometimes through California.

Lane had a hard time reaching Schneider, who had since left Ellery over a salary dispute. First Schneider wouldn't return Lane's calls, then he wouldn't agree to visit Lane's office. But the lawyer persisted. "I finally called him and said, 'Look, Lowell, you can either look very foolish on the stand, or you can sit down in my office and listen to the questions I will ask you at trial. You can do it the easy way, or the hard way, it's up to you.'"

The hippyesque computer engineer opted for the easy way. Lane sat him down, looked him in the eye, and asked: "Is Andrew Wang a criminal?" The notion made Schneider uneasy. He finally admitted that he might have given Wang permission to transfer the code for testing purposes. He couldn't remember for sure, but it was something he probably would have consented to.

After that admission, *United States* v. *Wang* might stagger on for a while, but it was legally dead. Serious criminal violations require what lawyers call "scienter": it means prosecutors have to prove a specific intent to commit a crime. If there is any room for reasonable doubt about the application of a law, a judge is required to instruct a jury to decide for the defendant. What

Schneider had admitted to Lane opened up plenty of room for doubt.[22]

In a normal case, Lane would have waited to spring his surprise at trial; but the lawyer was still deeply afraid of letting anything with even a hint of espionage attached to it get before a jury. "Who knows what a jury is going to do?" He made an offer to the prosecutors: If they would listen to his case, he would let them have an extremely unusual no-holds-barred pretrial interview with Wang.

Solano's lawyers couldn't pass it up. Wang was waiving his constitutional right not to testify. Here was an opportunity to get a preview of Lane's whole case. While the decision to drop *United States* v.*Wang* lingered for two more months of agonizing deliberations between Solano, his prosecutors, and officials in the FBI and the Department of Justice in Washington, the case really ended on October 9, 1995.

That day, in a private meeting at the FBI's office in Denver, Wang faced a battery of prosecutors, FBI agents, and a variety of other experts. He tried, again, to explain what had happened. The U.S. government brought its computer expert, and Good, acting as Wang's expert, participated via a conference call from California. As the day wore on, the engineers' techno-jargon baffled most of the lawyers, but the government's expert began to agree with Good: from an engineering point of view, Wang appeared to be telling the truth.

Eleven days later, the prosecutors deposed Schneider. He said what Lane said he would. Earlier, Schneider had signed a statement agreeing with Shaw's version—that Wang had nearly destroyed the company by stealing almost its entire commercial software source code. The prosecutors could have confronted him with the contradiction at trial.

But to impeach Schneider in front of a jury would have been suicidal. He was the Ellery's expert and the government's main remaining witness. "We would have been sawing off the branch behind ourselves," explained William R. Lucero, one of two trial prosecutors who handled the case.

Lucero and his fellow prosecutor, Mark J. Barrett, went to Solano and suggested that the Wang case be dropped. For Barrett, a florid-faced Irishman who had spent a year and a half putting the case together, it was one of the hardest decisions he has faced in fourteen years as a prosecutor. He had had calls from six other federal prosecutors wanting to know how to deal with computer fraud.

At this point, there wasn't much Barrett could tell them. As he put it, "In some cases, the law is nearly automatic. All I have to do is establish that a guy was in a car with $20,000 worth of cocaine and then say, hey, you explain it. But that wasn't the case here."

United States v.*Wang* can't take its place alongside Dowling and his bootleg Elvis Presley records in the nation's sparse Pantheon of landmark intellectual property rights decisions. That's because on December 6, 1995, Judge Sparr dismissed it "without prejudice," which means that, in terms of legal precedent, the case doesn't exist. Nobody was really happy with the outcome. Shaw, the chief executive of Ellery, continues to believe that Wang nearly destroyed his business.

Solano, the U.S. attorney, notes that some evidence in the case, such as Wang's murky dealings with Beijing Machinery, "was and is an appearance that remains suspicious."

As for Wang, who now runs a computer system for a small Denver company, he says: "There is still a shadow in my heart. I lost my job, my reputation both here and in China. I lost a big opportunity to sell my idea." Nonetheless, he intends to remain in the United States. Lane and Good, he notes, went out of their way to help him. "A lot of American people, when they saw the newspaper, hear all these things about me, they say, okay, Andrew is not this person. So I think this country is a good country. I still think this is the best country to live."[23]

If there is one lesson from the case that both sides agree on, it is the gross mismatch between the law and an exploding technology that now affects millions of people's lives. As Good, the NASA astronomer, puts it: "The laws are so far behind that it's not funny." Barrett, the prosecutor, won't argue with that. "We were trying to be creative here. It wasn't the easiest fit."[24]

FIFTEEN

Surviving

George B. Rathmann, a chemist, was in the middle of what he called "a war."

His company was one of over one thousand U.S. firms, most of them tiny, experimenting with biotechnology—the manipulation of living cells to create new drugs, agricultural products, and a host of other commercial inventions. Together, the biotechnology industry amounts to the crown jewel of post–Cold War U.S. research. It promises to be one of the engines that will drive America's economic growth by the year 2000.[1]

There were days in the summer of 1988, however, when Rathmann wasn't sure that his company, Amgen Inc., would make it to 1990, let alone 2000. Most of the basic research for the fledgling industry was American. It had spun out of billions of dollars of U.S. government–sponsored studies in the 1970s, but Japan's Ministry of International Trade and Industry had targeted the technology in 1981.

The Japanese government was spending only about a fifth of the amount of research money doled out by the United States, but big Japanese companies knew where to go to catch up. They were swarming all over the American market, buying some U.S. companies, working out partnership deals with others. Nearly 90 percent of the deals amounted to a one-way street for the fledgling technology to flow to Japan.[2]

When it comes to taking risks, biotechnology is Las Vegas dressed in a laboratory gown. Rathmann had made his own deal with a Japanese company: Kirin, the beer company, which was hoping to leap from brewing into pharmaceuticals.³ Together, the two companies had raised almost $250 million, betting that Amgen would be first to market a wonder drug called Epogen, that would later be in high demand for patients with kidney disease, AIDS, and those undergoing chemotherapy for cancer. Then Rathmann's main competitor, the Genetics Institute, bankrolled by a big Japanese drug company, Chugai Pharmaceuticals, claimed that it had developed the drug first.

After Rathmann sued the Genetics Institute, starting an expensive and long-enduring patent fight, Amgen's stock responded like a wounded duck, lurching sideways and then dropping from $18 to $3 a share. Rathmann's choices were stark: He would either have a billion-dollar company, or he would have nothing. He was brooding about all this one day, sitting in his office at Thousand Oaks, California, in the dusty, ex-urban foothills of Los Angeles, when a letter arrived from Gabriel Schmergel, the president of Genetics.

It said someone known only as "Pimpernel" was offering to sell Amgen's secret process for making Epogen to Genetics. Pimpernel would deliver Amgen's documents when the Cambridge company paid him $1 million in small, unmarked bills.

For Rathmann, it was a bolt out of the blue. Pimpernel, whoever he or she was, had access to his secrets. The Genetics letter included a sample document that Rathmann recognized as one removed from Amgen's research files. Rathmann was prepared to battle a competitor. He had installed expensive doorlocks tied to a magnetic pass card system to keep ousiders out of his labs. But he had no idea where to begin with an internal spy, somebody who could stroll out through his magnetic doors with Amgen's most prized formulas. His first instinct was to take the letter to the Thousand Oaks Police Department. "They told me I should take it to the post office."

At the post office, Rathmann was told to take the letter to the FBI. He remembers the FBI agent being cool, suave, and rather dubious. "He said we have to know if this case will involve a significant amount of money. Can you give me a number?" Rathmann's number had a few more zeroes on it than the FBI normally sees.

The mechanics of snaring Pimpernel were relatively simple. The letter had come from a post-office box in nearby Ventura. The FBI agent took a camera and hung around the post office until a man opened the box. *Snap.* The photo revealed one John S. Wilson, thirty-three, who had been hired for an entry-level research job at Amgen a year previously. He had just quit. Then FBI agents, posing as representatives of Genetics, arranged to meet "Pimpernel" in a Ventura restaurant. Wilson showed them five hundred pages of stolen Epogen documents. The FBI dickered the price down to $200,000. Pimpernel accepted. Then . . . *snap*. The FBI agents showed Wilson their handcuffs.

What Rathmann learned from that experience, however, is that securing a modern high-tech company from spies is no snap. And he knows a great deal about security. During the Cold War, Rathmann headed a top-secret Pentagon research project for the 3M Corporation. No foreign scientists were allowed into the labs. Researchers in the program were tightly compartmentalized. "No need to know" was the rule. It meant that mere scientific curiosity was not enough for a person to ask someone else a question. It meant researchers kept their mouths shut about their work.

With Amgen, none of this was possible. The man who invented Epogen is Fu-Kuen Lin, an immigrant from Taiwan and an expert in the diseases of plants. He appeared at Rathmann's door one day in 1981. At that point, Amgen consisted of ten people. There was no room in the company's tiny lab at the time, so Dr. Lin was put to work in a cramped library on an experiment that had been dropped by somebody else.

Two years later, Dr. Lin cloned a protein called erythropoietin, which stimulates the production of red blood cells in the human body. When it hit the market in 1990 as Epogen, Dr. Lin's drug took off, developing a $1.1 billion worldwide market for all those patients who need an artificial source to stimulate the formation of red blood cells.

And with Epogen, Amgen took off. There are now thirty-two other buildings clustered in the vicinity of the one where Dr. Lin made his breakthrough. As the company's director of biomedical sciences, Dr. Lin can hire anybody he wants. In his own personal laboratory, he has selected nine Chinese—four from Taiwan, five from the mainland; three Hungarians; and one American. "You want the diversity, otherwise you couldn't have the cross-fertilization that we need," explains Dr. Lin, a slender man now in his mid-fifties.

Overall, 30 percent of Amgen's workers are non-U.S. citizens and all Amgen researchers are encouraged talk to each other because that is how new products are born. "You have to have total free flow of information within the company," explains Dr. Rathmann, who has since retired from Amgen to form another biotechnology company.[4]

The matter of how to keep the information from flowing outside Amgen was a puzzle that he left for his successor, Gordon Binder, a tall, lean-faced engineer. There were some things about the Pimpernel case that were profoundly disturbing. Before he quit Amgen, Wilson had spent hours at the copy machine, copying the secret Epogen files. Nobody thought to question him.

When it comes to security risks, Binder is a man whose imagination can run wild. Before he joined Amgen, he worked for U.S. defense contractors who verged on paranoia. They put bars inside air vents. He remembers seeing office buildings overlooking the Pacific where the oceanside offices were required to be empty for security reasons. The fear was that an enemy submarine, bouncing laser beams off of the windows, could detect conversation within the offices from tiny variations in the reflected beams caused by vibrations. "You could drive yourself crazy," says Binder, looking out of his office window toward the busy freeway that runs along California's coast. "I'm not going to go down and live in some subterranean tank."

As the world's leading biotechnology company, Amgen now has a great deal more at risk. Eleven more major drugs are in various stages of research. The costs are stupefying: according to one industry study, it takes between $200–$350 million in research and clinical tests to bring each new drug to market.[5] Each is an all-or-nothing bet. "There's no insurance for this. It's very hard to prove a value for what somebody stole and what he did with it," explains Binder.

Binder shaped a novel theory of protection: He encouraged everybody to talk and think about risks. He hired William C. Boni, a former Army counterintelligence specialist, to be the company's security chief. Boni, who spent the early eighties looking for spies in South Korea, now makes it a point to sit down with each newly hired Amgen employee.

Old-time security people focused on locks, guards, and alarms. Boni works on awareness. He tells new researchers about Pimpernel, whose dreams of wealth netted him five years in prison. He tells them: "If that [Genetics] had been an unethical competitor, we could be a footnote in history." New workers are left with the strong impression that the value of their stock options and, indeed, their very jobs could disappear unless they develop an ability to spot and report suspicious behavior. The company has built close ties with the FBI, which comes in every two years to give a security briefing to top officers.

This all might sound routine, but it isn't. James A. Williams, the retired

Army general who headed the Defense Intelligence Agency in the 1980s, says many major American companies don't want to know about their vulnerabilties. "They have little knowledge of the research and development material that can get sucked out." Williams, who now runs a small consulting company, says corporate espionage is usually an unreported crime because the cost of talking about it is deemed too high.

"Company executives see no way to bring retribution, so they don't bring it up. They worry that if they do, their insurance rates will go up and their competitors will talk about it."[6]

"Most companies make no effort to protect their information," explains Robert Hildner, a senior consultant for The Fairfax Group, Ltd., a Washington-based private investigating firm that handles large corporate clients. "What causes part of the problem is the proliferation of computers. That leads to huge quantities of first drafts which go straight into the garbage. You can find an incredible amount about what's going on in a company just by going through stuff that people throw away. Some people specialize in this. 'Dumpster divers,' we call them. If you wear a suit and tie, you can walk into almost any office at seven P.M."[7]

Then there are companies that pay for security but don't quite get it right. A major bathroom-fixtures manufacturer hired Arthur Andersen & Co. to figure out why a competitor always managed to stay just a few cents under the company's sealed bids. Andersen's Chicago office discovered that the company scrupulously put its most sensitive documents, including price lists, into a shredder. But then it used the quarter-inch strips of paper that emerged as packing material for shipping products. In effect, the company was publishing its secrets in the form of a puzzle that somebody put back together.[8]

Amgen's next adventure with its secrets came in December 1993, when Binder received an anonymous letter from an employee, one of 3,200 then working for his company. It warned that a laboratory worker was planning to steal "cell lines," or the actual genetic material that goes into Epogen. It named the worker, an Asian, and said he was busy shopping for buyers overseas.

First, Boni had Kroll Associates, a large New York–based investigating firm, analyze the letter. A content and handwriting analysis indicated that the anonymous tipster was also Asian and highly educated. Next, Boni checked the suspect's telephone records and found he had made over seventy calls to his home country, a large Asian nation that Boni won't identi-fy. The calls, costing $1,200, went to dozens of different numbers.

Boni took the case to the FBI, but this time they rejected it. Unless Boni could show that the potential buyers included a government spy agency, the Feds would not take the case. There was no jurisdiction and, as yet, no crime. So Boni went back to Kroll. Using its Hong Kong office, Kroll traced some of the phone numbers and found that some of the calls had gone to government agencies. Kroll began interviewing employees and following the suspect. It discovered that he was still stockpiling the drug and related documents. Then another anonymous letter arrived, stating that the suspect was coming into the laboratory that very night with his outside accomplice.

When the two men entered the Amgen laboratory, planning to use the phones for more sales pitches to potential overseas buyers, Boni, a Kroll investigator, and a visiting FBI agent were waiting for them. Since nothing had been stolen yet, the employee was fired, but the incident was not for-gotten. It was highly publicized both inside and outside the company. Amgen's people had helped their company dodge another bullet.

There were more bullets to come. Amgen's Japanese competitors grow more aggressive and innovative. One, Hitachi Chemical Company, has built a $26 million, plum-colored research facility squarely in the middle of the University of California's campus at Irvine, just across the sprawl of Los Angeles from Amgen.

One of Hitachi's earlier innovations, a 1982 attempt to buy secret infor-mation on new IBM computers, embroiled the company in an FBI sting operation. FBI agents, expecting Russian spies, set up a meeting in a hotel room. What appeared on their videotape, however, were executives of Hitachi and Mitsubishi making illegal payoffs for secrets. Clips from the video are now highlighted in a new FBI training film entitled *Piracy in the 20th Century*.

Hitachi's biotechnology venture, called "Plum House," is legal. Accord-ing to an elaborate agreement worked out with the university, Hitachi researchers work with university students and professors, sharing facilities and equipment. Most of the research in biotechnology at the school is financed by two federal agencies, the National Science Foundation and the National Institutes of Health. Ideas born on the upper two floors of the building belong to Hitachi; those that are generated in the other areas belong to the university. Hitachi gets an advanced look at drugs being

developed at the university and can engage the university in joint marketing ventures.

Dr. Jack Jacobs, Hitachi's science director at Irvine, notes that the
Japanese company provides expensive lab machinery that the school can't
afford. He provides his services as a biochemistry teacher to first-year
medical students at no cost. In their spare time, Hitachi researchers lecture
on science at nearby public schools. "We're very strong in philanthropy,"
says Jacobs.[9]

Some countries don't use philanthropy as an approach to acquire U.S.
pharmaceutical technology. They just steal it, copy it, and sell it. In 1994,
the Pharmaceutical Research and Manufacturers of America singled out
the four worst offenders: India, Brazil, Argentina, and Turkey. Of those,
according to Dr. Harvey E. Bale, senior vice president of the trade association, India is in a class by itself: "No other country in the world has played
a more insidious and damaging role for such a long period of time in terms
of its total disregard for the norms of intellectual property protection, especially for pharmaceutical patents," Bale maintained.[10]

In December of that year, Amgen's next adventure emerged in the portly form of Subrahmanyam Kota, president of a Boston software consulting
firm. He was arrested in the process of selling some "bugs" to an FBI agent
next to a Dunkin' Donuts in Westborough, Massachusetts. The price was
$300,000.

The "bugs" turned out to be Epogen cell lines. According to the FBI,
Kota thought he was selling the drug to a KGB agent, and had expressed a
willingness to fly to Moscow to help set up a manufacturing operation for
the cells. The FBI agent had obtained a sample, which was sent for testing
at Amgen. While Kota had touted the "bugs" as being from Amgen, they
turned out to be a version made by Integrated Genetics, a Boston company
that had worked on the drug in the 1980s. According to the FBI, Kota had
obtained the cells from another Indian, Vemuri Bhaskar Reddy, who had
formerly worked for Integrated Genetics.[11]

Amgen's "war" continues. The Genetics Institute, which lost its first
patent challenge to Amgen's Epogen in 1991, has recently brought the matter back into court. The National Research Council, (NRC), which draws its
members from the U.S. academies of engineering and sciences and the
Institute of Medicine, sees the biotechnology industry growing from $2 bil-
lion a year in 1990 to as much as $70 billion by the year 2000.

While Amgen has learned much from its experiences, the overall health of the U.S. industry remains in doubt, according to the NRC. The birthing process of the U.S. industry, the council notes, has had a peculiar side effect: it has built a powerful competitor in Japan. Unless the United States, its universities and companies come up with a common strategy to get as much technology as they give to Japan, the question remains whether Amgen is the first or the last of the big U.S. companies to emerge in the field.

"There is no guarantee . . . that the U.S. will maintain a competitive edge," one report states.[12]

If there were guarantees of security in any business, you might think it would be in a business that makes state-of-the-art spy equipment for the U.S. government. At least that's what Bill Owens thought. He was tragically wrong.

Owens, who is in his early sixties, five feet seven inches tall and weighing in the neighborhood of three hundred pounds, still moves and reacts with the quickness of the Cincinnati Reds farm team ball player he once was. "He's an ex-baseball player that's carrying another baseball player on him," was how one company official described him.

Owens was one of Recon/Optical's key players: He moved and shook things. A gruff, straight-talking chemical engineer, Owens had a passion for the airborne surveillance camera business that impressed his colleagues and moved customers.

In 1986, Owens's company thought it was pretty secure. It had 1,200 employees working in two large buildings in Barrington, Illinois. At the height of the Cold War the folks at Recon/Optical were making one of the devices used every day: a long-range oblique photography (LOROP) camera that allowed U.S. planes to fly along the borders of the Soviet Union and peer in as far as seventy-five miles. Top-of-the-line LOROPs cost $4.5 million apiece; they work electro-optically, so that instead of storing their images on film, they create an electronic signal that can be displayed immediately on computer screens back at the base. Situations that Recon/Optical cameras caught could be dealt with instantaneously. It was a revolutionary device.

But it wasn't revolutionary enough for the Israelis. They signed a $45 million contract with Recon/Optical to push the state of the art: to develop a camera that could see 150 miles beyond a border. It was a tough assignment, but Recon/Optical took it on and put Bill Owens, then a vice president, in charge of the program, which was very sensitive.

Recon/Optical thought it had tight security. All the doors and windows were guarded and everyone had passes, including the three Israeli air force officers who set up an office inside the plant to keep tabs on the program.

One day in the spring of 1986, all that changed. A long-simmering contract dispute between Owens and the Israelis boiled over. Recon stopped work and Owens ordered the Israelis out of the building. He warned the security guards not to let the Israeli officers bring out anything besides their personal belongings. Under the contract, all of the property rights to LOROP technology belonged to Recon/Optical.

The Israelis tried to bring out fourteen boxes, many of them filled with papers written in Hebrew. Owens ordered them confiscated and had them translated. What emerged was evidence of a year-long Israeli effort to steal the technology. Some of it had already been sent over the company fax, again in Hebrew.

A four-year, secret, bitterly fought dispute followed before a panel of arbitrators in New York. Recon had evidence that the Israeli officers passed their information to a competing Israeli company, El Op Electro-Optics Industries Ltd. The panel finally decided that Israel had been "perfidious" and had illegally stolen some of the Illinois company's secrets. It ordered Israel to pay Recon $3 million in damages.

But that was only the beginning of the damages for the company and the agonies of Owens, whose rage has driven him to become a kind of poster boy for the FBI's security awareness program. Owens volunteered despite the fact that the U.S. government—his top customer—gave him no help when he desperately needed it. "I used to have black hair," he explains.

Israel has had espionage operations aimed at U.S. technology since the early 1960s, but they were artfully done. In one case, the suspected theft of nuclear weapons material from a small company in Apollo, Pennsylvania, separate investigations were ordered by three successive administrations. They came up mostly dry, though there were Israeli footprints all over the Apollo plant.

Owens had hard evidence, but neither the Reagan administration nor Owens's senators wanted any part of a fight with the nimble Israelis and their bruising lobby in Congress. "We begged people [in Washington] to help us, but we got nothing but their back," Owens says. As for the Israeli government, the arbitration panel discovered that it later disciplined the three air force officers involved, but not for the theft. They were punished for getting caught.[13]

If Recon/Optical was a publicly held company, it would have died right there. Its largest contract was in dispute; its top management team was stymied for months giving testimony in New York; its legal bills were running in what Owens calls "the double-figure millions."

But the Illinois company was privately held by a California owner, who decided to give Owens another chance. In 1988, two huge new Pentagon reconnaissance programs were about to be launched, each worth $1 billion. Recon/Optical, a company with a seventy-five-year-old track record, had only two competitors. In a normal year, it would have had a good shot.

But things weren't normal. Pressing the Israeli arbitration case was like carrying a giant leech. As Owens explains, "It depleted all of our cash, and when you're bidding a program like this, in the final stages of a proposal the customer will ask you for a best and final price. We had to retain our profit margins at such a level that there wouldn't be any risk at all in any program that we took on." Recon/Optical's competitors took risks and won. Owens had just watched $1 billion worth of work fly out the window.

Meanwhile, Recon/Optical became like the Cheshire Cat: There wasn't much left but its smile. Sales dropped 40 percent. The workforce was cut by two-thirds. The owner finally decided to put the company on the block. It was humiliating: A high-tech company with a product that was the envy of the world was sitting dead in the water. "We were parading all kinds of companies through our operations, including the competition's. That wasn't a very healthy era here," recalls Owens.

There were no buyers, though, just curious people with notepads. In 1991, the owner of Recon/Optical told Owens that he would be the new president. A small stream of research and development money appeared and Owens took the only pathway he knew: he would try to to invent himself out of the hole.

The Gulf War intervened. One hundred and sixty three Recon/Optical cameras performed well in Desert Storm. After the war, Owens got the Pentagon interested in his new idea, which was a "framing array system," a camera that can shoot an entire ten-mile-wide target zone in 2.5 seconds. It was a life-saving device for reconnaissance pilots because it takes surface-to-air missiles at least four seconds to target them.

It was also life-saving for Recon/Optical. Although the company has lost over eight hundred jobs, it now has a fighting chance. But the scars and the pain of Owens's long battle are still evident as he walks in his cavernous, mostly empty plant and looks at the deserted parking lot outside.

"This is unbelievable. I've got 400,000 square feet here and I need 85,000."

As one of a handful of U.S. company managers willing to talk about losses from economic espionage, Owens has achieved a sort of odd celebrity. The FBI approached him to give private talks to other companies as part of its awareness program. Owens remembers his first response. "I said, hey, you guys are a little late."

But Owens later reconsidered. That's how he got the starring role as the good guy/victim in the FBI film *Piracy in the 20th Century*. (Israel, the bad guy/villain, is identified only as "the customer.") Owens is determined that nobody will ever steal his company's secrets again. He is still outraged by his experience, and he gets a kind of perverse pleasure out of watching other executives fidget when they hear it.

"Anybody who thinks the government is gonna do this for you ought to have their heads examined," Owens says vehemently. "You gotta do it yourself. You gotta be smart up front. It's amazing. I get in front of these companies, big companies, and the naivete is the same as it was here. Then they start thinking. They start asking questions and it's really an awakening. It's like, 'Wow. That really *happens* to you?'"[14]

SIXTEEN

Fighting Back

"It's one thing to lose jobs to a democratic country that happens to pay low wages; it's quite another thing to lose jobs to the People's Liberation Army."
—Jeffrey L. Fiedler

Jeff Fiedler's spy campaign against the Chinese army began quietly one day in January 1993. A thin, bearded man, Fiedler has a rumpled, slightly wild look about him, like a high school English teacher who has seen too much bad punctuation. He was standing in the aisle of a Wal-Mart in the suburbs of Washington, D.C., staring at a "color-coordinated, mini-venetian blind."

The price tag said $4.29: a bargain. Most Americans would have snapped it up without a thought. Fiedler snapped it up, but his wheels were already turning. "It was inconceivable to me that you could make these things anywhere for that price."

Fiedler took the blind back to his office and punched the name of the New Jersey company that distributed it into his computer. It imported the blinds from another company: China North Industries. Who was that? Fiedler did some more pecking on his keyboard. His databases revealed a very odd company: it made T-80 tanks and Teddy bears; self-propelled 120-mm. mortars and fancy oak toilet seats; multiple rocket launchers and color-coordinated mini-blinds. China North Industries, otherwise known as NORINCO, had gone through a strange transformation. In the 1970s, it was known as China's Ministry of Machine Building and Electronics; before that, it was the Ministry of Ordnance. It was still the chief weapons maker for China's People's Liberation Army (PLA).

As young man drafted into the Vietnam War, Fiedler wound up in Hue working in a U.S. Army intelligence unit. A lot of what he did was piecing together odd bits of information to reveal the larger picture. Fiedler found he loved puzzles, especially when they involve Asia. The mini-blind was one piece, and Fiedler, now forty-seven, began finding others. He started making long charts that spilled over his messy desk and onto the floor.

He pieced together some of NORINCO's three hundred odd subsidiaries and revealed a pattern: NORINCO was selling millions of dollars of cheap manufactured goods in U.S. discount stores. At the same time, NORINCO was modernizing China's army. That meant that when Fiedler's Aunt Minnie went down to buy a color-coordinated mini-blind at her local Wal-Mart, she didn't know it, but she was making a small contribution toward China's future defense needs. Maybe she was helping to buy a new long-range tactical missile or an imported Russian submarine.

Some days Fiedler just sits in his office, chain-smoking Carltons, and rages about it, wreathed in a halo of smoke: "Here's a country that won't allow a real labor union to exist! Here are the people who are the occupiers of Tibet! Yet we allow them to do business in the U.S. What the fuck are we doing? Have we no perspective? No sense of values? No policy?"

Labor unions mean everything to Fiedler. After Vietnam, he spent twenty years working as a union organizer and an investigator for the Food & Allied Service Trades division of the AFL-CIO. As a young field operative, he learned the ropes from the Old Bulls who built the U.S. labor movement. While he worshipped some of them, Fiedler had no illusions about what his job was going to be. His mentors had grown up organizing strong unions. The role of Fiedler's generation would be a desperate rearguard action as union membership plunged, factories closed, and millions of U.S. jobs were exported overseas.

Fiedler's office in AFL-CIO's headquarters, just two blocks north of the White House, is a strange, messy place. The outer door is usually locked— one last barrier against process servers, Fiedler explains. "Basically what we do here is start fights," he says, leading the visitor down a narrow corridor stacked to the ceiling with plastic picnic coolers. The coolers contain samples of food bought from a local supermarket chain, part of a fight over whether the stores sold perishable items beyond the dates stamped on them. In Fiedler's office, a picture of AFL-CIO founder George Meany stares somewhat quizzically at one of Sam Walton, the founder of Wal-Mart.

This is Fiedler's war room. He has already had one battle with China. In 1991 he met Harry Wu, a political dissident who had spent much of his life in China's forced labor camps. Wu drew Fiedler a map showing which camps were exporting prisoner-made goods into the United States, and Fiedler used it to mount one of his campaigns. In a joint appearance before an investigating committee in Congress, he and Wu exposed how U.S. consumers were, in effect, subsidizing shocking, subhuman conditions in China's gulags, called *laogai*. One result was that the Bush administration got China to sign an agreement saying no more prison-made goods would be sold in U.S. stores.

Now Fiedler wanted to run a similar campaign on PLA-made goods, but his earlier venture with Wu created a problem: Fiedler was in China's database. If he went to China to find which PLA factories were making consumer goods, Fiedler was sure he would be followed everywhere he went. Fiedler lit up another Carlton and stared at the ceiling. Then it came to him. Why not beat China at its own game? He would make up a front company and hire a spy.

The front company would be called Missouri Overseas Traders, and it would supposedly be on the verge of buying a chain of three hundred U.S. discount stores that had gone into bankruptcy. Missouri Traders was lining up wealthy U.S. investors to take over the discount chain. They had a sure-fire formula for success: The chain would import huge quantities of goods from China, but only from trading companies that owned their own factories. That way Missouri Traders could assure quality and prompt delivery.

That was Fiedler's pitch. Now he needed to find somebody to make it. He settled on a fellow union organizer, Mark Atkinson, who was between jobs at the time. A slender man in his thirties with dirty blond hair, Atkinson shared Harry Wu's strong sense of outrage over China's human rights violations. As Fiedler describes him, Atkinson was also a man with a "silver tongue." He could have the PLA's front companies quivering with expectations.

The quivering phase started in July 1993, when Atkinson and Fiedler arrived in Hong Kong with a large database of suspect companies in Fiedler's laptop. They picked two major PLA units: NORINCO, the former Ministry of Ordnance; and the Xinxing Corporation, a branch of the PLA's General Logistics Department. Xinxing once confined itself to making uniforms for the army and China's security agencies. Now, like NORINCO, it had blossomed into one hundred subsidiaries that exported drugs, camping equipment, even human blood to the United States.[1]

While Fiedler hung around the hotel, Atkinson, in his role as senior vice president of Missouri Overseas Traders, started making calls on PLA front companies, starting with one called Rex International. Within two days, Atkinson began receiving invitations to visit factories in China's interior. Atkinston's hosts at places like Guangzhou and Dalien thought it odd that he always brought a video camera with him, but he insisted he needed videotapes of the Chinese factories to make a report that would satisfy his rich U.S. backers.

Atkinson taped PLA weapons factories that made stuffed toys, ceiling fans, automobile jacks, lighting fixtures, and venetian blinds. If he decided to buy, he told his solicitous hosts, he would buy for all three hundred stores at once. To check out Atkinson's bona fides, room service at the NORINCO-run hotel in Guangzhou included a daily, surreptitious search of his luggage, but Fiedler had prepared him for that. All the searchers found were Missouri Overseas Traders brochures.

In October, Atkinson returned to China for a further look with one of his "rich U.S. investors"—one Brian Ross. Ross, who also brought a colleague toting a video camera, was most interested in NORINCO's line of "sporting rifles," which turned out to be modified versions of the AK-47, the PLA's rugged assault rifle. NORINCO had already poured a million of the weapons into the United States, but Ross and Atkinson found the company was eager to sell more at less than one-tenth the cost of similar weapons made in the United States. Salesmen were hanging on their every word.

The public phase of a Fiedler campaign usually begins with a big splash in the media, and Ross—in reality a reporter for the prime-time *Dateline NBC* news magazine—did not disappoint. His show, which aired the following March, opened with a shot of a Chinese freighter entering the port of Los Angeles carrying a load of "sporting rifles." Not many Americans had heard of NORINCO, Ross noted, but its products "have now left a trail of blood across America."[2]

What followed was a collection of grisly scenes from recent shootings, including a massacre of children in a Stockton, California, schoolyard and two men who were gunned down outside a Wal-Mart in Oklahoma—all the work of NORINCO rifles.

Ross's report shocked a lot of people. In May 1994, President Clinton signed an executive order banning further imports of guns from China. In July, the House Ways and Means Committee held a hearing on a bill that would deny most-favored-nation import status for all consumer goods made by the PLA. Representative Nancy Pelosi (D–CA), led the attack, charging:

"The huge profits and hard currency earned through these sales are bankrolling the massive modernization and expansion of China's military and the proliferation of weapons of mass destruction to rogue regimes."[3]

The Clinton administration found itself in a difficult position. Big American discounters like Wal-Mart thrive on selling cheap Chinese goods, and major U.S. corporations like McDonnell Douglas and Boeing have a substantial business stake with partners in China. While Fiedler and Pelosi pushed from one direction, the companies lobbied against them.

Ultimately the U.S. government, with its enormous intelligence resources, pleaded ignorance. Ambassador Charlene Barshefsky, then deputy U.S. Trade Representative on dealings with China, explained that U.S. Customs agents had "neither the resources nor the ability" to identify products made by the Chinese government. As for PLA companies, "So far, U.S. analysts have been able to identify three for which there are identifiable products for export."[4]

After she testified, Fiedler, in one of his rare appearances wearing a suit and tie, took the witness stand and gave the committee a pile of Chinese documents that he and Atkinson had collected. They included the names of over one hundred PLA exporting companies and locations of their subsidiaries in places like Atlanta, Georgia; Secaucus, New Jersey; Southfield, Michigan; and Orange County, California.

Representative Pelosi's bill failed, but Fiedler had some satisfaction in knowing he had helped cut off the $200 million PLA's "sports rifle" business in the United States. The ban, like many agreements the United States has made with China, developed loopholes that were quickly found and exploited.[5] Congress later exempted weapons already in transit when the ban was imposed. The U.S. Treasury estimated the exemption would cover 12,000 weapons, but importers claimed 440,000.[6] A year after the ban, in May 1995, U.S. Customs agents discovered that, somehow, 75 million rounds of assault rifle ammunition had been illegally imported into the United States from sources in China and Russia.[7]

U.S. officials continue to argue that there is no way they can penetrate China's labyrinth of front companies to identify PLA fronts. "Who are you kidding?" one official asked a *Wall Street Journal* reporter. "We don't have access to their registration records to show who's the true owner. It would be impossible to identify who's doing what."[8]

NORINCO, on the other hand, had little trouble figuring out who is doing what. It hired a U.S. private investigating firm that found out Missouri

Overseas Traders was a mail drop with a fax machine in Columbia, Missouri. The investigator, claiming to be Missouri Traders, then called the local telephone company and complained about a billing error. Obligingly, the phone company gave him phone numbers of calls made on the machine, including one to Fiedler's office in Washington. Then Fiedler's office in the AFL-CIO's headquarters in Washington got a call from a man claiming to be from Federal Express. He said he had a package to deliver, but couldn't read the address because it was smudged. A secretary gave the caller Fiedler's address. Later Fiedler received a copy of a starchy memo that the private investigator had sent to his client in China.

> It would appear that Mr. Atkinson 'duped' NORINCO into get-
> ting pictures of your factories. What you wish to do with the
> above information in China [i.e.: disseminating it to trade offi-
> cials] is your decision.

It had taken Fiedler months to penetrate NORINCO's operations in China. NORINCO had uncovered Fiedler's business in the United States with a few swift phonecalls that revealed his identity, his phone number, and location. This was a gross abuse of his privacy, but Fiedler is one of those rare people who understands how tough business in America can be when the competition is the Chinese army.

Fiedler tucked the memo away for future reference. He is a man who knows good intelligence work when he sees it. "Far be it for me to be out-raged by any of this."[9]

(The lesson that someone in the United States might be watching seems to have been lost on NORINCO, which was trapped in a sting operation mounted by the U.S. Customs Service a few months later. It had allegedly shipped 2,000 fully automatic AK-47 assault rifles to the United States in a container marked "tools." A spokesman for the State Department made light of the matter. "I don't see why this needs to complicate U.S.-China relations at all," he said.)[10]

If a casting director was ordered to find the antithesis of Jeff Fiedler, he or she would have to give serious consideration to Glenn P. Hoetker, a shy, Quaker-educated librarian in his late twenties; a man who admires Japanese flower arrangements and freshly raked gravel. Hoetker doesn't pound the table, swear, smoke, or scheme, but in his own quiet way he, too, knows how to get under an enemy's skin.

The matter of how Hoetker became the sparkplug of a trade war that set two multi-billion-dollar companies at each other's throats and rattled the political crockery in Tokyo and Washington is an odd story. Hoetker himself still finds it amazing.

Hoetker fell in love with Japan at tiny Earlham College in eastern Indiana. Earlham is a Quaker school, and in the 1980s it offered one of the richest Japanese studies programs of any small college in the United States. For Hoetker, a tall, pale mathematics major curious about how high technology flows around the world, learning Japanese seemed like a ticket to a busy, lucrative career. Tens of thousands of English-speaking Japanese roamed the United States looking for markets and technology. Only a relative handful of Americans knew Japanese well enough to perform the same function in Japan.

During the late 1980s, as Japan developed into an economic and technological powerhouse, Hoetker figured that U.S. Fortune 500 companies involved in international trade had to be desperate for information about Japan. During his junior year, he went to live with a family in rural Morioka, Japan, and gained fluency in Japanese. In 1988, Hoetker used a postgraduate scholarship to visit high-tech facilities in Asia. After that, he got a master's degree in library and information science at the University of Illinois.

From there, it seemed, he had it made. Hoetker signed on with a newly formed Washington, D.C., company, SCAN C2C, that was the answer to his career dreams. A joint venture between Japan's Fuji Photo Film Company and an affiliate of Xerox, it ran a computer database that offered quick searches for and translations of excerpts from 185 technical journals published in Japan. No one else provided such information in the United States. Hoetker was sure that American companies would beat a path to its door.

But an earlier, more robust database started by University MicroFilms International, Hoetker discovered, had fizzled for lack of interest. In 1991, as he worked on SCAN C2C's computer terminals, Hoetker realized that that had not been a fluke. "There were entire days when we got no calls for research or document delivery or translation."

In 1992, Hoetker switched to the National Aeronautics and Space Administration, which had a huge database on foreign technology. There, he discovered a familiar pattern. Not many people used the Japan section of the database and progressively deeper budget cuts had spawned rumors that it might be abandoned altogether. Part of Hoetker's job was to attend academic conferences on how to use Japanese information. "At some of them I found more Japanese than Americans. They just wanted to know how we do it."

By early June 1994, Hoetker was back pounding the pavement, still looking for his dream job. He was seriously worried, but he hadn't given up. There had to be somebody in business who wanted to know about Japan. He went to visit a lawyer in the Washington office of Dewey Ballantine, a big, venerable Wall Street law firm. The lawyer had represented the semiconductor industry, which had been heavily battered by Japanese competitors. Hoetker was sure someone in Silicon Valley needed a Japanese information specialist.

But the lawyer was dubious. He would pass Hoetker's résumé around, he said without much conviction. The next day, however, lightning finally struck. Another lawyer at the firm, Thomas R. Howell, spotted the résumé, grabbed the phone, and hired Hoetker on the spot. Howell, Hoetker discovered, was the man he had been looking for since college: Here was someone who truly was desperate for information about Japan. One of Dewey Ballantine's larger clients, Kodak Company, had a big trade problem in Japan and was willing to spend the money to explore it. Howell had combed through every English database he could find. They offered few clues.

Kodak had been trying to crack Japan's film market since 1889. It had built an elaborate distribution network, hired over three thousand Japanese, flown blimps over Tokyo flashing Kodak's name along with a picture of a carp—a Japanese symbol of strength—sponsored national sports events, and recruited dazzling young ladies to give away free Kodak film. Kodak had tried so hard for so long that it was among ten U.S. companies singled out by Japan's Chamber of Commerce as models of "success."[11]

But after all that, in Japan Kodak was still only a minnow. Fuji enjoyed 70 percent of the film market. Kodak's slice was 9 percent and had been steadily shrinking since 1983, after Japan's tariff barriers against outside film had been dropped.[12] Kodak dominated Fuji all over the world—but not in Japan. When Kodak cut prices to its Japanese wholesaler, prices on its film went up in the stores. Something was seriously wrong. But what it was Kodak didn't know. Howell needed more information.

The lawyer quickly loaded Hoetker on a plane to Tokyo. Hoetker recalls Howell's marching orders: "I don't speak the language. I don't know the resources over there. We hired you because you do. Come back with good stuff."

After a fourteen-hour flight, Hoetker found himself checking into Tokyo's

Akasaka Prince Hotel. He was jet-lagged and weary, but he had this strange, almost titillating feeling: "All of a sudden I had the time, the resources, and the cause to apply everything I'd learned. I felt I'd finally been let loose."

Of the relatively few Americans who conduct serious information searches in Japan, most wind up in the hands of experienced *gaijin*-handlers. These are Japanese consultants whose main skills consist in speaking English and in determining what foreigners (*gaijin*) want to see. Hoetker simply bypassed them. Through his experience at SCAN C2C and NASA, he had learned that Japanese companies and trade associations often publish gossipy newsletters and annual reports.

Hoetker knew who could find them. Tokyo is packed with first-rate investigative firms. Using gumshoes is a national pastime in Japan. Companies use them on each other; families even use them to scope out prospective sons and daughters-in-law. Some of the most innovative firms are small and they don't speak English. Hoetker hired four, admonishing each one: "If you can't get it ethically, I don't want it."

After briefing his consultants, Hoetker spend a lot of time poking through periodicals in Japanese libraries. Japan's press, he discovered, had also been curious about film prices. One economics magazine called Fuji the "Gulliver of the business world" and asserted that it had muscled small camera stores to charge as much as four times the price of film sold in the United States by threatening to remove its advertising support for the stores.[13] Hoetker shipped over a thousand documents back to Washington, including trade association reports from film wholesalers and retailers going back to the 1960s. He had found some eye-popping stuff, including admissions of repeated efforts within Japan's trade association of photofinishing laboratories to fix prices.

Their newsletters contained New Year's greetings, executives' speeches, meeting notices, and an occasional exhortation such as: "This would be a good opportunity for us to get their [retailers] cooperation in raising the price, so let's make effort without passing it up." In another newsletter, the head of a chain of camera stores bragged about how he had stared down officials of Japan's equivalent of the U.S. Federal Trade Commission. The officials summoned the camera-store executive for a grilling about price fixing. "Are you doing this?" one official asked. "I know all about it, and am doing this," grunted the executive, adding: "Are you interrogating me without knowing my circumstances while you sit in this nice warm room?" The officials suddenly remembered they had to leave for other appointments. The morale of the story, according to the camera-store executive, was: "It is not necessary to lower your head [bow] to clueless government officials."[14]

Howell was beside himself. "It was just like hitting a gusher. . . . We had thirty years of these reports and we began to see the whole system function." Kodak's president, George M. C. Fisher, was enthusiastic and began signing roughly $1 million worth of checks to enable Dewey Ballantine to mount a full-scale investigation and legal assault on Fuji. At one point the law firm had a dozen translation companies—nearly all the available talent it could find in the United States—working to translate Hoetker's papers.

Thomas Howell, a curly-haired, energetic man in his mid-forties, spent his undergraduate days at Harvard studying history. He has a peculiar filing system, plastering books and documents all over the floor of his office. He and a team of six economists and support staff tiptoed among them, looking for the pieces of a trade law violation. Howell wanted to use as many Japanese sources as he could find. He'd waged similar trade battles with Japanese companies in steel and semiconductors and found American experts, especially academic economists, to be almost useless.

Up to the 1950s, according to Howell, American economists followed international trade flows by talking to traders and companies. After that, though, a new breed of economist took over the field, using free market theories and macro-level computer models. "The basic assumption in this town [Washington] is that everyone functions like the Americans. They say this or that couldn't happen, and then that becomes the reality. We come back with all this weird stuff and they'd say, 'That couldn't be happening, it doesn't show up in the gross numbers.'" Howell calls it "an American intellectual failure."[15]

Dewey Ballantine, former New York Governor Thomas E. Dewey's old law firm, loves big fights. It grew to over four hundred lawyers and spawned a half-dozen other major law firms following the old-fashioned dictum of one of its founders, who declared in 1921: "Prompt work, letters answered, clients pursued when in default, no mistakes, no personal engagements, clients' troubles carried on the train, on a walk, to bed . . . these will not get all the business in the world, but are guaranteed to get some business with unfailing regularity."[16]

To Howell, that meant don't spare the horses. He hired more Japanese-speaking troops, including Charles D. Lake II, a former special counsel to the U.S. Trade Representative (USTR). Because Lake grew up in Japan and his mother is Japanese, Japanese became his first language. *Gaijin*-handlers, trained to gush over any effort by an American to speak Japanese, always amuse him. "I say good morning and they say, 'Oh, your Japanese is wonderful.'"

Lake had a lot more to say than good morning. In May 1995, Dewey Ballantine filed a thick brief with the office of the U.S. Trade Representative. Using 256 different Japanese sources, it charged Fuji with manipulating four major wholesalers to jack up film prices in rural areas in Japan, creating a $10 billion war chest to fight Kodak overseas. Lake and Howell held lengthy sessions explaining their case to Japanese reporters. The result was that the Japanese reporters did some digging on their own. One later quoted an industry official describing Fuji's price structure as one of "the seven wonders in the photographic film industry."[17] "If you've got a story to tell and take the effort, you will find the Japanese press receptive," explains Howell.

Fuji did not take all this sitting down. It was jumping up and down, screaming. It hired another Washington law firm to produce a doorstop-sized book calling Kodak's claims "complete fabrications." Its most oft cited source was Fuji, but it made up for the shortfall in outside documentation with outrage. As a preface to Fuji's response, Minoru Ohnishi, president of Fuji, said that Kodak had "violated all the standards of business ethics."[18] Later, speaking to the Foreign Correspondents' Club in Tokyo, he accused Kodak of "vilification and slander."[19] An unnamed official of a photographic trade association took Ohnishi's shrill rhetoric a few notches higher, telling a trade magazine reporter: "Give me a goddamn break, I would like to say. Kodak's charge is prejudice against a colored race, and it is an arrogant view."[20]

Kodak's assault on Fuji is now regarded as a classic, a case likely to rumble on for years, both in Washington and in Geneva. "On a scale of one to ten, I'd rate it a twelve," says Clyde V. Prestowitz, Jr., the former USTR Japan specialist.

Meanwhile, Glenn Hoetker, the man who started all this, goes back to Tokyo regularly to hunt for more ammunition. For a Japanese-speaking American researcher, this is an exciting time. Hoetker, ever the optimist, thinks the Kodak-Fuji fight will wake up other American companies:

"This system [the alleged price fixing in Japan] was designed to be invisible to outsiders. Different businesses would find different problems. But if you are doing business over there, wouldn't it be nice if you knew about it?"[21]

SEVENTEEN

Winning

In the summer of 1954, heat waves shimmered on the white concrete runways at Nellis Air Force Base in Nevada as newly minted Air Force pilots were given a final test. John Boyd, a tall, broad-shouldered captain with a voice like a cement mixer, sized them up. Picking the cockiest fighter jocks, he offered to go one-on-one with them in a dogfight, flying F-100 Super Sabrejets. As the planes began to maneuver in the parched desert air, Boyd would either be on the pilot's tail within forty seconds or he would buy his adversary a steak dinner.

Boyd never lost. Dozens of pilots had the humbling experience of watching "Forty-Second Boyd" materialize, on schedule, in their rearview mirrors. In a real dogfight, that meant death. Boyd's F-100 had six 50-caliber machine guns. Each one could saw an airplane in half.

It was Boyd's way of taking some of the swagger out of the arrogant ones. He hoped the experience might introduce some wisdom that would one day save their lives. Boyd had been trained by World War II aces. Flying missions during the Korean War, he had seen the losers in dogfights—men who had made split second errors—drill holes into hillsides at almost the speed of sound. Winning wasn't just a possibility with Boyd. It had to happen.

On his retirement as an Air Force colonel in 1976, Boyd took up residence in the Pentagon's basement library and read everything he could find about military strategy. He started with Heinz Guderian, the architect of Germany's Blitzkrieg in World War II, and that led him back into history until he came to the father of all warrior-strategists, Sun Tzu, who advised warlords in China in 400 B.C.

In Asian cultures, as we have seen, Sun Tzu is still revered. For many years, Japanese business planners have used him as their "Bible."[1] Marrying his fighter pilot experience with his synthesis of the classics of military strategy, Boyd came up with a theory of combat that, he felt, made sense for America in the late twentieth century. He made it into a slide briefing, an art form in the Pentagon, where officials often have time to read little else.

Boyd made up a catchy sound bite: OODA-Loop. It meant that a pilot who could Observe, Orient himself, Decide, and Act faster would almost always win, because he was flying inside his enemy's Loop. Boyd is nothing if not persistent. He gave hundreds of briefings. Generals, congressmen, two future secretaries of Defense, stray reporters who showed even a glimmer of interest, all got Boyd's hours-long slide briefing on OODA-Loops.[2]

Soon, people were talking about OODA-Loops all over the Pentagon. Planners began applying them to the behavior of armies and fleets, not just to pilots. The Marine Corps adapted Boyd's ideas for its new theory of maneuver warfare and ordered privates to carry Sun Tzu in their backpacks. Like the rain coming in through a leaky roof, Boyd's ideas thoroughly permeated the winning strategy of U.S. forces during the Gulf War, which was based on speed, maneuver, and stealth. Later, generals and admirals borrowed liberally from Boyd's unpublished "Discourse on Winning and Losing" to explain their theories on information warfare. Some of them even passed off Boyd's ideas as their own.[3] Now, "Boydian" ideas have crossed over into business, where making quick, accurate decisions and moving faster than a competitor can react has become one of the theories *du jour*.[4]

Good thing, too, because the overused metaphor about "leveling the playing field" in trade wars needs to be trotted off to the locker room. It always limped, especially in matters involving high technology, where our competitors have been thinking and acting in warlike terms for decades. What was really being leveled was not the "playing field" but America's economic future, as ideas and technology were stolen and high-paying, blue-collar jobs were exported. Meanwhile, business people and politicians, riding on the lazy momentum brought about by world market dominance in the 1960s and 1970s, lost track of the competition.

In the late 1990s, the decline in the nation's economic competitiveness has become a national security issue. The question being wrestled with in Washington is how to address it. In the approaching twenty-first century, it is hard to think of a U.S. administration adopting a defensive strategy—rebuilding Fortress America. America's economy has spent much of its 220-year history growing strong behind protective barriers of tariffs and oceans, but that era seems mostly gone. Post–Cold War markets are global. Over the last twenty years, waves of illegal immigrants have literally changed the demography of the nation, yet Americans have stubbornly clung to the notion of openness as part of our birthright, which indeed it is. So, building a new wall around our economy doesn't sound very attractive, either politically or economically.

Perhaps an offensive strategy might be a better fit. While it has Asian roots, there is something very American about Boyd's theory. It requires intelligence, rapid movement, agility. It offers something that business people and watchers of action films and combat videos can all appreciate: losers die. The OODA-Loop provides a useful way to think about what might be necessary to take the offensive.

John Boyd, now in his late sixties and living in uneasy retirement in Del Ray Beach, Florida, has been thinking about the problem for some time. Mention Japan, and "Forty-Second Boyd" is already up in the air and maneuvering: "We're so goddamned arrogant," he rasps. "In the end in Vietnam, we had to leave. If we're going to compete against Japan, we're going to have to understand the enemy's culture and not just mirror-image him. They come over here by working in our culture. They've got a one-sided advantage over us. That's the game they're playing, and it's a very interesting game, I might add. They'll suck us dry, but whose fault is it? Is it their fault, or our fault? It's our fault."[5]

As the French have already started to discover, the culture of Western nations is a key part of the problem. They have begun to consider how theirs must change so that French companies can compete with "Japan Inc." In order to begin to carry out a Boyd-style OODA-Loop against America's economic competitors, our culture will have to change, as well, and nothing about it will be easy. Four disciplines will be necessary: Observe, Orient, Decide, and Act.

THE NEED TO OBSERVE

The United States employs between 70,000 and 80,000 people in its various intelligence agencies, and in the economic sphere they have not exactly covered themselves with glory.[6] As first demonstrated by the case of

"Farewell" (see chapter 6), they all wear different sorts of blinders. The ones supposed to watch overseas (the CIA, NSA, and the military) can't see an adversary who has imbedded himself in the United States and if they did, some of them have rules against warning the victims. Moreover, the vast majority of U.S. intelligence operatives are in the military, where knowledge of foreign languages and other necessary spy skills have long been regarded as a dead-end career path for aspiring generals and admirals. The domestic observers (the FBI and the Treasury) have had a hard time seeing, understanding, and coping with economic threats coming from overseas, even from tiny island tax havens a few miles offshore.

Since many of these intelligence jobs were created to keep watch on the forces of the Warsaw Pact, some will soon be eliminated, and others will undoubtedly be shifted into the economic sector where the new action is. But merely flipping switches in the federal bureaucracy won't solve the problem, because a good part of it resides within the American business community, which has steadfastly resisted the use of intelligence tools.

In the arena of competition, most American companies are John Wayne against the Indians. They act individually. The opposition sometimes acts and thinks by drawing on the resources of a nation. American companies don't go sniveling to government agencies for advice. It is an image that readily blends into the American dream—the Frontiersman, the Lone Ranger—except that it is an image of the past. Lately, the "Indians" have been winning. There are a few intelligent cowboys out there, like Motorola and Amgen, that have set up their own internal intelligence operations. The rest are like the United States before Pearl Harbor: there are plenty of clues about the competition around, but no one has the time or the responsibility to collect and analyze them.

What would John Wayne—or for that matter, the Indians—think about a U.S. company that has to hire a Washington consulting firm, like Leila Kight's Washington Researchers Ltd., to interview its own employees to find out intelligence about a competitor? It happens.

In describing his adventures during the seventies as a business consultant, Ira Magaziner recalls telling a group of U.S. steel executives that Japan was building factories to make steel more efficiently. They might take over U.S. markets, he warned. The steelmakers—many of whom later saw their companies annihilated by a flood of cheap Japanese imports—rejected Magaziner's report out of hand.

Magaziner recalled leaving the meeting feeling bewildered. "It wasn't that the American steelmakers weren't smart," he wrote, "but they had a different way of seeing the world than did the Japanese. The Americans were convinced that domestic forces were all that mattered. The Japanese, on the other hand, based their plans on the world."[7]

This is a problem that Magaziner, now President Clinton's domestic policy adviser, still worries about. The John Wayne mentality still runs strong, and Magaziner suspects that it will lead most U.S. companies to lobby against any large movement of U.S. intelligence manpower into economic intelligence. Magaziner believes the lack of economic intelligence is crippling U.S. business chances, especially in new markets opening up in Europe and Asia, where Japanese companies are quicker to move, invest, and set up distribution networks.

One way to fill the intelligence gap, he thinks, might be to encourage U.S. trade associations to expand their roles. In the United States, they mostly lobby. In Germany and Japan, they collect and share information among their member companies about overseas markets and foreign competition. Moreover, unlike government intelligence agents, agents from trade associations would have a better appreciation of the "real world" needs of a specific industry. "I think it might be more culturally acceptable in this country," says Magaziner, who has been working with an intergovernmental task force to help President Clinton develop a strategy for economic competitiveness.[8]

THE NEED TO ORIENT

In John Boyd's dogfight—or in any competition—knowledge of one's position in relation to the adversary is a critical piece of information. In this competition, we aren't even close. While U.S. companies might think they're John Wayne and American officials can brag about "the last remaining superpower," in trade matters America stands about three feet tall. Japan's ministries are filled with careerists who know American culture intimately, and Japanese companies see Washington as a relatively weak government, an easy game that can be manipulated by hiring of lobbyists and making generous contributions to Washington think tanks. The contrast with the U.S. side of the trade battleground is stark indeed. "The U.S. government is virtually flying blind in terms of the competence of its diplomats, trade and military officials to deal with Japan," says Chalmers Johnson, the dean of American Japan specialists. And American economists "are in the dark partly because they do not read Japanese and have made no empirical investigation of Japanese economic history."[9]

Assuming they wanted to, U.S. companies and trade associations will have a hard time fielding teams that can effectively find and win access to new overseas markets. Most U.S. job applicants are not really equipped or oriented to compete in the world. There is something about superpowers that makes them insular. The *National Geographic* discovered this in 1989. In a survey that asked people from ten nations to identify places on a world map, residents of the former Soviet Union did not do well at all. They did much better, however, than Americans in the age eighteen to twenty-four group, who scored dead last.[10]

Much has been written about the decline of the U.S. public school system. Sometimes it seems as if we prefer to wallow in our own dumbness, with each book and each newspaper article finding something more shocking than the last. It is as if education were a spectator sport—a poor showing on the playing field doesn't really hurt the fans. But in terms of global competition, especially against Asians, why Johnny can't (or doesn't) read will quickly translate into why Johnny's country can't win.

U.S. companies now spend some $25 billion each year on remedial education for employees. One study shows that American students, measured against Chinese and Japanese equivalents, start out roughly equal in kindergarten, and then go steadily downhill. The study, published in 1992, surveyed first- and fifth-grade students in two U.S. schools against those in similar communities in Japan and Taiwan. The highest-scoring American schools fell below the lowest-scoring Asian schools. Among the top-scoring one hundred students, eighty-eight were Japanese, eleven were Taiwanese, one was an American.[11] Later, when students from schools in Beijing were added to the study, the lowest-ranking Chinese students in math had scores that registered near the average for American students.[12]

Asian students buckled down because their teachers emphasized their obligations toward each other as a group and hammered home the message that "accomplishment depends on dedication and hard work." American students spent 20 percent of their classroom time running around out of their seats.[13] Asian mothers, especially Japanese, were quite skeptical of what went on in the classroom and kept a watchful eye on teachers. American mothers had the serene feeling that, whatever was going on in the classroom, their children were "above average."[14]

Results like this are not funny to U.S. aircraft manufacturers, who are already in a dogfight. By being artfully cajoled into sharing U.S. technology with Japanese and Chinese companies, they have bet their companies' futures on being able to stay one generation of aircraft being designed by newly emerging competitors. "We have a concern about kids coming down on the shop floor who can't read," explains Joel Johnson, a vice president of Aerospace Industrial Association in Washington, D.C. "I tell that to somebody in Toyota and they say, 'Oh yes, we have an illiteracy problem too.' Illiteracy for them, it turns out, is someone who can't do basic software programming."

The nation's science and engineering schools have tended to finesse the problem. As American applicants dwindle, the schools fill up with foreign students, especially bright ones from China. This seems to fit with another enduring dream in the American culture: whatever we do, we will always be saved by the American melting pot. "Immigration becomes ever more vital to the future of the U.S. economy," argues George Gilder, in an op-ed piece in the *Wall Street Journal* entitled "Geniuses From Abroad."

But the evidence is mounting that most of Gilder's "geniuses" are returning home—some to build competitors, some, in China, to build potentially competitive weapons systems. This is not Gilder's beloved free market at work here. Nor is it the quest for pure science, a theory that seems ever-compelling to U.S. university dons (especially when it gives them bright students to help write their papers and do their teaching and lab research). Very often it is state-sponsored technology transfer.

Since the days when the KGB's Line X learned how to mine MIT and other U.S. universities for weapons technology, government spy agencies have had a field day on American campuses, placing students, placing "guest scholars," and pressuring both to come home with informational goodies. U.S. companies that hire such "geniuses" do so at the peril of their trade secrets.

China, Japan, Taiwan, and lately South Korea have all used student placement as part of a national economic espionage strategy. South Korea's Ministry of Science and Technology, for example, has mounted a "Brainpool" project that offers leading scientists abroad a higher salary and airfare to return home. Before getting the better-paying job, the scientists spend six months getting debriefed at a Korean government science and technology facility. During the first year of the program, in 1994, fifty-seven foreign specialists were given offers; most of them were South Koreans working in the United States.[15]

A final and necessary part of our orientation will be to realize that—as seen by our adversaries—we are the empire with no clothes. Our information, computer, and telecommunications systems are naked to the whims of eavesdroppers, hackers, and spy agencies that inflict great damage. We have developed powerful encryption systems that can protect them, but our ability to use these codes to protect private enterprise has been stymied by our law-enforcement and intelligence agencies.

They also thrive in this openness and push the White House and Congress to limit the private use of code. But a new study, commissioned by Congress, argues that we would all benefit if government changed its policy and promoted encryption. On balance, it concludes wider use of powerful codes by banks, corporations, and utilities can curb economic espionage and help law enforcement by better protecting the banking system, electronic power grids, public phone networks, and the air-traffic control systems that are now vulnerable to manipulation.[16]

Washington developed code to protect our vital secrets in wartime. In economic espionage, what we are experiencing is a war that does not end. Kenneth W. Dam, the University of Chicago law professor who headed the study panel, put in simply. The widespread use of encryption by private business, he believes, is "inevitable" and the government must "recognize this changing reality."[17]

THE NEED TO DECIDE

There are hundreds of decisions to be made if the United States wants to remain competitive in this environment. These decisions are like crabs in a basket—all tough and all hanging on to each other. Again, as in Boyd's dogfight, doing nothing will not be a pleasant alternative. Competitors in Japan and Germany raised themselves from the bomb-gutted ruins of World War II with such slogans as "Export or die." As a motivational tool, it worked. Now the United States needs a slogan. In 1989, a panel of MIT professors suggested one *"Export or See Your Relative Standard of Living Diminish."* They added that while this "is not a slogan to set anyone's heart on fire . . . it expresses the truth."

To follow the path outlined by the MIT dons, "companies will have to cultivate knowledge of other languages, market customs, tactics, legal systems and regulations." Like the generation of U.S. engineers and scientists who once prowled the world, "Americans must learn to look for and shop for the best technologies wherever they happen to be."[18]

That means that the public school system must be fixed. And it means that more U.S. students graduating from that system should be lured into careers in science and engineering. That could be expensive, but not nearly as expensive in the long run as paying to train future competitors. Until a system is devised to prevent foreign governments from cheap technology-siphoning tricks on our campuses, we should scale back on visas for foreign students in science and engineering. To be sure, bright foreign students are a vital stimulant to American education; but when they become the majority in U.S. technical schools and dominate teaching and research assistantships, we are exporting our future.

The U.S. government must decide whether to tighten immigration laws. While high-tech companies are lobbying for continuing loopholes for "geniuses from abroad," perhaps a tightening would shift their formidable lobbying powers to focus on the public school mess. It is a problem they will have to confront sooner or later. Why not sooner? This is not rocket science. Home-grown geniuses have more of a tendency to stay home.

It is not that U.S. companies don't know what needs deciding. In January 1994, Sandia National Laboraties in Albuquerque, New Mexico, unveiled a modified war game for a group of executives from companies in the Electronics Industries Association. Originally developed for the U.S. military, the game had been modified for economic warfare. There were two "Blue Teams," signifying U.S. players. Then there was a "Purple Team," which quickly became Japan.

The most enthusiasm in the game was generated by the American executives playing on the Purple Team. They quickly pushed for a strategy that sent more foreign students to U.S. universities, encouraged more U.S. openness to foreign researchers and participants in trade groups, sponsored research projects at U.S. schools and think tanks, subsidized sales to the United States, and targeted U.S. high-tech companies for acquisition.

The upshot: The Purple Team won. At a later session, in which another Purple Team took the same postions, a Sandia analyst asked them whether further weakening of the United States might harm its markets for Purple Team products. The Purple Teamers were unconcerned, saying, "The U.S. would continue to be a service-based economy selling those things that it could—primarily fluff."[19]

What was the game for? J. Pace VanDevender, one of Sandia's designers, says it was to get U.S. industry thinking a bit beyond their balance sheets. Sandia has a peculiar need for a robust, home-grown electronics industry because its mission is to design the electronic devices that fire and safeguard nuclear weapons.

"Also, it was a way of showing that it's the U.S. economic base that drives our whole system of enterprise. We didn't win the Cold War because our bombs were superior," VanDevender points out. "We won because our economy was superior."[20]

THE NEED TO ACT

Decisions are tough, but the matter of implementing them can be tougher. A president who decides to rev up the nation's economic competitiveness may have to put his hand on the throttle. That falls in the category of having a long-term industrial policy. Most developed nations have one, but in the United States that violates a right-wing taboo.

Some industries are for it. "In order to make the U.S. run faster, you have to change our habit patterns, our mores, and you've got to spend money," asserts Joel Johnson, the aerospace industry executive. "And you have to replace defense research and development through some other mechanism, a structure that would expand civilian research that would tend to favor American companies."[21]

During the Bush administration, this was rank heresy. It meant the government was "picking winners." Despite the fact that a cornucopia of U.S. high technology—computers, transistors, communications satellites, fiber optics, the Internet, prototypes of commercial airliners and helicopters—has been "picked" and financed by planners in the Defense Department, Bush administration officials, and the Reagan people before them, took an almost theological position against "picking winners."

George Lodge, a lifelong Republican and a professor at Harvard Business School, says Republican theology must be revised to square with economic and historic reality. "We did that [picking winners] for thirty years with defense technology and we were number one. . . . We can do it. We've just got to want to. We've got to see that commercial competitiveness is just as essential to our national security as technology is for our military."[22]

It isn't just the president who must act. Economic competitiveness is a leadership problem that runs across the spectrum of professions in the United States. CEOs of American companies must find a way to disengage with companies in the People's Republic of China until the United States can sort out which companies are part of China's military and gulag system and which are not.

If U.S. intelligence agencies can't figure it out, then imports from China would be a good candidate for punitive tariffs. The matter should not be left up to U.S. labor unions or consumers in Wal-Marts to struggle with. Feeding technology and mountains of hard currency directly into the maw of the modernizing army of a nation that enslaves its citizens, systematically sends its spies to steal our secrets, threatens U.S. allies in the Pacific, and then proliferates weapons of mass destruction around the world does not make economic sense, let alone political sense.

Lawyers have a lot to do. For better or worse, they are a major American resource: Dewey Ballantine, the New York law firm that represents Kodak against Fuji Film, has shown that a determined effort can expose Japan's hidden trade barriers and engage Japanese consumers in an internal debate over the wisdom of price fixing.

We also need a coherent, modern body of criminal law that deters economic espionage. Congress has made a good start with a new law that makes it a federal crime to steal proprietary economic information, such as trade secrets, and carries fines up to $10 million and fifteen years in jail. It also broadens criminal sanctions against computer hackers to cases involving blackmail and attacks that interfere with regional phone systems, electrical grids, air traffic controls, and other critical systems.[23]

Prosecutors should not have to spend months crocheting together fragments of old laws to fashion indictments for the theft of intellectual property such as trade secrets and computer software. These are our crown jewels: they will either be protected or stolen. More effective and predictable law would also help the FBI, whose agents have been stumbling around in economic espionage cases like the Keystone Kops. They could use more support.

Dr. James P. Chandler, a professor at George Washington University Law Center in Washington, D.C., asserts that the United States must press for an international regime because the loss of valuable innovation may not be replaceable in a future when defense and corporate research budgets are severely cut back. "It is impossible for the U.S. to continue to transfer its intellectual property out of this country into a no-man's land of laws that doesn't protect the technology once it's gone," he said recently.[24] To put it another way, why should products from nations who steal our ideas and mock our laws find their way onto the shelves at Wal-Marts?

America's bankers have been staring at one enemy and it is them. They need to help the U.S. Treasury develop a computer-tracking system that can follow the flow of criminal money throughout the United States and in and out of the convenient "laundries" offshore. In an era when clever researchers can dig out tons of information about average, law-abiding citizens, it seems obscene for the American Bankers Association to argue that it's too complicated to follow the multi-billion-dollar trails of cocaine dealers and Mafia scumlords. If Australians can do it—and do it with U.S. software—there are probably people on Wall Street who can figure it out. In a system that is ultimately grounded on faith, the growth and spread of dirty money besmirches us all.

Insurance companies can help protect major corporations including banks, utilities and, yes, insurance companies, from becoming victims of information warfare. As it stands, most corporations don't complain when hackers penetrate and damage their databases. Like so many of the other "rape victims" in economic espionage, they fall silent. Meanwhile, ignorance about proper "firewall" software and other useful defensive techniques is rampant. The result: a huge amount of vital data is at risk as hackers proliferate. Some computer experts compare the current situation in cyberspace to Chicago in 1871, before Mrs. O'Leary's cow set it ablaze. What happened then? Insurance companies moved into the charred void, set standards for fire protection and began insuring buildings. Do we need an equivalent disaster before insurance companies realize there is an enormous new market for them in insuring databases? Or should they act now?

Economists have to act. They must write and report about real world trading patterns, as they once did. If their models and graphs don't reflect what's really happening in Paris or Tokyo or Moscow or Cali, especially in high technology, then what are they doing? And why are they doing it? A 1991 report by the American Economics Association gave a glimmer of the sorting out that seems overdue in the so-called dismal profession. An "underemphasis" on links between economic tools and market activities in graduate-level economics courses, it says, "may be turning out a generation with too many idiots savants, skilled in technique, but innocent of real economic issues."[25]

Taxpayers and congresspeople need to take a hard look at the costs of some forms of openness. For example, if the Freedom of Information Act costs $100 million a year to operate and is used primarily as a window on U.S. businesses by their competitors, perhaps it might be put on a fee-paying basis, or even closed down altogether.[26]

In the nation's current situation, there are better ways to spend the money. I propose the establishment of a $100 million "Francis Cabot Lowell Memorial Fund," which would provide scholarships to enterprising U.S. students, businessmen, lawyers, and especially economists who want to learn Chinese, Korean, or Japanese, and who are prepared to spend some time studying in a university, think tank, or a business in Tokyo, Taipei, Seoul, or Beijing.

Lowell was the founder of America's Industrial Revolution. A memorial to this clever, self-effacing man would provide a constant reminder that good ideas do not grow on trees and that high technology is not necessarily always invented here. Our fathers, our grandfathers, and our great-grandfathers understood this. It is high time to renew the tradition. To paraphrase the late, great American jurist, Oliver Wendell Holmes, Jr., one generation of idiots savants is probably enough.[27]

Notes

PROLOGUE

1. Dalzell, Robert F., Jr., *Enterprising Elite. The Boston Associates and the World They Made* (Cambridge, MA: Harvard University Press, 1987), p. 5.
2. Jeremy, David J., *Transatlantic Industrial Revolution: The Diffusion of Textile Technologies Between Britain and America, 1790–1830* (Cambridge, MA: MIT Press, 1981) p. 36.
3. Harbulot, Christian, *La Machine de Guerre Economique* (Paris: Economica, Avis, 1992), p. 5.
4. Ibid., p. 11.
5. Among them was a network of spies run by Alexander Hamilton. Some specialized in recruiting expatriate English technicians. Others bought machinery and evaded British Customs officials by sending their contraband to France, where another technology maven, Thomas Jefferson, had them repackaged for shipment to the United States. For a fuller account, see Jeremy, op. cit., pp. 36ff.
6. Ibid., p. 37.
7. Dalzell, op. cit., pp. 6–7.
8. Appleton, Nathan, *Introduction of the Power Loom and Origin of Lowell* (monograph printed by H. H. Penhallow, Boston, 1858), p. 14.
9. Miller, Perry, *The Life of the Mind in America* (New York: Harcourt Brace & World, 1965), p. 290.

CHAPTER I

1. In 1788, after Joseph Hague, a Philadelphian, smuggled in one of the British textile industry's other crown jewels—a water-driven Arkwright Rotary Carding Machine—it was featured in a parade. See Jeremy, op., cit. p. 15.

2. As defined in the National Security Act by an amendment in 1992, the U.S. intelligence community includes: the Central Intelligence Agency; the National Security Agency; the Defense Intelligence Agency; the National Reconnaissance Office; the Central Imagery Office; intelligence units in the Army, Navy, Air Force, and Marine Corps; parts of the FBI; and parts of the Departments of Treasury, Energy, and State. See *Report of the U.S. Commission on the Roles and Capabilities of the U.S. Intelligence Community,* June 6, 1995.

3. This estimate, first made by Robert M. Gates, director of the CIA, before the House Judiciary Subcommittee on Economic and Commercial Law on April 29, 1992, remains the official CIA measure of the threat.

4. *Report on U.S. Critical Technology Companies, Report to Congress on Foreign Acquisition of and Espionage Activities Against U.S. Critical Technology Companies,* 1994, p. 5. ("NORFORN" is a level of classified information that is not releasable to foreigners.)

5. Knightly, Philip, *The Second Oldest Profession: Spies and Spying in the Twentieth Century,* (New York: W. W. Norton & Co., 1986), p. 5.

6. *Report on U.S. Critical Technology Companies,* p. 23.

7. Ibid., p. 25.

8. *High-Stakes Aviation: U.S.-Japan Technology Linkages in Transport Aircraft* (Washington, D.C.: U.S. National Research Council, National Academy of Sciences Press, 1994), p. 88.

9. Interview with Chris MacMartin, July 1995.

10. Both companies testified before the House Judiciary Committee's Subcommittee on Economic and Commercial Law on April 29, 1992. Neither would elaborate outside the meeting room.

11. See "Minutes of Meeting Held in Director's Conference Room" and related documents, declassified by the CIA on March 20, 1991.

12. Interview with Gerard P. Burke, September, 1995.

13. Turner, Stansfield, "Intelligence for a New World Order," *Foreign Affairs* (Fall, 1991), p. 152.

14. Interview with Michael Sekora, August, 1994. Sekora's company is Technology Strategic Planning Inc., located in Stuart, Florida.

15. Florida, Richard, *The Breakthrough Illusion,* (New York: Basic Books, 1990), p. 20.

16. *Report of the U.S. Commission on the Roles and Capabilties of the U.S. Intelligence Community,* p. 12.

17. "Soviet Acquisition of Western Technology," April 1982, exhibit no. 1. Hearings before the Permanent Subcommittee on Investigations of the Senate Committee on Governmental Affairs, 97th Congress, 2nd session, hearings on May 4, 5, 6, 11 and 12, 1982.

18. Ibid., p. 6.

19. Interview with Interview with Jan P. Herring, August 1995.

20. See *U.S.-Japan Strategic Alliances in the Semiconductor Industry* (Washington, D.C.: National Research Council, National Academy of Sciences Press, 1992), pp 4–8.

21. Tyson, Laura D'Andrea, *Who's Bashing Whom? Trade Conflict in High-Technology Industries* (Institute for International Economics, 1992), pp. 25 and 39.

22. Interview with Ira Magaziner, July 1995.

23. *U.S.-Japan Technology Linkages in Biotechnology* (Washington, D.C.: National Research Council, 1992), pp. 34–35.

24. North, David S., *Soothing the Establishment; The Impact of Foreign-born Scientists and Engineers on America* (Lanham, MD: University Press of America, 1995), pp. 78ff.

25. Eftimiades, Nicholas, *Chinese Intelligence Operations* (Annapolis, MD: Naval Institute Press, 1994), pp. 17 and 27.

26. Interview with James Lilly, March 1995.

27. Interview with Nicholas Eftimiades, who notes that his opinions are not necessarily shared by the Defense Intelligence Agency, for whom he works.

28. "New Brain Drain, Skilled Asians Are Leaving U.S. for High-Tech Homelands," *New York Times*, Feb. 20, 1995, p. A-1.

29. According to *International Organized Crime*, a report by the National Strategy Information Center (a private intelligence policy research group). 27,112 Americans died from drug overdoses between 1988 and 1991. By comparison, 27,704 U.S. soldiers died in combat during the three-year Korean War.

30. Response by former CIA director James Woolsey to questions from the Senate Select Intelligence Committee, Jan. 25, 1994.

31. Both men spoke at the International Security Systems Symposium held in Washington, D.C., November 16–19, 1994.

32. Heffernan, Richard J., and Dan T. Swartwood, "Trends in Intellectual Property Loss." American Society for Industrial Security, International, Arlington, Va., (March 1996), pp. 1–4 and 11.

33. Testimony by Louis J. Freeh, director of the FBI, before the Senate Select Committee on Intelligence, Feb. 28, 1996.

34. This was the issue in *United States* v. *Liaosheng (Andrew) Wang*, in U.S. Federal District Court in Denver. See chapter 14, Virtual Justice.

35. FBI deputy assistant director Roger P. Watson recently explained the dilemma to a business group: "Today what we see is that collection platforms targeted against U.S. companies are not necessarily from diplomatic establishments. Frequently they are not. So therefore when we see an individual, how do we know an individual is connected to a foreign power?"

36. Interview with Edward Miller, July 1995.

CHAPTER 2

1. The Sun Tzu quotes are taken from *Sun Tzu: The Art of War*, trans. Samuel B. Griffith (New York: Oxford University Press, 1971), pp. 77, 84, and 148.

2. The account of Wu's meeting at the Old Cadres' Club comes from the trial transcript of *United States* v. *Bin Wu, Jing Ping Li and Pinzhe Zhang*, CR 92-188-N, U.S. District Court for the Eastern District of Virginia, Norfolk, Va. The trial was held in May 1993.

3. Interview with Henry Brandon, April, 1995.
4. Eftimiades, op. cit., p. 67.
5. Interview with Nicholas Eftimiades, June 1995. The analyst's opinions are his own and not necessarily those of his employer, the DIA.
6. Interview with Robert Messemer, Jan. 1995.
7. As described by James A. Metcalfe, the assistant U.S. attorney who prosecuted the case against Wu.
8. Interview with Tom Rademacher, June 1995.
9. Interview with Bin Wu at Federal Correction Institution, Loretto, Pa., March 1995.

CHAPTER 3

1. The consortium includes British Aerospace PLC, Aerospatiale SA of France, Daimler Benz AG of Germany, and Construcciones Aeronauticas SA of Spain.
2. Barber, Randy, and Robert E. Scott, *Jobs on the Wing: Trading Away the Future of the U.S. Aerospace Industry* (Washington D.C.: Economic Policy Institute, 1995). p. 17.
3. "Western Lift for China's Air Plans," *New York Times*, Feb. 25, 1995, p. A-37.
4. Transparency International, a Berlin-based group dedicated to curbing corruption in international business transactions, ranks forty-one countries on a "corruption index," based on polls, reports of business people and business journalists. With a possible high score of 10, China scored 2.16, ranking it just above Indonesia, which was in last place.
5. Woolard made his remark in November 1995 at a symposium on international security issues at the State Department.
6. Interviews with Bob Aronson and Tom Williams, August 1995 and October 1995, respectively.
7. Barber and Scott, op. cit., p. 29.
8. "McDonnell Douglas China Program, Background Information," press release issued by the company in 1992.
9. *Civil-Military Integration; The Chinese and Japanese Arms Industries*, background paper published by the Office of Technology Assessment (a branch of the U.S. Congress) in 1995, p. 142.
10. *CATIC; United, Realistic, Competitive, Innovative*, brochure produced by CATIC, undated.
11. *Impact of China's Military Modernization in the Pacific Region* (Washington, D.C.: U.S. General Accounting Office, June 1995), p. 18.
12. Report by Ziegler to the director of the Strategic Investigations Division, U.S. Customs Service, Oct. 4, 1993.
13. Letters exchanged during the negotiation were later released by the Pentagon.
14. Interview with Tom Williams, October 1995.
15. Barber and Scott, op. cit., p. 1.

16. "Boeing Flies into Flap Over Technology Shift in Dealings with China," *Wall Street Journal*, Oct. 13, 1995, p. A-11.

17. "McDonnell Douglas in China," a slide presentation prepared by John Bruns, China Program Office, Douglas Aircraft Co., Long Beach, CA, June 7, 1994.

18. "China Swiftly Becomes an Exporting Colossus, Straining Western Ties," *Wall Street Journal*, Nov. 13, 1995, p. A-1.

19. *The Decline of the U.S. Machine-Tool Industry and Prospects for Its Sustainable Recovery* (Santa Monica, CA: RAND Corp., 1994), Vol. 2, Appendices, p. 106.

20. Max Holland, *When the Machine Stopped; A Cautionary Tale from Industrial America*,(Cambridge MA: Harvard Business School Press, 1989), p. 121.

21. Magaziner, Ira, and Mark Patinkin, *The Silent War: Inside the Global Business Battles Shaping America's Future*, (New York: Random House, 1989), p. 110.

22. Inaba, Dr. Seiuemon, *The FANUC Story: Walking the Narrow Path* (FANUC, 1991), p. 9.

23. *The Decline of the U.S. Machine-Tool Industry and Prospects for Its Sustainable Recovery*, Vol. 1, p. 12.

24. Interview with Norman Levy, October 1995.

25. Godwin, Paul, and John J. Schulz, "Arming the Dragon for the 21st Century: China's Defense Modernization Program," *Arms Control Today*, (December 1993), p. 3.

26. "Denial of McDonnell Douglas Machine Tool Licenses to CATIC," a memorandum prepared by Dr. Peter M. Leitner for Maloof.

27. China's position, according to Li Daoyu, its ambassador in Washington, is that it has "all along adopted a serious and earnest attitude toward the issue of non-proliferation and opposed the proliferation of all weapons of mass destruction pending their complete elimination globally." Godwin and Schulz, op. cit., p. 9.

28. "Background—CATIC Machining Co. Ltd.," part of McDonnell's application for an export license for the Plant 85 machinery submitted to the U.S. Commerce Department.

29. Interview with Barbara Shailor, October 1995.

30. "Boeing Flies into Flap Over Technology Shift in Dealings with China," *Wall Street Journal*, Oct. 13, 1995, p. A-11.

31. Ibid.

32. Interview with Fred Lassahn, August 1995

CHAPTER 4

1. *Rashomon*, released by Japanese film director Akira Kurosawa in 1950, is one of the most famous Japanese motion pictures ever made. Set in ancient Kyoto, it involves a samurai who has been killed, and his wife who has been raped. The tale is recounted in flashbacks by a variety of characters, none of whom agree.

2. *High-Stakes Aviation: U.S.-Japan Technology Linkages in Transport Aircraft*, p. 65.

3. Samuels, Richard J., *Rich Nation, Strong Army; National Security and the Technological Transformation of Japan* (Ithaca, NY: Cornell University Press, 1994), p. 63.
4. Ibid., p. 170.
5. Ibid., p. 171.
6. Taoka, Shunji, "No One Knew North Korea Had Test-Launched a Missile," *AERA Magazine* (Tokyo), Jan. 17, 1994, p. 26.
7. Under the terms of the interview, this official cannot be identified further.
8. *JETRO: The Japan External Trade Organization*, report by the U.S. Congressional Research Service for Congress, Dec. 20, 1985, p. 41.
9. The top twenty *sogo shoshas* are: C. Itoh & Co., Ltd.; Chori Co., Ltd.; Itoman Corp.; Iwatani International Corp.; Kanematsu Corp.; Kawasho Corp.; Kinsho-Mataichi Corp.; Marubeni Corp.; Mitsubishi Corp.; Mitsui & Co., Ltd.; Nagase & Co., Ltd.; Nichimen Corp.; Nissei Sangyo Co., Ltd.; Nissho Iwai Corp.; Nozaki & Co., Ltd.; Okura & Co., Ltd.; Sumitomo Corp.; Tomen Corp.; Toshoku Ltd.; and Toyota Tsusho Corp.
10. Estimate of Juro Nakagawa, professor of international marketing, Faculty of Commerce, Aichi Gakuin University, Japan.
11. Interview with Michio Hamaji, February 1995.
12. Samuels, op. cit., p. 64.
13. "The Truth About Big Business in Japan," *Business Tokyo* (April 1990), p. 22.
14. "Tilt-Wing: A Page from Aviation History . . . Writing the Next Chapter," undated Ishida Group press release.
15. Interview with Fred Dickens, September 1995.
16. A copy of the French report can be found in the *Congressional Record*, April 28, 1993, pp. 2104–2107.
17. Sato, Bunsei, and Kiyohide Terai, *The Heliport Highway 600: Japan's Fourth-Generation Transportation System in the 21st Century*, undated paper published in Tokyo by Sato, a member of Japan's House of Representatives.
18. Forman, Brenda, *The V-22 Tiltrotor 'Osprey': The Program That Wouldn't Die*, paper presented at the University of Southern California School of Engineering, 1994, p. 16.
19. Interview with William A. Jones, September 1995.
20. Interview with Charles Crawford, September 1995.
21. Interview with John Stowe, September 1995.
22. Interview with Dr. J. David Kocurek, July 1994.
23. "Aerospace Firm Reportedly Target of Spy Probe," *Dallas Morning News*, August 21, 1993, p. 1-A.
24. Interview with Hugh W. Ferguson, September 1995.
25. "Ishida and Kocurek Announce Dispute Resolution," press statement by Taiichi Ishidi's lawyers, Dallas, Jan. 16, 1995.
26. *Civil Tiltroter Development Advisory Committee, Report to Congress* (Washington, D.C.: U.S. Dept. of Transportation, December 1995), p. 75.
27. Interview with Cecil Haga, September 1995.
28. Interview with John Zuk, October 1995.

CHAPTER 5

1. In Tom Clancy novels, U.S. subs stick to the Russian subs they follow like glue. In reality, such as the appearance of an *Akula*-class submarine off the East Coast in the spring of 1995, the Russian sub's propellors were so quiet that it frequently evaded U.S. subs trying to locate it. Asked about the incident, Dennis Harman, deputy director of U.S. Navy Intelligence, said, "We used to know where they were all the time. I don't think we can say that any more."

2. Griffith, trans., *Sun Tzu: The Art of War*, p. 96.

3. The fees paid by Mitsubishi and the team's meeting in Sakurai's office are discussed in "Documents Related to the Investigation of Senator Robert Packwood," Senate Committee on Ethics, U.S. Senate, 1995, pp. 20–23 and 236–237.

4. Ibid., pp. 23–26.

5. In an affidavit, Hitoshi Kodama, a Mitsubishi engineer, recalled taking apart Fusion's lamp in 1977. He says he found the Fusion product "too costly and unacceptable" for Mitsubishi's purpose; he packed it up and threw it in a corner of Mitsubishi's laboratory. Four months later, he was part of a three-man team that "invented" Mitsubishi's lamp. Even if their patent application happened to claim parts of Fusion's product, Mitsubishi's lawyers argued, "it is nothing more than a mere coincidence." "Opinion on MELCO/Fusion Matter," Yuasa & Hara, a Tokyo law firm retained by Mitsubishi, April 28, 1988, p. 36 and Exhibit E.

6. He was Colonel R. C. Cramer, director general of the Economic and Science Agency, set up under General MacArthur. See Mishema, Yasuo, *The Mitsubishi: It's Challenge and Strategy* (Greenwich, CT: JAI Press, 1989), p. 323.

7. Quoted in Ayer, Fred, Jr., *Before the Colors Fade: Portrait of a Soldier* (Boston: Houghton Mifflin, 1964), pp. 165–166.

8. Interview with Thomas J. Murrin, October 1995.

9. *Industrial Groupings in Japan* (Tokyo: Dodwell Marketing Consultants, 1992), p. 217.

10. The study was made by Regis McKenna, an adviser to Apple Computers. It is cited in Pat Choate, *Agents of Influence* (New York: Alfred A. Knopf, 1990), p. 127.

11. *U.S.-Japan Strategic Alliances in the Semiconductor Industry*, p. 4. Additional detail on the transfer of the VCR, which Ampex partly developed and then rejected in 1970 as being unlikely to catch on as a consumer product, comes from a November 1995 interview with Richard J. Elkus, Jr., a Silicon Valley entrepreneur who worked for Ampex at the time.

12. Dertouzos, Michael L., *Made in America, Regaining the Productive Edge*, report of the MIT Commission on Industrial Productivity (Cambridge, MA: MIT Press 1989), p. 225.

13. Spero, Donald M., "Patent Protection or Piracy—A CEO Views Japan," *Harvard Business Review* (September–October 1990), p. 4.

14. Interview with Nancy Chasen, July 1994.

15. "Documents Related to the Investigation of Senator Robert Packwood," p. 30.

16. A 1993 survey by Congress's General Accounting Office shows that many American companies share Spero's dim view of Japan's patent process. Of 376 U.S.

companies surveyed, 65 percent reported at least one major problem obtaining patents in Japan. The level of complaints was three times higher than those dealing with patent problems in Europe or the United States. See "Intellectual Property Rights; U.S. Companies' Patent Experiences in Japan," GAO/GGD-93-126, pp. 1–3.

17. "Effect of the Japanese Patent System on American Business," hearing before the Subcommittee on Foreign Commerce and Tourism of the Committee on Commerce, Science and Transportation, U.S. Senate, June 24, 1988, p. 35.

18. "Documents Related to the Investigation of Senator Robert Packwood," pp. 63–72.

19. Ibid., pp. 96–7.

20. Ibid., p. 209.

21. Ibid., p. 204.

22. Interview with Ambassador Michael Smith, November 1995.

23. Prestowitz, Clyde V., Jr., *Trading Places: How We Are Giving Our Future to Japan and How to Reclaim It* (New York: Basic Books, 1988), p. 318.

24. Interview with Robert D. Deutsch, April 1995.

25. Interview with Clyde V. Prestowitz, Jr., February 1995.

26. Memo from P. Rubin to W. Lawrence, Feb. 14, 1990, found in exhibit B, *Pat Choate* v. *TRW Inc.*, CA 91-1719-TPJ, U.S. District Court for the District of Columbia.

27. Ibid., exhibit S.

28. Interview with James H. Lake, November 1995.

29. "Packwood Resigning Senate Seat," Knight-Ridder News Service, Sept. 8, 1995.

30. "GOP Lobbyist Admits Fraud in Fund-Raising," *Washington Post*, Oct. 24, 1995, p. A-1.

31. Interview with Steve Saunders, November 1995.

32. Interview with Donald M. Spero, November 1995

CHAPTER 6

1. The details of this account come from a September 1995 interview with Victor Budanov, one of the KGB officers who investigated the case.

2. *Soviet Acquisition of Militarily Significant Western Technology: An Update*, p. 4. This paper was published by the U.S. Central Intelligence Agency in September 1985, though the document doesn't mention its publisher.

3. Regnard, Henri, *The USSR and Scientific, Technical and Technological Intelligence* (Paris: Défense Nationale, December 1983), pp. 107–121. (Regnard is described as a pseudonym for a "high-ranking" French official.)

4. *Technology Transfer: Soviet Acquisition of Technology Via Scientific Travel* (Falls Church, VA: Delphic Associates, 1991), p. 73.

5. Moynihan, Daniel Patrick, "How the Soviets Are Bugging America," *Popular Mechanics* (April 1987), p. 104.

6. Interview with Maynard Anderson, September 1995. Anderson is currently president of Arcadia Group Worldwide, Inc., a security consultant to corporations.

7. Gordievsky, Oleg, *KGB, The Inside Story* (New York: HarperCollins, 1991), p. 11.
8. Interview with Stanislav Levchenko, June 1995.
9. *Soviet Acquisition of Militarily Significant Western Technology: An Update*, pp. 9–10.
10. Deriabin, Peter, and T. H. Bagley, *The KGB, Masters of the Soviet Union* (New York: Hippocrene Books, 1990).
11. Wolton, Thierry, *Le KGB en France* (Paris: Bernard Grasset, 1986), p. 247.
12. Brook-Shepherd, Gordon, *The Storm Birds: Soviet Postwar Defectors* (New York: Weidenfeld & Nicolson, 1989), p. 256.
13. Pierre Marion, then the head of the SDECE, was "shocked" about the arrangement, and still believes that "Farewell" was a ruse by the KGB to fool both the DST and the CIA. See Marion's *La Mission Impossible: A la Tête des Services Secrets* (Paris: Calmann-Lévy, 1991) pp. 56ff.
14. Budanov interview.
15. Gordievsky, op. cit., p. 12.
16. Budanov thinks that hypochondria may have had something to do with the antics of his old boss. Before his defection, Yurchenko was sure he was dying of cancer. Part of the bargain he struck with his CIA handlers called for a second opinion with leading specialist in Washington. The doctor gave Yurchenko a clean bill of health.
17. Interview with Kenneth DeGraffenreid, March 1995.

CHAPTER 7

1. Details of this account come from a September 1995 interview with Victor Budanov.
2. Interview with Victor Yasminn, September 1995.
3. Waller, Michael J. "Police, Secret Police and Civil Authority," paper given at a symposium at the Russian Research Center, Harvard University, Nov. 22, 1994, p. 10.
4. Ibid., p. 13.
5. Remnick, David, "The Tycoon and the Kremlin," *The New Yorker*, Feb. 20 and 27, 1995, p. 133.
6. Interview with Michael Waller, September 1995.
7. *Global Organized Crime: The New Empire of Evil* (Washington, D.C.: Center for Strategic and International Studies, 1994). The incident comes from testimony of Robert Rasor, special agent in charge, Financial Crimes Unit, U.S. Secret Service, p. 26.
8. For a description of the scheme, see *Medicare: One Scheme Illustrates Vulnerabilities to Fraud* (Washington, D.C.: U.S. General Accounting Office, August 1992).
9. Statistics on Russian crime and fraud come from a presentation by James Woolsey, then the director of the CIA, given to the Center for Strategic and International Studies. See *Global Organized Crime: The New Empire of Evil*, pp. 140–141. In a January 27, 1993, press conference celebrating its first year of operation, the new Russian Security Ministry said it stopped over 1 million tons of oil and 100,000

tons of rare earth being illegally exported. It found that $1 billion worth of state-owned fertilizer—chemicals needed for next year's crops—had vanished after someone illegally gave forty companies the right to sell it.

10. Budanov, Victor. "Security Provision for Foreign Business in Russia," a presentation given to a business forum in Helsinki, Finland, September 1995.

11. Interview with Leila Kight, July 1995.

12. Interview with Keith Flannigan, August 1995.

13. Interview with Gerald P. Burke, September 1995.

14. Interview with Robert B. Wade, September 1995.

15. Interview with Dimitar Loudjev, October 1995.

16. President Yeltsin's remarks were reported by *Ekho Moskvy* and Itav-Tass on February 8, 1996.

CHAPTER 8

1. The nickname "La Piscine" comes from a large swimming pool in the neighborhood of DGSE headquarters.

2. "Corporate Spying May Not Be for Us," *Washington Post*, June 27, 1993, p. C-2.

3. De Vosjoli, P. L. Thyraud, *LAMIA* (Boston: Little, Brown & Co., 1970), pp. 310–312.

4. Ibid., p. 317.

5. De Vosjoli later returned to the United States and took up residence in the South, apparently using an assumed name. His exploits in the French Resistance and his Cold War adventures in Cuba and Washington were the basis for *Topaz*, a novel by Leon Uris, published in 1967.

6. Pacepa, Ion Mihai, *Red Horizons, the True Story of Nicolae and Elena Ceausescu's Crimes, Lifestyle and Corruption* (Washington, D.C.: Regnery Gateway, 1987).

7. De Marenches, Count Alexandre, and Christine Okrent, *The Evil Empire* (London: Sidgwick & Jackson, 1988), p. 41.

8. Ibid.

9. Marion, *La Mission Impossible*, p. 116.

10. Ibid., p. 123.

11. Ibid., p. 49.

12. Reibling, Mark, *WEDGE, The Secret War Between the FBI and CIA* (New York: Alfred A. Knopf, 1994), p. 33.

13. Carley, William M., "A Chip Comes in from the Cold: Tales of High-Tech Spying," *Wall Street Journal*, Jan. 19, 1995, p. A-13.

14. Riebling, op. cit., p. 395.

15. Brief of Texas Instruments in *Bull CP8* v. *Texas Instruments Inc.*, U.S. District Court for the Northern District of Texas, Dallas Division, Civil Action no. 3:93-CV-2517T.

16. According to a 1995 joint study by the Commerce Department and the CIA, U.S. companies operating overseas lost $40 billion over a two-year period because of bribes by foreign-based competitors, some of whom were allowed to deduct the

bribes from their taxes. Because it names the countries involved, the study was classified.

17. A response from the CIA to questions posed by the U.S. Select Committee on Intelligence. See "Current and Projected National Security Threats to the United States and Its Interests Abroad," a hearing by the committee on Jan. 25, 1994, p. 81.

18. A copy of the French report can be found in the *Congressional Record*, April 28, 1993, pp. 2104–2107.

19. Hughes's reaction was later summed up in a paper, "Industrial Espionage: Meeting the New Challenge of National Security," presented to the International Security Systems Symposium in Washington, D.C., Nov. 15, 1993. Armstrong, Hughes's chairman, had more than one reason to be incensed at the French. He headed IBM's overseas operations in 1989 when the FBI discovered a French mole sending company secrets out of IBM's Paris office.

20. Greve's story appeared in Knight-Ridder newspapers, such as the *Miami Herald*, on Sunday, April 18, 1993, along with a lengthy list of targeted companies.

21. Woolsey, R. James, "The Future of Intelligence on the Global Frontier," speech to the Executive Club of Chicago, Nov. 19, 1993.

22. Final versions of the study, prepared with the help of U.S. intelligence agencies, emerged in 1995. According to senior administration officials, it is based on cases where the U.S. company lost in situations where it had a better product at a lower price than competitors. The details of the study remain secret.

23. "Current and Projected National Security Threats to the United States and Its Interests Abroad," a hearing of the Senate Select Committee on Intelligence, Jan. 25, 1994, p. 21.

24. Harbulot, op. cit., p. 95.

25. Ibid., p. 152.

26. *Rapport du Groupe "Intelligence économique et stratégie des entreprises,"* Commissariat général du Plan, February 1994, p. 76.

27. Interview with Henri Martre, September 1995.

28. Interview with Rémy Pautrat, September 1995.

29. Interview with General J. Pichot-Duclos, September 1995.

30. *Le Point*, March 4, 1995, p. 37.

31. "C.I.A. Confirms Blunders During Economic Spying on France," *New York Times*, March 13, 1996, p. A-10.

CHAPTER 9

1. Molander, Roger, Andrew Riddile, and Peter Wilson, *Strategic Information Warfare: A New Face of War*, RAND Corporation, July 1995, p. 10.

2. "The Day After . . . In Cyberspace," scenario for the RAND war game, p. 11.

3. Molander, et al., op. cit., p. 18.

4. "The Day After. . . ," p. 21.

5. Interview with Leon Sloss, October 1995.

6. "Pentagon Studies Art of 'Information Warfare'" *Wall Street Journal*, July 3, 1995, p. A-20.

7. *Report on U.S. Critical Technology Companies*, pp. 45–46.

8. Interview with Rop Gonggrijp, August 1994.

9. Interview with James C. Settle, October 1985.

10. "The Latest Flurries at Weather Bureau: Scattered Hacking," *Wall Street Journal*, Oct. 10, 1994.

11. Interview with Jorgen Bo Madsen, January 1995.

12. Testimony of James Christy, Air Force Office of Special Investigations, given to the Center for Strategic and International Studies, *Global Organized Crime* panel, p. 51.

13. "X. Information Security; Computer Attacks at Department of Defense Pose Increasing Risks," U. S. General Accounting Office, May 1996, p. 24.

14. Defense Department press release, June 17, 1994.

15. Statement issued by Lola DeGroff, deputy public affairs officer, Defense Information Systems Agency, June 13, 1995.

16. Testimony of L. Dain Gary, manager of the CERT Coordination Center, which monitors hacker incidents on the Internet. Gary's testimony appears in the Center for Strategic and International Studies report on *Global Organized Crime*, p. 52.

17. Littman, Jonathan, "The Last Hacker," *Los Angeles Times Sunday Magazine*, Sept. 12, 1993.

18. Interview with Colonel Thomas Kuhn, June 1995.

19. "The Threat of Foreign Economic Espionage to U.S. Corporations," hearings before the House Judiciary Committee, April 29 and May 7, 1992.

20. Interview with Emmett Page, Jr., June 1995.

21. Interview with Major Clem Gaines, Air Force Public Affairs office, October 1995.

22. *NII Security: The Federal Role*, Office of Management and Budget, June 5, 1995, p. 16.

23. Interview with Don B. Parker, November 1994.

CHAPTER 10

1. *New York Times*, Oct. 14, 1995, p. 1.

2. An account of Fujisaki's remarks given by a spokesman from his embassy, October 1995.

3. Interviews with Michael B. Smith and Clyde V. Prestowitz, Jr., November 1995.

4. "Police Seize 166 Tapes of Wiretapped Conversations," *Mainichi Daily News*, Tokyo, July 22, 1994.

5. "Eavesdroppers Find Japan Easy to Bug," *Nikkei Weekly*, Tokyo, Sept. 12, 1994, p. 20.

6. "Affidavit of William E. De Arman," U.S. Customs agent, April 1, 1995, U.S. District Court, Southern District of New York, *In re Application for Arrest and Search Warrants*, p. 16.

7. Ibid., pp. 6, 18, and 19.

8. Ibid., pp. 14–16, 85.

9. Interviews with Dave McCall, August and October 1995.

10. Interview with Herman Kruegle, August 1995.

11. Bamford, James, *Puzzle Palace. A Report on America's Most Secret Agency* (Boston: Houghton Mifflin, 1982), p. 98.

12. The Washington, D.C.–based Cellular Telecommunications Industry Association advises phone owners: "Always remember that cellular telephony is a radio-based service. You should not discuss sensitive personal or business matters on an analog cellular phone. . . ."

13. The U.S. State Department's Overseas Security Advisory Council tells companies that have offices in bug-prone countries to install a "small, company-controlled switch" that can "help ensure that conversations are not transmitted through handsets that are 'hung-up,' and also can serve to decrease the threat of covert line access." See *Guidelines for Protecting U.S. Business Information Overseas*, Washington, D.C., 1995, p. 26.

14. Ball, Desmond, *Signals Intelligence in the Post Cold War Era* (Singapore: Institute of Southeast Asian Studies, 1993), p. 22.

15. Ibid., p. 129.

16. Ibid., p. 129.

17. Interview with Desmond Ball, November 1995.

18. Interview with Jan P. Herring, August 1995.

19. Interview with Noel Matchett, July 1995.

20. Ball, op. cit., p. 26.

21. Interview with Noel Matchett, July 1995.

22. Ball, op. cit., p. 39.

23. "Special Edition," Moscow Interfax, Nov. 12, 1994.

24. "Diplomatic Panorama," Moscow Interfax, Feb. 21, 1995.

25. Ball, op. cit., p. 22.

26. Kononenko, Vasiliy, "Who Is 'Keeping Tabs' on Whom in Russia?" interview with Colonel General A. Starovoytov, the head of FAPSI, in *Izvestiya*, Moscow, April 16, 1995, p. 5.

27. "Investors with Shoulder Boards Go to Telecommunications Market," *Kommersant-Daily*, Moscow, May 6, 1995, p. 1.

28. Baryshnikov, Ignat, *Secrets?* (Moscow: Sedognya, 1993), p. 7.

29. Kononenko, op. cit., p. 5.

30. Interview with Henri Martre, September 1995.

31. Interview with David Tostenson, July 1994.

32. Interview with Mark W. Goode, September 1995.

CHAPTER II

1. Since 1979, the White House's Office of Federal Procurement Policy has required corporate information from all companies selling more than $25,000 worth of goods or services to the federal government. The database housing the information is

maintained by the General Services Administration's Federal Procurement Data Center. In 1994, the center collected information from 74,228 separate companies that took part in 18 million government procurement contracts.

2. Interview with Mac McCutchan, April 1995.

3. Estimate of Paul F. Wallner, open source coordinator for the Defense Intelligence Agency. Found in "Open Sources and the Intelligence Community: Myths and Realities," *American Intelligence Journal*, National Military Intelligence Association, Washington, D.C., (Spring–Summer 1993), p. 19.

4. The estimate comes from the *Burwell Directory of Information Brokers—1996* (Houston, TX: Burwell Enterprises, Inc., 1996).

5. Interview with Norma Tillman, December 1995.

6. Interview with Rop Gonggrijp, August 1994.

7. "Technology Finds the Skeleton in Any Closet," *Tulsa World*, Oct. 2, 1993, p. C-18.

8. Interview with Helen Burwell, December 1995.

9. Interview with Eugene Garfield, July 1995.

10. *The U.S. Intelligence Community: A Role in Supporting Economic Competitiveness?*, Congressional Research Service, Dec. 7, 1990.

11. Interview with Richard Clavens, July 1995.

12. Interviews with Harold Relyea and Justice Department FOIA experts, December 1995.

13. Interview with Leila Kight, August 1995.

14. Carley, William M., "Oil Leaks: Global Spy Networks Eavesdrop on Projects of Petroleum Firms," *Wall Street Journal*, Jan. 6, 1984, p. A-1.

15. Interview with Alan W. Wolff, currently a Washington-based partner of the Dewey Ballantine law firm, December 1995.

16. *The Intelligence Community's Involvement in the Banca Nazionale Del Lavoro (BNL) Affair*, report prepared by the staff of the Select Committee on Intelligence, U.S. Senate, February 1993, p. 13.

17. Ibid., p. 15.

18. Ibid., pp. 17 and 76.

19. Remarks made by McConnell at a U.S. Naval Institute seminar on military intelligence, Suitland, Maryland, June 27, 1995.

20. Interview with Jan P. Herring, June 1995.

21. Interview with Robert D. Steele, August 1994.

22. The excessive secrecy during the Gulf War was detailed by William Colby, a former director of the CIA, at a Nov. 7, 1995, symposium on global security hosted by Open Source Solutions in Washington, D.C.

23. Excerpt from "War and Peace in the Age of Information," lecture given by Steele to the Navy's Postgraduate School, Monterey, CA, Aug. 17, 1993.

24. Interview with Admiral William O. Studeman, July 1995.

25. Cole, Jeff, "Eyes in the Skies, New Satellite Imaging Could Soon Transform the Face of the Earth," *Wall Street Journal*, Nov. 30, 1995, p. A-1. Among the new consortia are: Space Imaging Inc., of Denver, a combination of Lockheed Martin, E-Systems, Mitsubishi Corp., and Eastman Kodak Co.; EarthWatch Inc., Ball

Aerospace & Technologies Corp., WorldView Imaging Corp., and Hitachi Ltd.; and Orbital Sciences Corp, which is partly owned by EIRAD Co., of Saudi Arabia.
26. Sibbet made his presentation at the International Security Systems Symposium in Washington, D.C., on Nov. 17, 1994.

CHAPTER 12

1. "Federal Government's Response to Money Laundering," hearings before the House Committee on Banking, Finance and Urban Affairs, May 25, 1993, p. 32.
2. Dannen, Fredric, and Ira Silverman, "The Supernote," *The New Yorker*, Oct. 23, 1995, p. 53.
3. Interview with Jack Blum, March 1995.
4. *Information Technologies for the Control of Money Laundering* (Washington, D.C.: Office of Technology Assessment, Congress of the United States, 1995), pp. 2–3.
5. *Report on the Measurement of International Capital Flows*, International Monetary Fund, September 1992, pp. 1–5.
6. Pak, Simon J. and, John S. Zdanowicz, "A Statistical Analysis of the U.S. Merchandise Trade Database and Users in Transfer Pricing Compliance and Enforcement," *1994 Tax Management* (Washington D.C.: Bureau of National Affairs), May 11, 1994.
7. *International Narcotics Control Strategy Report* (Washington, D.C.: U.S. Department of State, Bureau of International Narcotics Matters, April 1994), pp. 368, 383, 516, and 522.
8. See the General Accounting Office's *Money Laundering: The Use of Bank Secrecy Act Reports by Law Enforcement Could Be Increased*, May 1993, p. 8.
9. Godson, Roy, and William J. Olson, *International Organized Crime: Emerging Threat to U.S. Security*, (Washington, D.C.: National Strategy Information Center, 1993), p. 36.
10. Interview with Stanley E. Morris, September 1995.
11. China has since liberalized its trading system.
12. The Bank of China's description of Sun Ming's activities is contained in *Bank of China* v. *Ming Sun, an individual also known as Sun Ming. . . .* , CV 93-5395-HLH, U.S. District Court, Central District of California, Los Angeles, June 6, 1994. In a meeting with the Bank's lawyers, Ming refused to respond to any of the charges, asserting his right against self-incrimination.
13. Interview with Robert Van Etten, March 1995.
14. Interview with Kawika Daguio, March 1995.
15. *Bank of China* v. *Sun Ming*, U.S. District Court, Central District of California, CV 93-5395-HLH (JRx), second amended complaint for damages, pp. 16 and 17.
16. Interview with Tim Sape, March 1995.
17. Interview with Richard Kendall, March 1995.
18. Interview with Florence Chan, March 1995.
19. Interview with Richard Rogers, March 1995.
20. Interview with Bob S. Platt, March 1995.

21. According to a text of his speech before the seventeenth Annual International Asian Organized Crime Conference in Boston on March 6, 1995, Louis J. Freeh said: "In one case, the FBI—along with the Immigration and Naturalization Service—assisted authorities from the People's Republic of China in connection with a massive fraud scheme. Ultimately, the main subject was arrested in the United States and deported to China to stand trial. In addition, American investigators recovered millions of dollars stolen through the scheme and returned that money to China."

22. Interview with Graham Pinner, March 1995.

23. "Clinton Urges Global Effort Against Crime," *Washington Post*, Oct. 23, 1995, p. A-1.

24. Interview with Stanley Morris, July 1995.

CHAPTER 13

1. Dertouzos, Michael L., *Made in America: Regaining the Productive Edge*, (Cambridge, MA: MIT Press, 1989), p. 67.

2. Interview with Harvey Pollicove, November 1995.

3. Interview with Richard Samuels, May 1995.

4. "Barriers and Benefits: How U.S. Colleges and Universities View Opportunities for Students and Faculty to Study and Teach in Japan," Institute of International Education, New York, (Spring 1992), pp. 6–7. A more recent report, *A Census of U.S. Students in Japan: 1995 Update*, published by the Laurasian Institution, Atlanta, GA (March 1995), notes that even the results of having a small number of U.S. students studying in Japan may be overstated because about a third of them have instructors who teach in English (p. 12).

5. Dalton, Donald H., and Manuel G. Serapio, *U.S. Research Facilities of Foreign Companies: An Update*, U.S. Department of Commerce, Technology Administration Asia-Pacific Technology Program, October 1995, p. 10.

6. *National Critical Technologies Report*, prepared for the White House Office of Science and Technology Policy, March 17, 1995, p. xv.

7. Interview with Donald Dalton, May 1995.

8. Epstein, Stephanie, *Buying the American Mind* (Washington, D.C.: Center for Public Integrity, 1991), p. 4.

9. Interview with Dr. Allan Bromley, October, 1995.

10. *Foreign Participation in U.S. Academic Science and Engineering: 1991*, special report by the National Science Foundation, February 1992, pp. 28 and 85.

11. Some come from China's military elite. General James A. Williams, former head of the Defense Intelligence Agency, recalls a chat with a number of lieutenant colonels in the People's Liberation Army during a visit to Beijing in 1983. They spoke with American-accented English and talked about their days on U.S. college campuses. When he returned to the United States, General Williams, now retired, had their names checked against U.S. immigration records. There were no records. "All I can figure is that they must have come in under different names," said Williams in an interview, September 1995.

12. Interview with William C. Norris, August 1995.

13. Interview with Ronald A. Morse, October 1995.

14. Interview with Joe Allen, September 1995.

15. *Is Science for Sale?: Transferring Technology from Universities to Foreign Corporations*, report by the Committee on Government Operations, Oct. 16, 1992, pp. 8–10 and 15.

16. *The International Relationships of MIT in a Technologically Competitive World*, report by MIT faculty study group, May 1, 1991, p. 16.

17. Ibid., pp. 6, 10.

18. Interview with Dr. Charles M. Vest, July 1995.

19. Interview with INS spokesman, April 4, 1994.

20. Interview with Michael Finn, September 1995.

21. North, *Soothing the Establishment. The Impact of Foreign-Born Scientists and Engineers on America.*

22. Interview with Dr. Frank L. Morris, Sr., August, 1995.

23. Estimate made by U.S. Embassy in Tokyo, November 1995.

24. "Universities Yank Welcome Mat for Longtime Foreign Faculty," *Science*, (July 1995), p. 26.

25. Interview with Ivan Hall, April, 1995.

26. Interview with Dr. Allan Bromley, October 1995.

27. Interview with Dr. Eugene Wong, September 1995.

28. "Asian Countries Aim to Boost Research," *Wall Street Journal*, Oct. 24, 1995, p. A-10.

29. *Report on U.S. Critical Technologies*, p. viii.

30. Interview with Robert Sullivan, October 1995.

31. Interview with Dr. Fang Chen Luo, September 1995.

CHAPTER 14

1. The accusation was made by FBI agent John Gedney in Denver's Federal District Court. See "Software Theft Suspect Under House Arrest—Loss of Code Threatens National Security," *Seattle Times*, April 16, 1994, p. D-1.

2. Testimony by FBI director Louis J. Freeh before a joint hearing of the Senate Select Committee on Intelligence and the Senate Judiciary Subcommittee on Terrorism, Technology and Government Information, Feb. 28, 1996.

3. Remark from a speech by Roger P. Watson, the FBI's deputy assistant director for operations, at the International Security Systems Symposium, Washington, D.C., Nov. 16, 1994.

4. "Global Intrigue on Information Highway; Local Case Alleges Chinese Piracy," *Denver Post*, April 24, 1994, p. A-1.

5. *United States* v. *Liaosheng Andrew Wang*, 94-CR-59-S, U.S. District Court for the District of Colorado, "Superseding Indictment," p. 3.

6. *1995 Report on Global Software Piracy* (Washington, D.C.: Software Publishers Association, 1995), pp. 4–6.

7. Interview with James P. Chandler, September 1995.

8. Interview with Andrew Wang, December 1995.

9. Interview with David Lane, December 1995.

10. Ming Yue, Unidata's founder, went on to have his own adventures in the U.S. legal system. In 1993, after he sold Unidata to a U.S. investor, the investor won a $1.35 million default judgment against a Hong Kong company, allegedly set up by Yue, for receiving an allegedly fraudulent payment from Unidata for the company's proprietal software. In 1994, Ming Yue, who denies setting up the Hong Kong company, sued Unidata for a breach of contract and won $500,000 in a settlement. Lawyers for Unidata and Yue refused to talk about details of the latter dispute.

11. Interview with John Good, December 1995.

12. "Global Intrigue on Information Highway," *Denver Post*, April 24, 1994, p. A-1.

13. "Software Theft Suspect Under House Arrest," *Seattle Times*, April 16, 1994, p. D-1.

14. Interview with Good, December 1995.

15. Interview with David Lane, December 1995.

16. Case file, *United States* v. *Wang*, April 4, 1994.

17. Ibid., April 27, 1994.

18. Interview with Wang's prosecutors—Henry L. Solano, Mark J. Barrett, and William R. Lucero—December 1995.

19. Case file, *United States* v. *Wang*, letter from Elizabeth Betancourt, Office of Citizens Consular Services, Department of State.

20. Opinion of Judge Richard G. Stearns, *United States* v. *La Macchia*, CA9410092-RGS, U.S. District Court of Massachusetts.

21. Interview with Wang's prosecutors, December 1995.

22. In his motion to dismiss the case, Solano, the U.S. district attorney, cited Schneider's testimony as the main factor. "If a juror views the evidence in this case as reasonably permitting either of two conclusions—one of not guilty, the other of guilty—the juror must, of course, adopt the conclusion of not guilty."

23. Interview with Andrew Wang, December 1995.

24. Interview with Good and with Wang's prosecutors.

CHAPTER 15

1. *Gaining New Ground: Technology Priorities for America's Future* (U.S. Council on Competitiveness, 1991), p. 6.

2. In a study by the National Research Council in 1992, researchers examined 231 linkages between large Japanese companies and small U.S. firms. In 90 percent of the cases, the report notes, the flow of the technology was from the U.S. to Japan. See *U.S.-Japan Technology Linkages in Biotechnology*, pp. 17 and 22.

3. Because Kirin contributed to Amgen's manufacturing technology, the Amgen-Kirin joint venture is considered one of the rare cases where the U.S. company benefits from Japanese research. See *U.S.-Japan Technology Linkages in Biotechnology*, p. 24.

4. Interview with George B. Rathmann, October 1995.

5. *Biotechnology Drug Products* (Washington, D.C.: Biotechnology Industry Organization, undated).

6. Interview with James A. Williams, August 1995.

7. Interview with Robert Hildner, July 1994.

8. "Security Experts Advise Firms to Avoid Panic, Excess Zeal in Probing Data Leaks," *Wall Street Journal*, Sept. 20, 1991, p. B-1.

9. Interview with Dr. Jack Jacobs, June 1995.

10. Testimony by Dr. Bale before the Subcommittee on International Trade of the Senate Finance Committee, June 24, 1994.

11. Facts of the case are taken from a press statement made by the U.S. Attorney's Office, Boston, Dec. 15, 1994. Both defendants denied the charges.

12. *U.S.-Japan Technology Linkages in Biotechnology*, p. 12.

13. "Inquiring Eyes: An Israeli Contract With a U.S. Company Leads to Espionage," *Wall Street Journal*, Jan. 17, 1992, p. A-1.

14. All of Bill Owens's remarks are from an interview with him in August 1995.

CHAPTER 16

1. Solomone, Stacy, "The PLA's Commercial Activities in the Economy: Effects and Consequences," *Issues & Studies, a Journal of Chinese Studies and International Affairs*, Institute of International Relations, Taipei, Taiwan (March 1995), pp. 27–28.

2. Transcript, *Dateline NBC*, March 15, 1994, 10:00 P.M.

3. "H.R. 4590, United States–China Act of 1994," hearing before the Subcommittee on Trade, Committee on Ways and Means, House of Representatives, July 28, 1994, p. 8.

4. Ibid , pp. 104–105.

5. The U.S. Commerce Department's National Trade Data Bank estimates that $208 million worth of arms and ammunition were imported into the United States from China between 1990 and 1993.

6. "Chinese Weapons Flow into U.S. Despite Clinton's Ban," Dow Jones News Service, April 7, 1995.

7. "Ammunition Seized," Associated Press News Service, May 4, 1995.

8. "Selective Trade Sanctions Against China Would Be Hard to Enforce, Critics Say," *Wall Street Journal*, May 19, 1994, p. A-10.

9. Interview with Jeff Fiedler, June 1995.

10. "U.S. Agents Say Tanks, Rockets Offered," *Los Angeles Times*, May 24, 1996, p. A-1.

11. *Japanese Market Barriers in Consumer Photographic Film and Paper*, Vol. I, published by Dewey Ballantine for Eastman Kodak, Co., November 1995, p. 92.

12. *Privatizing Protection: Japanese Market Barriers in Consumer Photographic Film and Consumer Photographic Paper*, published by Dewey Ballantine for Eastman Kodak Co., May 1995, pp. 3–7.

13. "'Invincible Arrogance'—Fingers Point to Fuji Film," *Jitsugyou Kai* (March 1994), pp. 24–27, cited in *Japanese Market Barriers in Consumer Photographic Film and Paper*, Vol. II, November 1995, p. 19.

14. *Japanese Market Barriers*, Vol. II, pp. 66–67.

15. Howell's position is gaining support among economists. Professors at Berkeley are leading the charge for studies that emphasize "real world economics." See "Back to the World; Berkeley's Economists Attack Policy Issues with Unusual Gusto," *Wall Street Journal*, Dec. 1, 1995, p. A-1.

16. *The Bull: Seventy-Fifth Anniversary Edition*, an in-house newsletter published by Dewey Ballantine, Jan. 24, 1995, p. 4. The quote comes from Emory R. Buckner, one of the firm's founders.

17. "A Study of Corporation—Fuji Photo Film—The Trick Behind Its 70 Percent Domestic Market Share," *Senaku* magazine (September 1995), cited in *Japanese Market Barriers*, Vol. II, p. 8.

18. *Rewriting History, Kodak's Revisionist Account of the Japanese Consumer Photographic Market*, published by Willkie Farr & Gallagher for Fuji Photo Film Co., July 31, 1995, p. ii.

19. Cited on p. 16 of *Japanese Market Barriers*, Vol. II

20. "Zenren Counterargues Kodak's Complaints Charging It Is Under Konica and Fuji's Control," *Camera World*, Aug. 5, 1995.

21. The information in the second half of this chapter is based on an interview with Glenn P. Hoetker in December 1995.

CHAPTER 17

1. See "Intelligence, Trade and Industry, Strategic Information Systems in Japan," a paper by Juro Nakagawa, professor of marketing, Aichi Gakuin University, Nissin City, Japan.

2. Dick Cheney, President Bush's Defense secretary; Les Aspin, the first Clinton administration Defense Secretary; and Newt Gingrich, later to become Speaker of the House, were among Boyd's fans on Capitol Hill.

3. Boyd, a self-taught intellectual, says he doesn't mind the widespread plagiarism of his "Discourse on Winning and Losing," a more elaborate version of his slide briefings, which he finished in 1987. "My whole idea was to get them to steal it and embrace it. I went into that with my eyes open. Go steal the son of a bitch, I say. It's for your use."

4. See, e.g., Romm, Joseph J., *Lean and Clean Management* (New York: Kodansha International, 1994), Richards, Chester W., "Riding the Tiger: What You Really Do with OODA Loops," *Handbook of Business Strategy* (New York: Faulkner & Gray, 1994); Stalk, George, and Thomas Hout, *Competing Against Time* (New York: The Free Press, 1990); and Meyer, Christopher, *Fast Cycle Time* (New York: The Free Press, 1993).

5. Interview with John Boyd, July 1995.

6. The estimates vary, depending on how certain jobs and agencies are counted. This one comes from Richard Haver, a CIA official who headed the team that assessed the damage caused by Rick Ames, the KGB's mole. Haver spoke at a seminar on military intelligence at the U.S. Naval Institute, Suitland, Maryland, in June 1995.

7. Magaziner, *The Silent War*, p. 5.

8. Interview with Ira Magaziner, September 1995.

9. Johnson, Chalmers, *Japan: Who Governs? The Rise of the Developmental State* (New York: W. W. Norton & Co., 1995), pp. 99 and 102.

10. Sweden came top, with a score of 11.9. The United States came bottom, with 6.9, well behind Mexico, which had an 8.2. See Grosvenor, Gilbert M., "Superpowers Not So Super in Geography," *National Geographic* (Dec. 1989), p. 816.

11. Stevenson, Harold W., and, James W. Stigler, *The Learning Gap*, (New York: Summit Books, 1992), p. 33.

12. Ibid., p. 222.

13. Ibid., p. 148.

14. Ibid., p. 118.

15. Articles from Seoul's newspaper *Maeil Kyongje Sinmun*, June 10, Sept. 1, and Dec. 3, 1994, translated by the U.S. Foreign Broadcast Information Service. These and other articles showing the "particular mechanisms South Korea uses to obtain foreign technology without paying for *it*," can be found in an FBIS publication: *South Korea: Indirect Technology Transfers*, May 5, 1995, p. 17.

16. "Cryptography's Role in Securing the Information Society," Computer Science and Telecommunications Board, National Research Council, Washington, D.C., May 1996, p. ES-3.

17. "U.S. Strategy Should Promote Computer Codes," *Wall Street Journal*, May 31, 1996, p. B-5.

18. Dertouzos, *Made in America: Regaining the Productive Edge*, pp. 143–143.

19. Berman, Marshall, and J. Pace VanDevender, *Sandia Report, Prosperity Games Prototyping*, Sandia National Laboratories, August 1994, pp. 41–43 and 50.

20. Interview with J. Pace VanDevender, September 1995.

21. Interview with Joel Johnson, September 1995.

22. Interview with George Lodge, July 1995.

23. For a full account of the "Economic Espionage Act of 1996," see p. S12202 of the Oct. 2, 1996 *Congressional Record*.

24. "Intellectual Property and National Security," unpublished speech by Chandler.

25. See "Back to the World; Berkeley's Economists Attack Policy Issues with Unusual Gusto," *Wall Street Journal*, Dec. 1, 1995, p. A-1.

26. This will, of course, raise a howl from my own profession: journalists. Though we may have helped originate the FOIA, we are now minor players in the arena, constituting only about 5 percent of the action. My own experience, after some twenty-five years of using FOIA, is that the system is so overloaded with lawyers' requests that agencies can easily wait out journalists. FOIA requires a response within ten days. I recently received a reply from one agency that had been pending for ten years. If FOIA was a horse, we would have shot it long ago.

27. Holmes's much-abused quote comes from *Buck* v. *Bell*, his decision in a 1927 Supreme Court case (274 U.S. 200, 207), in which a state's right to cut the Fallopian tubes of a mentally defective woman from a family with a history of mental defectives was challenged. Holmes wrote: "The principal that sustains compulsory vaccination is broad enough to cover cutting the Fallopian tubes. . . . Three generations of imbeciles are enough."

Index

INDEX

INDEX